# THE DAYS OF THE MARTYRS

# THE DAYS OF THE MARTYRS

A history of the persecution of Christians from apostolic times to the time of Constantine

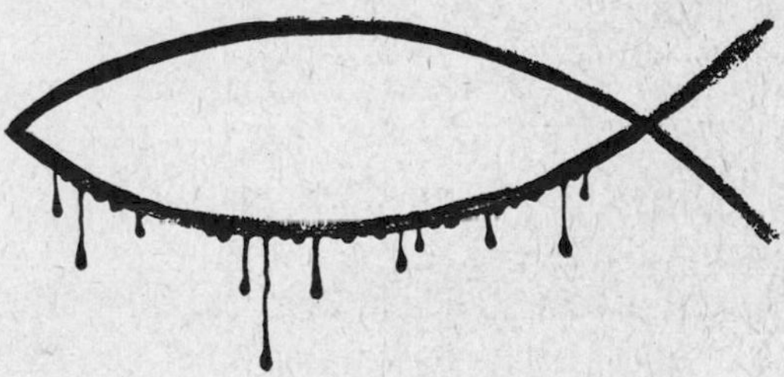

C. BERNARD RUFFIN

Our Sunday Visitor, Inc.
Huntington, Indiana 46750

Our Sunday Visitor, Inc.
200 Noll Plaza
Huntington, Indiana 46750

International Standard Book No.: 0-87973-595-3
Library of Congress Catalog Card No.: 85-60517

Cover design by James E. McIlrath

Printed in the United States of America

595

# Acknowledgments

The author and publisher wish to acknowledge the following:

Yale University Press, for *The Christians as the Romans Saw Them*, by Robert L. Wilken. © 1984. Reprinted by permission.

The Society for Promoting Christian Knowledge (SPCK), for *The Ecclesiastical History and the Martyrs of Palestine*, by Eusebius. © 1954. Reprinted by permission.

Glencoe Publishing Co., a division of MacMillan Publishing Co., Inc., for *The Days of the Martyrs*, by Guiseppe Ricciotti, translated by A.E. Wallis Bull. Reprinted with permission of Macmillan, Inc. © 1959 by The Bruce Publishing Co.

Oxford University Press, for *The Early Christian Fathers*, edited and translated by Henry Bettenson. © 1969. Reprinted with permission.

Penguin Books Ltd., for excerpts from *The Annals of Imperial Rome* (revised edition, 1977), by Tacitus, translated by Michael Grant. Reprinted by permission of Penguin Books Ltd. © 1956, 1959, 1971 by Michael Grant Publications Ltd. Additional thanks to Penguin Books Ltd., for excerpts from *Lives of the Later Caesars*, translated by Anthony Birley. Reprinted by permission of Penguin Books Ltd. © 1976 by Anthony Birley.

The Division of Christian Education of the National Council of the Churches of Christ, for the use of Scripture quotations taken from the *Revised Standard Version Bible, Catholic Edition*. © 1965 and 1966 by the Division of Christian Education of the National Council of the Churches of Christ in the U.S.A., and used by permission of the copyright owner.

# Dedication

**This book is dedicated with gratitude to Ernst and Louise Helmreich, who in my college days nurtured and expanded my love of history.**

# Table of contents

# Introduction

The word "martyr" comes from the Greek word *martus*, which means "witness." From its earliest days, the Christian Church has honored individuals who witnessed to their faith in Christ by choosing to die rather than compromise that faith. The Christian martyrs demonstrated that serving and loving Jesus was more important than anything life could give them. By voluntarily accepting death when they could have saved their lives simply be repeating a seemingly innocuous formula, the martyrs testified not only to the centrality of Christ in their lives but also to their faith in the Resurrection and the life of the world to come.

As far back as records exist, the Christian community held in special veneration those people who gave up their lives to witness their belief that Jesus is the Son of God. The graves of these men, women, and children were given special attention, and it soon became the custom to erect altars above them for the celebration of the Holy Mass. In fact, in the Apocalypse, the Apostle John sees in his vision "under the altar the souls of those who had been slain for the word of God and for the witness they had borne" (Revelation 6:9).

In this book we shall recount the history of the Christian martyrs from the time of Christ to the time of Constantine. To conclude our history at the year 325, when the "Peace of the Church" became nearly universal within the Roman Empire, is purely arbitrary. The history of martyrdom by no means came to an end at that time. Throughout every century until the present day millions of Christians have willingly surrendered their lives for their Lord, but to do justice to them would entail a work of many volumes that the efforts of a single lifetime might be insufficient to compile.

The chief sources for the story of *The Days of the Martyrs* in the first four centuries are the writings of the Palestinian historian Eusebius Pamphili (c.260-c.340), and those documents known as the writings of the "Ante-Nicene Fathers," which comprise those authentic Christian writings which date from the first century to the Council of

Nicaea, which was convened in 325. In approaching these works I have not attempted to introduce any new scholarship or any novel interpretations, but have generally accepted the ancient witnesses at face value. There may be some facts that suggest exaggeration, but with the lack of any other reliable documentation to shed light on the recounted facts, I consider that the extant accounts are the closest thing we have to the events in question, and disputing them serves no useful purpose except in those rare cases in which one incident is described by more than one source, and these conflict. Most often, however, there exists only one primary source for a given event in ancient Church history. Certainly, if *The Ecclesiastical History* of Eusebius had been lost, we would know almost nothing of the history of the Church from the time of the apostles to the time of the Emperor Constantine. There may be in Eusebius some accounts or descriptions that sound farfetched. Perhaps Eusebius exaggerated or relied upon unfounded gossip. But how does one know for sure? The modern historian is in no position to say, "Well, I don't think this could have happened." If some ancient writer was mistaken, after so great a passage of time there is seldom any way of determining this. The twentieth-century historian is certainly in no position to judge the work of his third- and fourth-century predecessors, since primary sources were available to them that are not extant for him.

The "Acts" (or histories) of individual martyrs are a different story. It was customary for Christians in given communities to commit to writing the story of men and women in their locality who surrendered their lives as martyrs and to send these accounts to congregations in other parts of the Roman world, as a source of inspiration to believers everywhere. Some of these accounts have come down in the form in which they were originally written. The histories of the martyrdoms of Polycarp, Perpetua, and the Christians of Lyon are in this category. The originals of most of the martyrs' acts were, however, lost long ago, and the versions that have survived are fragmentary, numerous, conflicting, and late, often dating no earlier than the early Middle Ages. Over the years there have been a number of attempts — many of them quite fanciful — to reconstruct them. In the case of the stories of individual martyrs, which come from late and fragmentary sources, I have attempted to rely upon common sense in putting together from the different versions an account that seems most logical. This does not mean that the events of sixteen hundred years ago necessarily transpired in the manner that a man in his thirties sitting at a typewriter in Alexandria, Virginia, thinks they must have happened. It is perhaps better to devise a coherent account than to create a tedious and unreadable "scholarly" book by setting forth a collection of different versions, attempting, without any sound reason for doing so, to judge which fragments of which versions (if any) are most likely to be true.

In reconstructing most of these martyrs' lives, I have generally relied on the work of an Anglican priest named Sabine Bering-Gould, who died at the age of ninety in 1924. Baring-Gould is most familiar for his popular hymn "Onward, Christian Soldiers," but he spent years poring over various *Actae* of saints and martyrs and other documents in Latin and Greek to compile an impressive sixteen-volume *Lives of the Saints*, which was published in England in 1898. I have taken the liberty of paraphrasing his heavy Victorian language into English more intelligible to most readers today. I do hope I shall not meet with the good Father Baring-Gould's displeasure when I meet him in the next world.

In the next two hundred pages or so there appears the story of the persecution of the Church of Jesus Christ during the first three hundred years of her existence, highlighted by the stories of individual men, women, and children who willingly laid down their lives rather than deny that faith. I have not attempted to include or even mention every martyr of whom some mention has been made in available sources, but have tried to prepare a reasonable selection of martyrs who are familiar, or whose stories are particularly interesting or edifying.

The first chapter in the story of an imaginary second-century Christian presents an overview of the life of a "typical believer'' (if there ever was such a creature), to enable the reader to relate more easily to the historical accounts that follow in the ensuing chapters. Wherever I have quoted the Bible, I have used the *Revised Standard Version Bible, Catholic Edition.*

*—C.B.R.*
Alexandria, Virginia
Feast of the Conversion of St. Paul, 1985

# 1

# A day in the life of a Christian

It is the year of Our Lord 178, the year 930 since the foundation of Rome. Life in Rome begins at dawn, but while it is still more than an hour away, Quintus the shoemaker and Felicitas, his wife, our fictional characters, have important business to do before they commence the routine of daily life. Making the sign of the cross, they kneel beside their beds and thank their God for watching over them during the night and for giving them health and strength to begin the work of another day. Quintus and Felicitas are members of the rapidly growing community of Christians, a "sect" maligned as a "detestable superstition," but which nevertheless exerts an undeniable fascination and attraction for their pagan neighbors. While ridiculing Christians as superstitious fools on the one hand, on the other hand they seem to be drawn in greater and greater numbers to join in their meetings to find peace in the consolation of their sacred mysteries.

Felicitas was born in Rome some fifty years earlier, to Christian parents. Quintus was, however, born a pagan. Always warned by his mother to beware of Christians because they kidnapped children to chop them up alive for food at their banquets, it was only when he met Felicitas that Quintus learned that these tales were lies. When Quintus went to Felicitas' father, Apelles, to ask for her hand in marriage and learned that Christians were not to mate with unbelievers, he began to attend Christian services of worship. There he met with the leader of the community, an Egyptian named Paul of Thebes, to prepare for baptism.

This new religion appealed to Quintus. Religious as his mother was, she believed that everything depended upon Fate, the movement of the stars; everything was determined from the beginning of time. The gods, if not distant, were angry. According to Quintus' father, death was the end of everything. His mother, however, believed that the dead became ghosts, languishing in a gloomy void. Angry and envious of the living, they had to be soothed. Quintus used to go with his mother to offer sacrifices of warm milk on the graves of his grandparents and his sister Phibia. Failure to do so, he was taught, would lead to terrifying hauntings. "The most loving soul on earth could become the most menacing phantom after death if not properly appeased!" Quintus' mother had told him.

But Paul of Thebes taught a different doctrine. "Christians," he said, "are not the slaves of fate or chance, but are guided by the hand of a loving God. God loves every member of the human race. Not even a sparrow falls from the sky without the consent of the merciful maker of heaven and earth. Though He may give or He may take, the Father of our Lord Jesus will never forsake His children. Whatever happens is part of His loving purpose." Paul of Thebes would read from the writings of another Paul, a Jew from Tarsus who had been beheaded some eighty years before when the cruel tyrant Nero was emperor. This Paul, who had suffered very much, had written, "All things work together for good for those who love God."

The old priest spoke about Jesus, the God-Man who had died for the sins of the world. "Now this Jesus was not a 'son of a god,' like Hercules, who was the offspring of an adulterous union of a god and a mortal woman, but rather He is the 'Son of God,' in the sense that the one true God — in a holy way, a pure way, an invisible way — entered the womb of a holy virgin to beget one who was both Man and God. This Jesus promises that those who believe in Him will never die. The just man will go on to a better world, reclothed in a body that can never die, to live forever with Jesus in joy and gladness unending."

Every evening, along with three other men, Quintus went to the apartment where Paul of Thebes lived, to be instructed in the Christian faith. Paul kept with him copies of the writings of some of Jesus' apostles, including some which he called "Gospels," that told about the life of this man called "Christ," or "Savior." Paul of Thebes made sure that Quintus and the other men, none of whom could read, memorized key passages. Other practical instruction came from a document called *The Teaching of the Twelve Apostles*. Quintus learned much of it by rote. He learned, "There are two ways, one of life and one of death; and great is the difference between the two ways. This is the way of life: 'First you shall love God who made you, secondly your neighbor as yourself, and whatever you would not like done to you, do not do to another.'"[1] The *Teaching* warned against a number of practices that were common at the time:

> You shall not commit murder. You shall not commit adultery. You shall not corrupt boys. You shall not practice fornication. You shall not steal. You shall not practice magic. You shall not practice sorcery. You shall not kill an unborn child or murder a newborn infant. And you shall not desire the goods of your neighbor.[2]

Quintus was taught, moreover, to "flee from" jealousy, quarrelsomeness, and irritability and not to give away to "evil desire," use "obscene language," or let his "eye wander." The witchcraft and astrology so widely practiced were absolutely forbidden. On the other hand, Quintus and his colleagues were exhorted to cultivate meekness, patience, guilelessness, mildness, and gentleness.[3]

At last Quintus was ready to be baptized. He had to fast for three days before midnight on the morning of Easter, then he was led to a large pool in the mansion when the congregation met. Paul of Thebes poured water three times over Quintus' head and declared, "I baptize you in the Name of the Father, the Son, and the Holy Spirit." How happy Quintus had been that morning, clad in his white robe, singing the praises of his risen Lord!

Life had not been easy for Quintus. When they learned of his Baptism, his parents turned against him and refused to speak to him. Quintus set up a shop of his own a short distance from the street where they lived, but they never came to see him until they were old and ill, and then it was left to Quintus and Felicitas to nurse them until they died. Quintus' surviving brother, who had been close to them throughout the years, never lifted a finger for his parents once they became incapacitated. Felicitas bore Quintus four daughters, but three of them died as babies. Only Prisca, a lively, intelligent girl, the joy of her parents' hearts, survived into childhood.

An epidemic broke out in Rome in the year 166. Although many of the pagans abandoned their sick for fear of infection, Christians, as a rule, not only tended their afflicted, but saw to the care of the non-believers as well. During the epidemic the carpenter next door, terror-stricken, left his sick wife and children alone in their apartment and fled Rome. Felicitas went to stay with them and nursed the woman and two of the children back to health, although five of the children died and Felicitas herself caught the infection and was laid low for weeks.

The neighbor woman had previously been hostile to Christianity, but afterwards began to attend services of worship with Quintus and Felicitas and was eventually baptized.

Prisca had fallen sick and lost her sight as a result of the pestilence. Her health was so weakened that she died two years later. Christians did not cremate their dead, like many of the heathens. Not only did the flames suggest the fires of hell, it was felt more appropriate for the body to return gradually to the earth from which it had originated. Prisca was buried in one of the underground cemeteries that had been built at the direction of Flavia Cornelia, the rich woman who put her home at the disposal of their congregation. And so Prisca's remains were committed to a niche in a communal burial vault, the plastered walls of which were painted with such symbols of Christian hope, as harps, palms, crowns, and figures of the Resurrection like Jonah, Daniel, and the three Israelite children in the "Fiery Furnace." As Prisca was laid to rest, the congregation sang a hymn like this one:

> No more, ah, no more sad complaining,
> Resign these fond pledges to earth;
> Stay, mothers, and thick-falling tear-drops,
> This death is a heavenly birth.
>
> Take, Earth, to thy bosom so tender,
> Take, nourish this body. How fair,

How noble in death! We surrender
These relics of man to Thy care.

This, this was the home of the spirit,
Once built by the breath of our God;
And here, in the light of his wisdom,
Christ, Head of the risen, abode.

Guard well the dear treasure we lend thee,
The maker, the Saviour of men
Shall never forget His beloved,
But claim his own likeness again.[4]

"No one should be made sad by death," Paul of Thebes said, "since in living is labor and peril, but in dying, peace and certainty of the Resurrection." Quintus and Felicitas ever afterwards referred to the day of their daughter's death as the day of her heavenly birth. On her grave they inscribed the words, "To Prisca, our dear and worthy daughter, who lived 18 years, 4 months. Live in Christ."

Quintus and Felicitas thought of her as they walked through the narrow and filthy streets, carrying a torch to illuminate the way to the home of Flavia Cornelia, where the congregation met. Although many neighbors of Quintus and Felicitas knew that they were Christians, thus far the couple had been let alone. Since the time of the Emperor Trajan, who had died shortly before Quintus was born, it had been understood that even though being a Christian was a capital offense, authorities were not allowed to hunt Christians down, but rather take action only when the followers of Jesus were denounced formally as a public menace by people willing to come forth and make the charges, not anonymously, but in person.

Like most Christian houses of prayer, the place where Quintus and Felicitas worshipped was a converted residential mansion. Flavia Cornelia and her husband had been converted many years ago and placed the mansion at the disposal of Paul of Thebes. Flavia's husband had been killed shortly after his conversion. He was a high official in the court of the Emperor

Antoninus Pius. Someone wanted his job and thus formally denounced him to the emperor.

Quintus and Felicitas entered the passageway leading to the house church. On the floor there had once been a mosaic of a dog, with the inscription *Cave Canem* ("Beware of Dog"). Lately, Flavia replaced it with a picture of a fish. Christians knew what that stood for, if pagans did not. The Greek letters spelled "fish," standing for Jesus Christ, Son of God, Savior.

They entered into a large open courtyard, called an "atrium," surrounded by pillars and lighted by skylights. It was there that the worshippers gathered for divine services. Looking straight ahead, Quintus could see a room called the "tablinum," separated from the "atrium" only by a pair of steps. This had been the place where Flavia's husband's parents had their family shrine. The altar had been reconsecrated to Christ, but Flavia retained the large throne-like chair, designed for the patriarch of the clan, for use by the bishop when he worshipped with them. Beside it were chairs for the priest, or presbyter, Hermes, who came to them five years ago when the aged Paul of Thebes died, and for the deacons Peter and Gnaeus and the deaconess Olympas. There was also a reading desk and a large lampstand. To the left of the "atrium" was a pool called the "impluvium." Flavia had converted this into a baptistry. A dining room, called the "triclinum," to the right of the "tablinum," and unseen from where Quintus stood, was used for community feasts.

Today was the first day of the week, "Dies Solis," or Sunday, simply another working day for Romans, but the day on which Christians celebrated the Resurrection in their principal service of the week. The service began with the traditional Jewish mutual exchange of blessings. "The Lord be with you," declared Hermes, to which the worshippers, the men standing on one side and the women on the other, replied, "And with thy spirit." This reply by the congregation was an acknowledgement of the special grace that the Holy Spirit bestowed on all priests at ordination.[5]

Readings from Scripture followed. There existed at this time no handy volume called "The Bible." The books that now comprise our Sacred Scriptures were found on scrolls of papyrus, kept and jealously guarded by the lectors, men able to read and write, whose task it was to read from the Scriptures during services of worship. No other members kept the Scriptures in their homes. Everything had to be copied by hand, and there were just not enough copies to go around.

The first lesson was taken from the Jewish Scriptures, from the book of Daniel; the second from the writings of the apostles (in this case, from a letter St. Paul wrote to the Romans); and the third from the Gospel of St. Luke. Since a large number of Christians worshipped in Flavia Cornelia's atrium, the lector Damasus stood on the step of the tablinum and chanted, so that his voice could carry further and be heard throughout the hall. In between the lessons, psalms were sung in their entirety. A cantor, singing an elaborate melody, alternated with the congregation. The signal for the people to join in was the cantor's cry of "alleluiah." Then Hermes, sitting behind the altar, delivered a "prophetic" message, stating unequivocally what the Lord was saying to the people that day. After the sermon, all those who had not yet been baptized were dismissed. Various intentions were announced, for which the people prayed successively on their knees, first silently as individuals, and then with the deacon Peter, who summed up all the petitions in a short prayer known as the "Collect." After this, every member of the congregation brought up to the tablinum a gift, not only for the sustenance of the clergy, but for the relief of the poor as well.

The gifts were mostly in kind rather than coin: oil, cheese, vegetables, fruits, and flowers, as well as the bread and wine to be consecrated in the Eucharist.

Hermes then blessed the bread and wine, and cried out to the worshippers, "Let grace come and let this world pass away. Hosanna to the Son of David! If anyone is holy, let him come! If anyone is not, let him repent. Maranatha. Amen!"[6] When the congregation had partaken of the consecrated bread and wine, they were dismissed with the simple words *Ite missa est* ("Go, you are dismissed").

When Quintus and Felicitas reached their home, it was

daybreak and time to begin work. Quintus had a small shop on the lower level of the apartment house where he lived. After eating a piece of bread, which constituted the typical breakfast for the Roman poor, he worked until midday, not only repairing, but actually constructing shoes and sandals. Felicitas sat, spinning. At noon, the couple ate their "prandium," a meal of eggs, vegetables, mushrooms, and fruit, washed down with some wine mixed with water. Afterwards they faced Jerusalem, knelt, and prayed.

Early in the afternoon was the time for the siesta. Nearly everything in Rome came to a halt during the heat of the day. Later in the afternoon, when the wealthier Romans went to the public baths or engaged in other forms of recreation, such as the games or the theater, Quintus returned to his shop. Felicitas went with some of the ladies of their congregation to visit some sick people. During the afternoon, some of Quintus' friends stopped to talk with him. They talked about the terrible reports concerning the extermination of almost the entire Christian population of Lugdunum, Gaul (now Lyons, or Lyon, France). Gaul was many days away, and Quintus had never been there (in fact, he had never been outside Rome, for that matter), but there was a man in his congregation, Urban, a retired soldier and a native of Asia Minor, who had a sister living in Lugdunum. Although he had no way of confirming his conviction, he was certain that she and her family were among those who "made their robes white in the blood of the lamb." When Quintus groped for a word of comfort, Urban replied, "Why should I grieve as those who have no hope? Why should we be sorry for those now in the presence of God?"

Quintus wondered whether he could ever have the courage to die for his Lord, but he remembered what Paul of Thebes had told him years before, that God never allowed a person to be tempted beyond his strength. "If the time should come when you have to face the trial of martyrdom," the old presbyter had said, "then the Lord will supply you with the strength to endure it. To worry about it now is not good, for you would be trying to solve a problem for which God has not sent you the strength to cope."

Just before sundown, or "the time when the lamps are lit," Quintus and Felicitas sat down to their largest meal, the "ientaculum." For dinner they had soup, vegetables, fruit, and, today, a little pork, which was supplied by a Christian farmer known to a member of their congregation. Christians normally did not eat meat, even if it was available, on Wednesdays and Fridays.

Since the lamps available to the poor gave forth but a dim, sputtering, smokey light, the day ended at sunset for Quintus and his wife. Before they retired, they knelt, crossed themselves, faced the east toward Jerusalem, and said their evening prayers. After emptying the slop-jar out the window, they retired for the night, closing the window shutters. Sleep in Rome was often difficult because of the rumbling wagons that brought food from the countryside. Wagon traffic was banned during daylight hours because of the congestion it caused.

Quintus and Felicitas had not been asleep long when they were awakened by the sound of a determined knocking on the door. What could this be? Could old Aurelia be worse? Perhaps some brethren from Macedonia had arrived and needed accommodations. But as soon as Quintus unlatched the door, he was struck in the face, knocked down, manacled, and hurried away into the darkness of the night by two furious-looking soldiers. It all happened in a shorter time than it took to say an Our Father. As soon as the soldiers disappeared with her husband, Felicitas ran to the home of some members of her congregation who lived across the way. Quintus, a few hours later, came to his senses in total blackness and overwhelming stench. Almost overwhelmed by the fetid, suffocating heat, he could scarcely believe that this was happening to him. "The thing that I have most feared has come at last," he said to himself.

Sliding about on the slimy floor of his prison cell, Quintus did not know whether he was waking or sleeping. What was it like to be killed by a lion or a bear? He pictured in his mind the evil brutes rushing at him, opening their terrible mouths to engulf him in their jaws. He could almost smell their foul breath and feel the grisly teeth ripping into his flesh. But then, soon it would be all over and he would be with his Savior. But perhaps he might not be thrown to the beasts, like the people of Lyon had been. Perhaps he would be crucified like the young Antoninus, the baker's son. What would it be like to be stripped naked, and have the hands and feet penetrated by iron spikes, and then hang for hours, perhaps days, unable even to keep the flies from settling upon the crusted wounds from the scourging that would precede this final punishment? Quintus now thought of Gaius Cornelius Scaevola, a physician and aristocrat, who was strung up by his hands and flogged until his skin hung in ribbons. Perhaps the common people might give up their mad superstition if so eminent a man repudiated Christ, the authorities thought. Scaevola, however, refused to renounce his Lord and was chained to a red hot grate. Then, still obdurate in his allegiance, he was taken from the griddle, smoking and stinking, and dragged away, leaving a trail of bits of charred flesh, to be decapitated. Scaevola was a Roman citizen, so he was entitled to an "easy" death. Quintus was also a Roman citizen, so he would probably be decapitated rather than crucified. But to what tortures would he be subjected beforehand?

Quintus was praying the Our Father when the doors opened and two young soldiers brusquely ordered the prisoner to follow them immediately. Filthy, barely able to walk, Quintus was led into a large public building called a basilica.

"Are you Quintus Sutor?"

Quintus looked up and saw an insignificant-looking man whose visage he searched in vain for signs either of benignity or malevolence. "I said, are you Quintus Sutor?"

"I am, your excellency."

"Where do you live?" demanded the magistrate.

"On the Lane of the Three Taverns, beside the public pump."

"What is your occupation?"

"I am a shoemaker, like my father and grandfather before me."

"Very well. Now, Quintus, I wish to make this brief. You have been accused of being a Christian." A man stepped forward whom Quintus recognized as a shoemaker who had a shop on his street. He hardly knew the man, whose name was Avitus and who had come forward to denounce Quintus for invoking the Christian God to cast a spell to take away his customers. Quintus knew the reason why Avitus had so little business. It was because his work was inferior. Avitus spent most of his time drinking.

"This charge is preposterous!" Quintus insisted.

"Perhaps it is," said the magistrate. "But all you have to do is take a pinch of incense and burn it here on the tripod in front of Caesar's statue, and you are a free man."

"But I would never do that!"

"And why not? Are you saying that you *are* a Christian?"

"Yes, I am a Christian, your excellency."

"Look, my friend," said the magistrate, "we aren't out to destroy men's lives. Caesar is concerned that everyone show their proper reverence toward the gods of Rome, especially now that our borders are gravely threatened by barbarians. All you have to do is show your allegiance to your country and to your emperor by burning incense in front of this little statue."

"But I am a Christian."

"You *are* aware, Quintus, that being a Christian is punishable by death. Are you not aware of the Neronian Institution, that 'It is not lawful to be a Christian'? We do not take pleasure in hunting people down. All we want you to do is burn some incense in front of Ceasar's statue to show us that you are a loyal citizen of Rome."

"I pray for Caesar every day," retorted Quintus, "but to offer incense before his image is to honor him as a god, and it is written in our sacred writings, 'Thou shalt have no other gods before me.' "

The magistrate replied, "Respect your gray hairs. I know that you are an honorable man. You have never in your life been afoul of the law. And, I must say, I have never known a member of your sect who was not an ideal citizen — except in the stubborn refusal to honor the emperor and the gods of Rome! You are aware, my good Quintus, that if you refuse I will be constrained to order your immediate execution?"

"I understand this, your excellency. I choose to accept the consequences. I cannot be unfaithful to my Lord."

"I do not care to have your blood on my hands. I hereby order that the defendant remain in custody for three days so as to have time to reconsider his decision."

"That will not be necessary," said Quintus. "I cannot, I will not renounce Christ my Lord."

It was strange. Quintus had never been a particularly courageous man, but now, as he had been taught long ago, the Lord was supplying the strength. He was led out of the basilica back to the prison. He was able to catch a fleeting glance of the weeping Felicitas who, with several other women, was standing outside the basilica. Whisked by, he had time only to point upward toward heaven.

Quintus was led into a small chamber inside the prison. As one of his guards handed a written order to the officer in charge, Quintus could see in front of him, on the stone floor, a block of wood, reddened with gore.

The officer in charge said, "The executioner will be here momentarily. I must blindfold you and lead you to the block. You understand that we are merely soldiers, carrying out orders. We know how to do as we are told — unlike you."

Quintus handed the officer a gold coin. "Yes, I understand, and forgive you. This is for the executioner."

"No, we don't want it. I'll give it to your wife when she comes for your body. You're a brave one, old man. You must have a great God. If I didn't have nine children, I. . ."

So Quintus was blindfolded and led to the block. The officer announced, "The soldier who is under orders to end your life is on his way. You may take the few minutes that remain to you to pray to your God."

And so Quintus stretched out his hands and prayed, "Lord, into Thy hands I commend my spirit."

Quintus, Felicitas, and everyone else we have mentioned in the last few pages existed only in our imaginations. Their story is not, however, dissimilar to that of millions of other Christians who lived between the time of Christ and the Emperor Constantine. The following pages will tell the true story of their conflict and their victory.

# 2

# 'We must obey God and not men': The Church in Israel

Most of the thousands of Christian believers who, in the first three centuries after the coming of Christ sealed their commitment to their Lord with their blood, were, like our fictitious Quintus, victims of the Roman government. During the first three decades of the Church's existence, however, the primary instigators of persecution were not the Romans, but the leaders of the Jewish nation.

From all existing documents, the fact is that for the first thirty years of the Church's existence one would have been hard put to locate a Roman official who knew what a Christian was. The celebrated North African Christian writer, Tertullian (c.150-c.240), believed that Tiberius, the emperor during whose reign Christ was crucified, read the reports of Jesus' life and miracles and even considered asking the Senate to enroll Him among the gods of Rome. If Tertullian was in receipt of accurate information, it meant only that the emperor Tiberius, a cruel, suspicious man in his seventies, was sufficiently impressed by Jesus' reputation to toy with the notion of making him one of the hundreds of gods whom it was permissible for the peoples of the empire to worship, if they so chose. Such an idea was, at most, only a passing fancy, as no such decree was ever promulgated. Certainly none of the emperors or high officials in the first century had the slightest idea of what Christianity was all about. Some individuals may have regarded the Founder as a rebel, others as a good teacher, perhaps even as a holy man worthy of religious devotion, but few if any residents of the Roman Empire had any understanding whatsoever of the main points of Christian teaching.

Were we to go back in time and interview the Emperor Caligula, who governed the Roman world violently and incompetently from 37 to 41, during the time that the faith was making its first inroads in the empire, his response would likely have been, "Who? Oh, you mean the Nazarenes or Nazirites or something like that. Their leader was put to death in the reign of my predecessor! They say He was a magician who worked miracles. They were right to kill Him because you never know what men like that are liable to do! It is always best to kill! But, the Christians . . . why, they're just a sect of those d--d Jews! None of them are loyal Romans! They think they're too good for our gods. I'm going to teach all of those jokers a thing or two when I get good and ready!" This, roughly, would probably have been the attitude also of Caligula's successor, the more moderate and balanced Claudius I, who reigned until 54.

If Christians encountered any hostility on the part of the Romans in these years, it was because of their identification as Jews. Judaism was one of the recognized religions of the Roman Empire. It was not confined to Palestine, but had adherents and converts throughout the empire. Jews were allowed to worship in their magnificent Temple in Jerusalem, and hold services in their synagogues throughout the Roman world. They were allowed to make converts, and their men, because of their religious scruples, were exempted from service in the imperial army. As long as the Roman government saw Christians as Jewish sectarians, there was no direct persecution of the followers of Jesus because of their religion. Any violence inflicted on Christians by the Roman state was because of political, rather than religious, activities on the part of the group with which they were associated.

The Romans tolerated the Jewish religion, but rather grudgingly. As we will see in the next chapter, although Romans were not religious people — at least from a Jewish or Christian standpoint — they were superstitious, and believed that unless the guardian spirits of the Roman state were appeased with sacrifices, the Roman world was threatened with disaster.

Although Jews were allowed to satisfy their obligation to appease the gods of Rome simply by praying for the emperor in their Temple, there were many Romans who felt that toleration of such "atheism" was dangerous and could have serious repercussions if Rome's tutelary spirits should get "riled up" over the lack of attention shown them by an increasingly large percentage of their client population. However, the considerable violence used by the Romans against the Jews during these years was ostensibly for political, rather than religious, reasons. Since Palestine had been absorbed into the Roman Empire in 63 B.C., Jews had bitterly resented Roman rule, and almost every year, in the hundreds that passed between Jerusalem's occupation by Pompey the Great and the crucifixion of Christ, had seen some act of rebellion or terrorism. Thus, when the leaders of the Jewish nation condemned Jesus to death and asked Pontius Pilate, the Roman procurator, to carry out the sentence, they implied that He was a revolutionist. Had Jesus been such, Pilate would have been only too glad to comply with their request to have Him crucified. When it became apparent to Pilate that Jesus was no revolutionary, that His "kingdom is not of this world," he wanted to free the controversial rabbi, and was persuaded not to do so only when a riot threatened to break out. Had such a disaster occurred, Pilate could easily have been accused of incompetence and recalled; so, like millions of other bureaucrats to the present day, he crumbled under pressure to save his job.

In A.D. 33, the year when Our Lord was crucified and rose from the dead, Jerusalem was a city in the Roman province of Judaea. It was not the capital. The center of government had been removed many years before to Caesarea, where the largely non-Jewish population were considered better hosts for Roman officials and troops. Roman authority in Judaea was in the person of an imperial appointee called a "procurator," who was nominally subject to the governor of Syria. The procurator had charge mainly of financial and military matters. The local government was under control of the high priest and an assembly of seventy men, known as the Sanhedrin, a body with both judicial and legislative authority. It could sentence a man to death, but could not carry out the sentence. They could only recommend to the procurator that the sentence be carried out. The Sanhedrin was composed of members of the high priestly family, or chief priests; lay leaders known as the elders; and canon lawyers known as the scribes. Many of the latter belonged to a sect called the Pharisees, who were concerned with a strict observance of the Law of Moses, and believed in a spiritual world, in the existence of angels and demons, and in rewards and punishments beyond the grave. Most of the chief priests and elders, on the other hand, were members of a sect known as the Sadducees, vehemently denied the existence of a spiritual world and of the possibility of a life beyond the grave.

The Sanhedrin opposed Jesus and His followers on both spiritual and political grounds. The Pharisees were generally the most favorable to Christian teaching. Two of them, Joseph of Arimathea and Nicodemus, were Christians. The famed Rabbi Gamaliel, universally respected, took a moderate position. Other Pharisees, however, like Saul of Tarsus (later known as Paul), whom some scholars believe was then a member of the Sanhedrin, were bitterly opposed to Jesus because He claimed to be God. For pious Jews this was the ultimate blasphemy, punishable by death.

The Sadducees were opposed to Jesus and His followers not only because He claimed to be God and because He taught about things (like angels and devils and the Resurrection), in which they did not care to believe, but especially because they perceived the carpenter from Nazareth as a political threat. If Christians became too numerous, the power of the Sadducees would diminish and order would break down, and then the Roman government would feel threatened and use the existence of this movement of renegade Jews as a pretext for withdrawing the privileged status of Judaism as a recognized, legal religion. This, in turn, might prove the pretext for the removal of local government.

Flavius Josephus, the first-century Jewish historian of pro-Roman sympathies, in his *History of the Jewish Wars*, leaves an account, including information not recorded by the evangelists, which further illuminates the attitude of the Jewish ruling class both to Jesus as well as to the Romans. According to Josephus, the Sanhedrin, having met under the chairmanship of the high priest to discuss Jesus, expressed their fear that His followers were going to proclaim Him king. "We are utterly incapable of resisting the Romans," they decided. "But, as the blow is about to fall, we'd better go and tell Pilate what we've heard, and steer clear of trouble, in case he gets to know from someone else and confiscates our property, puts us to death, and turns our children adrift."

So, representatives of the Sanhedrin went to Pilate, who reacted by sending his troops to "butcher many of the common people," apparently as a warning against any thought of revolt. Life was cheap to Pilate and his associates. The procurator arrested Jesus and held an inquiry, but, for the moment, released Him, convinced that "he was a benefactor, not a criminal or agitator or would-be king." One reason for the leniency on the part of an official who earned a reputation for brutality was Pilate's conviction that Jesus had cured his wife "when she was at the point of death." Josephus recounted that the crowds around Jesus grew larger than ever and "the exponents of the law were mad with jealousy." Josephus further maintained that the Sanhedrin eventually bribed the reluctant Pilate to order Jesus' execution.[1]

We see here that the antipathy of the Sanhedrin to Jesus and His disciples was due both to selfish fear of loss of influence, as well as a genuine patriotic concern that the Nazarene's popularity might lead to anti-Roman rioting that Jesus Himself would not be able to control, and subsequent repression by the Romans. Thus, after Jesus was crucified, the apostles and other disciples of Jesus were in grave danger. The Sanhedrin hoped that Jesus would be quickly forgotten, but, of course, did not count on the Resurrection and Pentecost. So, when the "sect" began to grow dramatically, they began to take steps to repress it.

Within a few days after the Holy Spirit descended on several dozen worshippers as they met to pray, the numbers of the faithful had grown to approximately three thousand. One day the Apostles Peter and John were going, as was their daily wont, to pray at the Temple. At an entrance known as "The Beautiful Gate," there was a crippled beggar. This man had been a fixture there for many years. Everyone knew him and was aware that his legs were genuinely and obviously crippled, unable to walk a step. As he did with everyone who passed him, the beggar solicited alms from Peter and John. He must have been startled when, instead of digging for coin, or simply ignoring him, Peter said, ". . .Look at us. . . . I have no silver and gold, but I give what I have; in the name of Jesus Christ of Nazareth, walk" (Acts 3:4-6).

It is a wonder that the beggar did not turn on the apostles, retorting indignantly, "What's the matter with you? Can't you see that I'm crippled?" On the contrary, the beggar allowed the apostles to raise him to his feet. Immediately he found that he could now walk normally, and, "walking and leaping," he entered the Temple with Peter and John, praising God.

This created an immediate sensation, since everyone knew that his handicap was not feigned. When the sight of the ex-cripple drew a huge throng of the curious, Peter used the miracle as an opportunity to proclaim Christ Jesus. He declared that it was through faith in the name of Jesus, Whom God had raised from the dead, that the beggar was brought to perfect health. He explained that Christ had been foretold by all the prophets from Samuel on. Christ was the "prophet" foretold by Moses, of whom it was written, ". . .Every soul that does not listen to that prophet shall be destroyed from the people" (Acts 3:23). Christ was indeed the seed of Abraham through whom the world was to be blessed, "in turning every one of you from your wickedness" (Acts 3:26).

Members of the Sanhedrin of the Sadducee Party, were, upon hearing Peter's address, furious because 1) they considered Peter and John unauthorized teachers, 2) the apostles were proclaiming a man to be God, and 3) the apostles were teaching the reality of the Resurrection. Summoning the Temple police, the Sadducees had Peter and John arrested and held in prison overnight. Nevertheless, as a result of the miracle and Peter's declaration, approximately two thousand more people became Christians that very day.

Peter was questioned the next day by the irate high priest Annas. "By what power or by what name did you do this?" he demanded. Peter replied that it was done in the name of Jesus of Nazareth, "whom you crucified, whom God raised from the dead," that the man was healed. "There is salvation in no one else, for there is no other name under heaven given among men by which we must be saved" (Acts 4:12).

The high priest conferred with members of the Sanhedrin and decided that the miracle was so public and so obvious that it would be pointless and foolish to try to deny it. They simply ordered Peter and John not to proclaim that Jesus was Christ. The apostles were not theologians. They were simple fishermen. Surely they valued their lives and safety. They had seen what the wrath of the Sanhedrin did to their Master. They could be cowed by the august authority of so many learned and eminent men. "We'll let you go," they said, "but we don't want you to speak or teach at all in the name of Jesus. We forbid you."

"Whether it is right in the sight of God to listen to you rather than to God, you must judge, for we cannot but speak of what we have seen and heard," said the apostles. (Acts 4:19-20).

How could Peter and John have escaped being condemned to death there and then? The fact was that in recent days the Apostles had gained so much support that the Sanhedrin dared not take any punitive action, for fear of a riot and the bloody intervention by Pilate that they so dreaded.

Healings and other miracles continued and were interpreted as proofs of the power of Christ. People even carried their sick out into the streets and laid them there in beds and cots so that at least the shadow of Peter might fall on them. Crowds swarmed into Jerusalem from the neighboring countryside, bringing not only those physically afflicted, but also those possessed by evil spirits. St. Luke stated that they were *all* healed.

Boiling with rage, the Sadducees ordered their police to round up all twelve of the apostles and throw them into prison. The next morning the captain of the Temple police was told that "the men whom you put in prison are standing in the Temple and teaching the people." The apostles insisted that an angel from God came to them at night and opened the doors of the prison. Once again the Twelve were arrested and hauled before the Sanhedrin. Annas, tremendous in his wrath, roared, "We strictly charged you *not* to teach in . . . [Jesus'] name, yet here you have filled Jerusalem with your teaching and you intend to bring this man's blood upon us" (Acts 5:28; emphasis added). In other words, they said, "You're trying to blame us for the misfortune of your leader."

Peter's rejoinder was that "we must obey God rather than men." He went on to declare that "the God of our Fathers" had "raised Jesus whom you killed by hanging Him on the cross," and God elevated Him to His right hand as Ruler and Savior, to give Israel repentance and forgiveness of sins.

Once again, the apostles had accused the Jewish leaders of killing Jesus, once again they had proclaimed this crucified carpenter as Savior and Lord, the Messiah of Israel. Many members of the Sanhedrin were "convulsed with rage" and ready to sentence the Twelve to death, but were talked out of such a violent course of action by Gamaliel who, citing two cases of pseudo-Messiahs whose followings had petered out after their death, urged his colleagues to let the apostles alone. ". . .If this plan or this undertaking is of men, it will fail; but if it is of God, you will not be able to overthrow them. You might even be found opposing God" (Acts 5:38-39). So the Sanhedrin gave in to the advice of its most respected member and let the apostles go, but not before it ordered that each be tied to a pillar and lashed thirty-nine times with a whip tipped with bone.

The Church continued to increase, and things moved to a head. Most of the converts to Christianity were Jewish, but, of these, some were from the ranks of the Jerusalem Jews, who were very strict about observing the Law and very much influenced by the teaching of the Pharisees. Others were "Hellenists," who were partially assimilated into the Greco-Roman culture and much more liberal about observing the Law of Moses. These two groups normally did not get along, and tension continued even after conversion. The Christians, of course, set aside goods for the support of the poor, and eventually the Hellenist Christians complained that the widows of the Jerusalem faction were favored over those of their own group. It was at this point that the apostles decided that they could not devote themselves to "prayer and the ministry of the Word" if they had constantly to be involved in matters of finance and administration. Therefore, they appointed seven men (Stephen, Philip, Prochorus, Nicanor, Timon, Parmenas, and Nicolaus) as deacons, to look after the administrative end of the Church.

The most outstanding of these men was Stephen, who was sufficiently energetic that he had time not only to attend to business matters but to preach as well. Luke described him as "full of faith and the Holy Spirit . . . full of grace and power," relating "great wonders and signs among the people" (Acts 6:5, 8). In those days, not only did Christians in Jerusalem meet each day in private homes to pray, to listen to the apostles teach the words of Jesus, and to partake of the Eucharist, they also went to the Temple and to the synagogues with other Jews. In the synagogues they used to debate the rabbis concerning the Lordship of Christ. Stephen, a powerful speaker, blunt and outspoken, tended to infuriate his opponents. Eventually, members of five local synagogues, resenting Stephen because he had made fools of their rabbis, denounced the deacon to the Sanhedrin as a blasphemer. The assembled fathers gladly had Stephen arrested and brought to trial. The deacon was told that he stood accused of predicting that Jesus of Nazareth would destroy the Temple and change the customs that Moses handed down to them.

Stephen made a long defense in which he argued not only that Jesus was the fulfillment of Moses and all the prophets, but also that the rulers of Israel, like their ancestors, were just too proud and hardheaded to understand. After recounting God's dealings with Abraham, Isaac, Jacob, Moses, David, and Solomon, he pointed out that the Jews always made it a point of opposing the bearers of God's word. "You stiff-necked people, uncircumcised in heart and ears, you always resist the Holy Spirit. As your fathers did, so do you. Which of the prophets did not your fathers persecute? And they killed those who announced beforehand the coming of the Righteous One, whom you have now betrayed and murdered, you who have received the law as delivered by angels and did not keep it" (Acts 7:51-53).

It is not difficult to understand how Stephen's critical (if entirely justified) words were taken by his hearers as insulting and inflammatory. The majority of the Sanhedrin were gnashing their teeth in rage when Stephen gazed into heaven and declared, "Behold, I see the heavens opened and the Son of Man standing at the right hand of God." He had come to his point: Jesus was God. This was too much for the Sanhedrin. They stopped their ears and rushed at him. Apparently they were so enraged that they did not have him seized by the police; they grabbed him themselves and dragged him outside the city limits to stone him to death.

As the first stones from the angry leaders and the crowd that followed them began to strike him, Stephen prayed, ". . .Lord, Jesus, receive my spirit." Then, kneeling amidst the hail of missiles, gashed and bloody, he prayed audibly, ". . .Lord, do not hold this sin against them" (Acts 7:57-60).

Thus Stephen became the "Protomartyr," the first person of whom there is record who was killed because he proclaimed that Jesus was Lord of all humanity and that salvation alone was through Him, and who could have saved his life by denying Him. His death was followed by a "great persecution" against the Church in Jerusalem. We do not know the names of any other victims, except Prochorus, another deacon, who is mentioned by the Church Father Hippolytus. It is almost certain that there were other professors of Christ who were stoned as blasphemers, since nearly the entire Christian community — more than five thousand people — fled Jerusalem. Only the apostles remained.

One of the most vehement persecutors was Saul of Tarsus, an influential rabbi of the Pharisee faction, who directed the police to make searches of houses and imprison all those suspected of being followers of Jesus of Nazareth. Saul certainly was not the only prominent Jewish leader who wanted to destroy the Christian community. An indication of the violence and the bitterness toward Christians that existed among the Israelitic leaders of that time is that after Saul was converted to the New Faith, his colleagues did everything they could to kill him. His Christian brethren had to lower him in a basket from the city walls of Damascus in the dead of night, so that he could escape assassination.

Shortly after that the persecution died down, and the Christians who had fled to the towns and villages of Judaea, Galilee, and Samaria were able to win many converts from the people there. This persecution had taken place in A.D. 37, when there was no procurator in Judaea. Pilate had used excessive violence in suppressing a local uprising and had been recalled. During the time between his dismissal and the arrival of Marcellus, his temporary replacement, the Sanhedrin had a free hand in pursuing their anti-Christian policy. After Marcellus arrived, and, especially, after he was succeeded by Marullus, Pilate's permanent replacement, things got back in hand. The Roman government doubtless saw the violence on the part of the Jews as the beginnings of a civil war among the eternally innumerable factions of the Middle East, a war that could be avoided only if Rome stood by to take a firm hand.

Persecution was renewed, however, five years later, when Herod Agrippa became king of Israel in A.D. 42, succeeding to the control of all the territories when his grandfather, Herod the Great, had ruled before his death in 4 B.C. Agrippa, who was fifty-one, had been reared at the Imperial Court in Rome and was a lifelong friend of the current emperor, Claudius. Agrippa was popular with the Jews, not the least because he had saved them from the "Abomination of the Desolation" planned by Caligula.

As we have seen, Rome permitted Jews to exercise their religion and exempted them from the obligation to sacrifice to the National Gods. Caligula, a vicious, unbalanced egomaniac, succeeded to the throne in A.D. 37 and was determined that the Jews, if they were unwilling to worship Jupiter, Apollo, Mars and other traditional Roman gods, would nevertheless worship him! It had been the custom, in the preceding half-century, to worship the emperor's "genius," or protecting spirit, but an emperor enrolled as a full-fledged "god" only after death.

Caligula was the first emperor to insist on being worshipped personally as a god during his own lifetime. Around the year 40 he made plans to have a statue of himself erected in the Temple in Jerusalem. Then he would compel the Jews to offer sacrifice to him as well as to their Jehovah. The emperor's advisors warned him that such an action would lead to revolution. Should Caligula abominate the Temple of the Jews, bedlam would break loose in Palestine, and the inevitable rebellion could be suppressed only with such violence and bloodshed as would cause the emperor's name to stink forever. Unwilling to listen to reason, Caligula sent orders to Petronius, governor of Syria, to erect the statue. Petronius immediately replied that his conscience forbade him to comply with such an ill-advised command.

In the meantime, Herod Agrippa staged a lavish banquet for Caligula, a magnificent spread of the kind that the extravagant prince loved. Caligula, flushed with wine and high spirits, bade Agrippa ask him for a boon. As Agrippa's uncle Antipas had declared to his stepdaughter Salome a decade earlier, Caligula said, "I'll give you anything you desire. Just name it." Agrippa asked Caligula to respect the wishes of the Jews and not place his statue in their Temple. Caligula was taken aback, but felt that he could not go back on his word. Agreeing to forego his pet project, he vented his wrath on the uncooperative Governor Petronius, whom he ordered to commit suicide. Happily, before that message reached Syria, Petronius received word that, along with his wife and daughter, the tyrant had been butchered by his bodyguards on January 24, 41.

Claudius I, who succeeded Caligula, granted his old friend Agrippa control of his grandfather's old dominions. Upon his arrival in Israel, Agrippa did everything possible to ingratiate himself to the Jewish leaders. He moved the capital back from Caesarea to Jerusalem, and, at least in public, scrupulously observed the Jewish Law. In his aim to please the most influential of his new subjects, Agrippa began another persecution of the Christian community. The new king felt that he needed the support of the high priestly House of Annas as well as that of the rich and powerful Sadducees. Although he probably could not have cared less about the teachings of Jesus, in order to consolidate his base of power Agrippa began to take action against the Christians.

In A.D. 43 he arrested James, the son of Zebedee, one of the Twelve. The former fisherman was hauled before the Sanhedrin and tried for blasphemy. Witnesses declared that the prisoner had preached for years that God had made Himself known in human flesh in the person of a carpenter from Nazareth named Jesus. The legislative assembly quickly sentenced the apostle to death. Evidently a Roman citizen, James was condemned to die by decapitation rather than crucifixion.

As James was being escorted to the place where his head was to be struck from his body, one of the witnesses at his trial appeared. "Will you please forgive me, sir, for bringing about your death?" James was silent for a while, then embraced the man and declared, "Peace be with you, my brother." The repentant witness was, of course, arrested. He declared himself a convert to Christianity and was executed along with the apostle.

Peter was also arrested, and Herod Agrippa intended to kill him, too, but the leader of the apostles mysteriously escaped from prison and disappeared from Palestine. Agrippa probably intended to comply with the wishes of the high priests and Sadducees in eradicating the followers of Jesus from his dominions, but he was stayed in his unhallowed plans by the hand of death. In the spring of 44, Agrippa presided over thanksgiving celebrations for his friend Claudius' successful military campaign in Britain. Several days of Roman-style games were planned in Caesarea. On the second day of the games, the king entered the stadium dressed in glittering cloth of silver and was given a resounding ovation by the spectators, most of whom were pagans. Without any objection from the king, the crowds hailed him as a god. Shortly after he was seated, Agrippa was seized with violent abdominal pains and had to leave. Five days later he died, apparently of gangrene of the bowel.

With Agrippa's death, his domains were reorganized into

the procuratorial province of Palaestina. The new governor, Cuspius Fadus, took no action against the Christian community, which began to recover. Indeed, for eighteen years the Christians were left in peace. The head of the Christian community in Jerusalem was James the Righteous, a man known as "the Lord's brother." Protestants believe that James was a son of Mary and Joseph, born after Jesus. The Catholic Church teaches the perpetual virginity of Mary, and describe him as a cousin. Eusebius believed that James was Jesus' stepbrother.

James was an extraordinarily holy man. The second-century historian Hegesippus related that he was, in fact, "holy from his birth." Like John the Baptist, James drank no wine or any alcoholic beverage and was a vegetarian. He never cut his hair or beard and never bathed. He spent so much time on his knees in prayer that his knees grew hard and calloused like a camel's.

Like the young Paul, James was a devout Pharisee, and he was at first embarrassed and angered by Jesus. It was only after the Resurrection, when Jesus appeared to James, that the "Righteous One" was converted. Even then, he strongly insisted that new Christians keep the Jewish Law and its attendant regulations. He had several run-ins with Peter and Paul, who demanded to know how he could ask converts from paganism to keep a Law with which neither they nor their ancestors could successfully comply. In A.D. 49, it was agreed, when all the surviving apostles met in ecumenical council in Jerusalem, that converts to the faith from paganism would be required to keep only the laws forbidding immorality, apostasy, and murder, but that converts from Judaism were bound to the entirety of the Judaic legal system, including the practice of circumcision.

James not only was zealous for the Law of Moses, he was also enthusiastic in his devotion to the Blessed Virgin Mary, who must have gone to her heavenly home during this period. In the fixed portion, or *ordinary, of the liturgy*, which James allegedly composed for the Jerusalem Christians, is the prayer, "Hail, Mary, highly favored: the Lord is with thee; blessed art thou among women and blessed is the fruit of thy womb, for thou didst bear the Savior of our souls. Hail in the highest, our all-holy, pure, most blessed, glorious Lady, the God-mother and ever-virgin Mary."[2]

James' insistence that Christians in Jerusalem keep all the Jewish ritual laws was part of his attempt to keep peace with the increasingly hostile Jewish community. Now that Christianity was spreading through the Roman world, the apostles and other evangelists were encountering considerable hostility from the Jewish populations of cities throughout the empire. Luke recorded that Paul and Barnabas were driven out of Pisidian Antioch in Asia Minor (now Turkey) by Jewish mobs, and shortly afterwards were stoned by hostile Israelites in the city of Iconium. When the two apostles moved on to Lystra, another city of Asia Minor, crowds of Jews from Pisidian Antioch and Iconium followed them and stoned Paul, leaving him for dead. In addition, the apostles encountered riots by Jews in other cities where there were numerous conversions to Christianity. When Paul came to Jerusalem in 58, James stressed to him that if he did not want any trouble there he should, like the local Christians, show that he was a model Jew and go to the Temple to observe the traditional rites of purification. Paul complied. Even so, he was mobbed in the Temple by a crowd of Jews who chanted, "Kill him! Kill him!" The apostle was saved from death only by the intervention of the Roman authorities. Even then, when it became known that forty fanatics had made a vow not to eat or drink until they had killed Paul, the Roman authorities had need of two hundred infantrymen, seventy horsemen, and two hundred troops to move Paul out of Jerusalem in the dead of the night to the relative safety of Caesarea.

While no major persecution was in progress in Palestine at the time, the hostility of the local leaders was growing. The smoldering fire of hate blazed into a raging conflagration in 62, when procurator Porcius Festus died. Before his successor arrived from Rome, Palestine came under the control of Ananus the high priest, a Sadducee who has been characterized as a man of "vindictive insolence." Ananus immediately began to arrest Christians. One of his first victims was, of course, James.

"Restrain your followers," Ananus insisted. "They have been acting as if they believed Jesus was the Messiah." Emphasizing James' unimpeachable credibility, he urged the bishop to declare publicly, on the Temple grounds, "the true facts about Jesus."[3]

Did Ananus and company really doubt that James sincerely believed that Jesus was the Son of God? Did they believe that James, under pressure, would disabuse his followers of the notion of Jesus' divinity? Did they really believe that this man, whose integrity of character was admitted by even his most implacable opponents, had been proclaiming a lie? Or did they feel that, under the threat of death, James, like everyone else they knew, would admit to anything?

The aged bishop was compelled to stand on the balcony of the Temple roof before the immense throng in the Temple courtyard, who were in Jerusalem to celebrate the Passover. Many of these, including a great number of influential and powerful people, had come to a profession of faith in Jesus. Ananus and other members of the Sanhedrin stood beneath the balcony, waiting for James' recantation. "Righteous One, in whom all of us ought to have confidence, for as much as the people are led astray after Jesus, a man who was crucified, declare to us what is meant by the expression, 'The Door of Jesus.' " Seeing so eminent and respected a man ready to address them, the crowds, unaware that James was a prisoner, pressed forward to hear him.

"Why do you question me concerning the Son of Man?" James proclaimed. "He is sitting in heaven at the right hand of the Great Power and is about to come upon the clouds of heaven!"

The high priest and his colleagues were taken aback. Even when threatened with death, this infuriating man would not renounce his faith. Now, after they had publicly declared that everyone was "obliged to accept" the word of the "Righteous One," hundreds of people were putting their trust in Jesus. The crowd was cheering James and shouting, "Hosanna to the Son of David!"

The members of the Sanhedrin conferred among themselves as James continued to proclaim Jesus as Lord and Savior. "We made a bad mistake," they said. "We had better go up and throw him down, so that they will be frightened and not believe him!" So they loudly interrupted James' speech. "Oh! Oh!" they shouted. "The Just Man is also in error!"

Immediately some of them rushed up the stairs and seized the old bishop and pushed him off the balcony. As James lay injured on the ground, hostile members of the Sanhedrin surrounded him and shouted to the crowd, "Let us stone James the Righteous!" They began to take stones (which they had brought just in case the Righteous One would not cooperate) and began to pelt James with them. Most of the crowd were outraged and horrified, but there was nothing they could do. James the Righteous was stoned by their indignant leaders and a group of thugs whom they had brought with them, just in case a little force was necessary to make their point.

Amid the hail of rocks, James knelt and prayed, "I entreat Thee, Lord God and Father, forgive them; they know not what they do."

"Stop! What are you doing? The Righteous One is praying for you!" yelled members of the crowd. But there was nothing they could do. As James lay on the ground, bruised and bloody, one of Ananus' hit-men went up to him and, with a heavy club, beat his brains out.[4]

Before Ananus and his supporters could create further bloodshed, Lucceius Albinus, the new procurator, rushed to Jerusalem, took charge, and deposed Ananus. Once again the Christian community in Jerusalem was saved.

Eight years later, to suppress a major revolt, Roman troops poured into Palestine, burned Jerusalem and the Temple, and slaughtered many thousands of inhabitants. After that the Sanhedrin no longer was a major force in the persecution of the Church, although Christians for many years had to experience much hostility and violence from Jews throughout the empire. From now on, however, the Church would have to face the might of a much more powerful opponent — the government of the Roman Empire.

# 3

# The light in the darkness: The Church in the pagan world

In the previous three decades, Christianity had made dramatic inroads into the Roman world as the apostles and their followers took the Gospel to the farthest limits of the empire and even beyond. Paul was instrumental in winning many converts, both Jewish and Gentile, in Greece and Asia Minor, but one must not nurture the misconception that the spread of Christianity was due to the single-handed efforts of this one apostle. In the first century, the Good News was carried by other apostles and their disciples to Italy, Gaul, Spain, Britain, North Africa, and even beyond the borders of the empire, into Persia and India.

In order to understand the appeal of Christianity to the inhabitants of the Roman Empire and the eventual hostility on the part of its rulers, it is necessary to understand the religious atmosphere that prevailed in those days. The National Religion of Rome was very different from Christianity, Judiasm, and most other modern religions. It was a public, not a private religion. It concerned outward acts rather than inward creeds and purity of heart. The position of the Roman government was that the state should expect prosperity and protection only if the spirits who were associated with the city of Rome, deities such as Jupiter, Mars, and Apollo, were shown the proper respect by all inhabitants of the empire. Rome had conquered many different civilizations with many different religious traditions. The government had no objection whatsoever if individuals continued to worship their traditional gods, so long as the gods of Rome were honored too. This reverence consisted only in the burning of incense before statues of the emperor and the National Gods on various ceremonial occasions.

The Jews alone were exempted from the obligation to worship the National Gods, but they were required to offer sacrifice and prayer to their God in their Temple in behalf of the emperor and the Roman state. Still, many Romans could not understand why members of this peculiar race were unwilling at least to go through the formalities of the National Religion, even if their hearts were not in it. Many Roman intellectuals were atheists and agnostics, but nevertheless complied with the trivial obligations of the National Religion, even endorsing the practice as a means of preserving a cultural and patriotic unity. As we have seen in the case of Caligula, there was periodic talk of rescinding the exemption and compelling Israel, too, to offer sacrifice to the gods of Rome.

After fulfilling one's obligations to the National Gods, an inhabitant of the Roman Empire was free to pursue any religion he chose, or none at all. The National Religion was concerned with the welfare of the state, not that of the individual. And so, to address the inner longings of their souls, the people of the empire turned to a bewildering variety of cults. There were so many of them that it is difficult to characterize what a "typical" Roman believed, if, in fact, there was such a thing as a "typical Roman."

Many intellectuals, as we have said, were outright skeptical of the existence of any personal gods. A writer of the school of Aristotle, who said that "God" is synonymous with "necessity," declared, "God is to us a law, evenly balanced, receptive neither to correction nor change."[1] Lucius Annaeus Seneca (c.4 B.C.-A.D. 65), the celebrated Stoic philosopher, wrote of the National Religion: "These observances a philosopher will maintain because they are imposed by law, not because they will please the gods." He went on to say that the "whole base throng of gods," the product of superstition, should still be worshipped, but only "to set an example, not because they exist."[2] Such intellectuals involved themselves in philosophical systems such as Stoicism, Epicureanism, Platonism, and Skepticism, which were generally concerned with personal conduct and man's relationship with the universe, but which seldom admitted belief in anything like a personal god.

Many ordinary people turned to what were called "mystery cults." These societies, nearly all of them imports from the eastern provinces, professed to impart a secret knowledge to the initiate which was supposed to guarantee him either eternal life or some other benefit in time or eternity.

One of the most popular of these cults was that of the Eleusinian Mysteries, which had its origins in Greece. This cult centered around Persephone, daughter of Demeter, the Earth Mother. Persephone was kidnapped by Hades, God of the Dead. Through the efforts of her mother, Persephone was ultimately accorded the privilege of returning to the world above for half of the year, while during the other half she was constrained to remain in the underworld as the bride of the death-god. This myth originally was associated with the mystery of the changing seasons, but eventually it was extended to the quest for eternal life. When, after a period of fasting and wandering about the seashore with lighted torches to imitate Demeter in her search for Persephone, the time came to be admitted to the Mysteries, the sacred object of the cult — an ear of corn, the symbol of life — was revealed to the initiates in a brilliant light enhanced by the use of mirrors. The initiates engaged in a ritual meal in which they professed to be participating in the life of the goddess Demeter. They insisted that eternal life was obtainable only through their prescribed rituals. "Thrice blessed are they who have seen these rites and then go to the gates of Hades, for they alone have life there, but all others have only woe."[3]

Although he professed a belief in a sort of immortality, the cultist in the Eleusinian Mysteries had no concept of a god who loved him unconditionally as a person, and whom he was to love in return. It was simply a matter of getting something out of the gods. The deities were seen as a source of benefits who, through the proper magical rites, could be manipulated.

Another popular mystery religion was Mithraism, which was limited to men and was popular among soldiers. This cult came from Iran. Its devotees believed that the good god Mithras, a benefactor and supporter of mankind, wrestled with the powers of darkness in the person of a cosmic bull and established civilization on earth before he ascended into heaven, from whence he aided his followers in their constant struggle against the evil god Ahriman. Mithraists therefore believed that God and the devil were equals. Observing a liturgy that one writer described as "a mass of occult hocus-pocus," Mithraists met in chapels called caves. There were seven levels of initiation: the Raven, the Bridegroom, the Soldier, the Lion, the Persian, the Courier of the Sun, and finally, the Father. Initiates had to undergo tests of endurance, such as ordeals of extreme heat and cold. They practiced a form of communion, partaking of bread and wine, through which they professed to participate in the life of Mithras. They believed in a world to come, but felt that its attainment was based solely on works. If a man's good deeds outweighed the bad, he was admitted into paradise.

Mithraism and the Eleusinian Mysteries were tame compared to other cults that found a popular following in the Roman Empire. There was, for instance, the Bacchanalian, or Dionysiac, Mysteries, which were likewise supposed to confer eternal life upon initiates. This cult centered around Bacchus, or Dionysius, the god of wine, and, needless to say, the consumption of strong drink was a very prominent feature of the worship. In fact, initiates drank and danced themselves into a frenzy and concluded their rites in a grisly sexual debauch. Whereas the sacred symbol of the Eleusinians was the ear of corn, for the Bacchanalians, it was the phallus. The eternal life which the initiates expected was seen as one great drunken orgy! The cult was so wild and had such a bad reputation that the Roman Senate banned it as early as 186 B.C. It went underground, however, and in the first century, the Bacchanalian Mysteries had many adherents.

Another cult that claimed to confer immortality upon its initiates was that of Isis. A female goddess first worshipped in Egypt, Isis was the wife of Osiris, who was killed and cut to pieces by his jealous brother. Isis was able to collect all the severed pieces and sew them together — except for the organ of procreation of his body — which she could not find. Then, by means of special incantations, she brought him back to life again to rule as king over the dead. The devotees of Isis, led by white-robed, cymbal-banging priests with shaved heads, practiced a sort of baptism. In it, according to some scholars, the initiate was held under the water until he was at the point of drowning and had an "out-of-the-body experience." Indeed, initiates professed to approach the bounds of death and be "carried through all the elements," to return again to the "upper air," after seeing the sun "glowing with brilliant light," and beholding in person the "gods of heaven and hell."[4]

Then there was the cult of Cybele, or the Great Mother. The priests castrated themselves, wore women's clothing, and bathed in ox blood.[5] The initiates likewise were baptized in the blood of a bull and partook of a sacramental meal of milk. In this way they professed to be uniting themselves with the Great Mother.

Whether or not the Romans belonged to one or more of these cults, nearly all inhabitants of the Roman Empire held one belief in common — Fate. British historian Michael Grant called this belief "one of the most terrible doctrines which has ever oppressed humanity."[6]

Nearly all Romans believed that the movement of the heavenly bodies — especially the seven planets and twelve signs of the Zodiac — controlled everything that went on, including human behavior. Moreover, it was almost universally held that if one properly studied the movements of the heavenly bodies, he would find there decreed everything that would happen in the future.

Along with this belief in astrology, the typical Roman believed in portents and omens. That is, an unusual occurrence was supposed to foretell some significant event in the immediate future. For example, the respected historian Cornelius Tacitus (c.55-c.120) wrote about the portents that supposedly foretold the assassination of Claudius I in 54:

> A series of prodigies indicated changes for the worse. Standards and soldiers' tents were set on fire from the sky. A swarm of bees settled on the pediment of the Capitoline temple. Half-bestial children were born, and a pig with hawk's claws.[7]

The upshot of all this is that most Romans believed that everything was predetermined. Free will was but an illusion. "Most men," wrote Tacitus, "find it natural to believe that lives are predestined from birth."[8] Moreover, it was widely believed that even the gods were subject to the Law of Fate, manifest in the stars.

Few people entertained any hope of an attractive existence in the hereafter. Many philosophers believed that the soul was absorbed into the Creator, to lose all individuality in a kind of Nirvana, such as is believed in to this day by the Hindus and Buddhists. A belief in reincarnation was also common among intellectuals. Some philosophers of the School of Plato believed that after one thousand years of penance and purification as a disembodied shade in the world below, the soul entered a new incarnation. After repeated incarnations, the soul was either purified to the point that it would be absorbed into the Divine Element or was so corrupted that it was finally condemned to eternal torment.

Most uneducated people believed that if the soul had any existence at all after death, it was as a ghost. Homer's famous lines, "Better to be a slave of a poor man on earth than reign as king over the dead," still reflected widespread belief in the first century of the Christian era. Common people believed that ghosts from the world below were constantly breaking through into the world above, and had to be appeased to prevent "hauntings" and other personal calamities, just as the National Gods had to be appeased to prevent public catastrophes. It was commonly believed that if the ghosts of family members were not appeased with soothing offerings of bowls of warm milk and goblets of blood, they would come and "get" the living. People would be struck dead, and legions of ghosts would rush howling through city streets.

There were no personal gods, lovingly concerned with people. On the contrary, mankind was menaced by evil spirits who had to be appeased to prevent disaster. Human choice and human will was illusory, nor was there hope for any happiness beyond the grave. Even members of mystery cults had no sense of anticipation of the joys of the hereafter. Except for the Bacchanalians and their absurd and obscene concept of eternal orgies, initiates may have believed in the survival of the soul, but only in a state far inferior than that which it had enjoyed on earth.

The epitaphs on Roman graves echo this lack of hope:

"I was not, I am not, I care not."

"I am ashes, ashes are earth, earth is a goodness. Therefore I am not dead."

"May the passerby who has seen these flowers and read this epitaph say to himself, 'This flower is Flavia's body.' "

"What I ate and drank I have with me. What I left behind I have lost."

"We are nothing, as we were before. Reader, consider how swiftly we mortals drop back from nothing to nothing."[9]

What a contrast there was between those inscriptions and others, from roughly the same period in time, which marked the graves of Christians. Typical Christian epitaphs were:

"Live in Christ."

"Petrolanus, who desired to see God now sees Him."

"Alexander is not dead, but lives above the stars, and his body rests in the tomb."

"Prima, thou livest in the glory of God and in the peace of our Lord Jesus Christ."

"To Cyriacus, sweetest son. Mayest thou live in the Holy Spirit."

"Our Lady, and Queen . . . we commend to thee our daughter . . . who lived 10 mos."

"Petronia, the wife of a Levite, the type of modesty. In this place I lay my bones. Spare your tears, dear husband and daughters, and believe that it is forbidden to weep for one who lives in God."

"Septimius Praetextatus Caecilianus, servant of God, who led a worthy life. If I have served Thee, O Lord, I have not repented and I will give thanks to Thy Name. He gave up his soul to God at the age of 33 yrs. and 6 mos."

"Come nigh unto me, my Lord and Saviour. Be Thou my guide, I entreat Thee, Thou light of them for whom the hour of death is past."[10]

In Judaism, which had considerable appeal before the coming of Christ, people were introduced to a religion which taught the existence of one holy God who governed the universe and required holiness and righteousness of all individuals. To become a Jew, however, a man had to submit not only to the painful and embarrassing rite of circumcision, but also to adhere to a confusing and burdensome body of laws and regulations governing every aspect of one's life. Moreover, some strains of Judaism offered no more hope of life beyond the grave than most pagan religions.

In Christianity, however, the inquirer was told not only of a God who created heaven and earth out of nothing, but a God who loved mankind so much that in the recent past He came to earth as a man to die to pay the penalty for men's sins, a penalty which even the most scrupulous attempts at righteousness and the most punctilious attempts to keep the Holy Law could not expiate. God loved every human being individually. Imagine the joy with which many pagans must have received the words of Jesus that declared, "Are not two sparrows sold for a penny? And not one of them will fall to the ground without your Father's will. But even the hairs of your head are all numbered. Fear not, therefore you are of more value than many sparrows" (Matthew 10:29-31). One can imagine the rapture with which the heathen heard, "Ask, and it will be given you; seek, and you will find; knock, and it will be opened to you. For every one who asks receives, and he who seeks finds, and to him who knocks it will be opened. Or what man of you, if his son asks him for . . . a fish, will give him a serpent? If you then, who are evil, know how to give good gifts to your children, how much more will your Father who is in heaven give good things to those who ask him!" (Matthew 7:7-11).

The inquirer learned that he *did* count, that he *did* make a difference, that he *did* have a choice in life. If he became a believer, he was baptized with the assurance that the God of heaven and earth was claiming him as His own and sending His Holy Spirit to dwell within him to guide and direct and protect him forever. He was then admitted to a sacramental meal in which he participated, not in the obscene existence of some demon-god, but in the very life of Christ Himself who claimed as His own all who put their trust in Him. Moreover, he was taught that life did not cease at death, nor was one reincarnated endlessly, nor did one become a specter floating through the void. He was taught that the sufferings of this life were "preparing for us an eternal weight of glory beyond all comparison, because we look not to the things that are seen but to the things that are unseen; for the things that are seen are transient, but the things that are unseen are eternal" (2 Corinthians 4:17-18). Instead of being stripped at death to enter an inferior existence, the Christian was further clothed in a better body, not subject to decay, and admitted into a better existence. "For while we are still in this tent, we sigh with anxiety; not that we would be unclothed, but that we would be further clothed, so that what is mortal may be swallowed up by life (2 Corinthians 5:4).

How joyful it was to know that one was not at the mercy of blind fate, that "God so loved the world that he gave his only Son, that whoever believes in him should not perish but have eternal life" (John 3:16). How wonderful to know that God was not an angry spirit who had to be appeased, but that He loved and desired the love of His children. How glorious to know that existence did not stop at the grave but was fulfilled and perfected in a glorious eternity in the presence of the Lord! No wonder Christianity spread like wildfire between Pentecost in 33 and the first attempts by the Romans to stamp it out in 64.

# 4

# Enemies of the human race: The persecution by Nero

By July 64, Nero Claudius Drusus Germanicus had been emperor of Rome for nearly a decade. Born in December 37, he had been only seventeen when he succeeded Claudius. His father, Domitius Ahenobarbus, was described as a man "hateful in every walk of life," so violent and cruel that he once killed a slave for refusing to drink as much wine as he commanded, and on another occasion gouged out a man's eyes after a slight disagreement. Nero's mother, Agrippina, was the sister as well as the lover of the detestable Caligula, and after the death of Ahenobarbus, she married her uncle Claudius, who subsequently adopted the twelve-year-old Nero. When Agrippina had Claudius killed and seized power in a coup in 54, she had her son proclaimed emperor and held the reins of power for five years until Nero, then twenty-two, decided that he wanted to rule in his own right and had her killed.

Nero was about five-feet, six-inches tall, with freckles and yellow blond hair. He enhanced the nearsighted vision of his grey eyes with a sapphire looking glass. At twenty-seven, after years of intemperate eating and drinking, the emperor had a bloated, jowly face, a pot belly, and skinny legs. He had first been married to his cousin Octavia, Claudius' daughter by one of his earlier wives, the adulterous and dissipated Messalina, but he had recently killed her and married the wife of his friend Otho. His present wife was Poppaea Sabina, who was then thirty-three years of age and rumored to be sympathetic to Judaism.

According to historian Gaius Suetonius Tranquillus (c.69-c.140), Nero's private life was characterized by acts of wantonness, lust, extravagance, avarice, and cruelty. He was fond of roaming the streets of Rome at night with his cronies, beating people up, robbing shops, raping women, and behaving like a common street thug. Eventually he was nearly beaten to death by a senator whose wife he had "handled indecently." Nero guzzled, gluttonized, and fornicated "from midday to midnight." According to Suetonius he "prostituted his own chastity" to the point that he "defiled every part of his body." After living in incest with his mother, he took to abusing not only married women, but children of both sexes. In fact, he castrated young boys to treat as women. For his amusement, the depraved emperor was wont to dress as a wild animal and hurl himself at men and women tied at stakes, there to "attack their private parts." Cynical, he often remarked that "no man was chaste or pure in any part of his body, but that most of them concealed their vices and cleverly drew a veil over them."[1]

As cruel and bloodthirsty as his uncle Caligula, "he showed neither discrimination nor moderation in putting to death whomsoever he pleased on any pretext whatsoever." He ordered one victim killed because he kept a bust of one of Julius Caesar's assassins in his home. Another he executed because he found the man's expression sullen. Certainly any senator, any public official against whom Nero entertained the slightest suspicion, was killed without the slightest compunction. "No prince has ever known the power that I have!" Nero exulted.

The emperor had nothing but contempt for most of the cults practiced in his empire. He once expressed an interest in the cult of the Great Mother, but later came to despise it so intensely that he publicly urinated on the statue of the goddess. Of course, he was very much concerned that all of his subjects remain loyal to him through the National Religion. Moreover, like Caligula, he insisted that he be reverenced personally as a god.

Nero was probably the first Roman emperor to have any meaningful knowledge of Christianity. Although the Empress Poppaea was said to be favorably disposed toward Judaism, one of Nero's concubines, Acte by name, was said to have been sympathetic to Christianity. Whether Nero ever took the time to discuss such exalted matters with these women is doubtful;

he must, however, have been aware of the activities of Peter, the leader of the new cult, who was frequently in Rome and was winning a number of converts.

Then too, several years earlier there had been brought from Palestine to Rome a most unusual person, a little Jewish man in his late fifties, with a bald head, a big Semitic nose, a long grey beard, and skinny legs. He was a merry little man with sparkling blue eyes, who was always smiling. His close friends called him Saul, but publicly he was known by his Roman name Paulus, or Paul. Paul had been arrested by Roman authorities in Jerusalem, where he appeared to be the cause of a riot. Originally they thought he was some sort of revolutionary, but even when the governor ascertained that this was not the case, the Sanhedrin at Jerusalem exerted so much pressure that Paul had been kept in custody for two years. After that time, certain that he could not get a fair trial in Jerusalem, Paul had "appealed to Caesar," which meant that his trial would be moved to Rome to be judged by the emperor in person.

Two years went by before Paul obtained his hearing before Nero. During that time the apostle was under house arrest, but was allowed to meet with members of the large Christian community at Rome. At last, around 62, he had his trial. No one is certain of its outcome, or even of the charges leveled against Paul. Most likely the charge was sedition. The Jerusalem ruling class, according to Josephus, normally had the ear of the empress, and it is likely that they used their influence with her to lobby Nero against Paul. Very possibly, they suggested to the emperor that this renegade rabbi was disloyal to the gods of Rome, and that he professed to work in behalf of a king whose aim it was to conquer the whole world.

Most scholars believe that Paul was acquitted. Probably Nero, like Pontius Pilate thirty years earlier, was convinced that the kingship of Christ, since it was "not of this world," was no threat to him. Whatever happened, it would have become clear to Nero that Christianity and Judaism were two distinct religions. If Christianity was a distinct religion, however, then it needed a government charter to exist. Since it had no such charter, it was illegal. For the time being, however, Nero made no effort to move against the Christians. Then, during the evening of July 19, 64, things changed dramatically.

Let Tacitus tell us what happened. The weather had been hot and dry, and that evening a strong wind was blowing when fire broke out in some of the shops near the Circus Maximus, which sold "inflammable goods."

> Fanned by the wind, the conflagration instantly grew and swept the whole length of the Circus. There were no walled mansions or temples, or any other obstructions which could arrest it. First, the fire swept violently over the level spaces. Then it climbed the hills, but returned to ravage the lower ground again. It outstripped every countermeasure. The ancient city's narrow winding streets and irregular blocks encouraged its progress.
>
> Terrified shrieking women, helpless old and young, people intent on their own safety, people unselfishly supporting invalids or waiting for them, fugitives and lingerers alike — all heightened the confusion. When people looked back, menacing flames sprang up before them or outflanked them. When they escaped to a neighboring quarter, the fire followed — even districts believed remote proved to be involved. Finally, with no idea where or what to flee, they crowded onto the country roads, or lay in the fields. Some who had lost everything — even their food for the day — could have escaped, but preferred to die. So did others, who had failed to rescue their loved ones. Nobody dared fight the flames. Attempts to do so were prevented by menacing gangs. Torches, too, were openly thrown in by men crying that they acted under orders. Or they may just have wanted to plunder unhampered.[2]

Nero was at Anzio when the fire broke out, and returned to find the fire menacing the imperial palace. Soon the entire area of Palatine Hill, with all the imperial apartments, was in flames. Nero acted competently and humanely. He opened the remaining public buildings as well as his own private parks to the homeless. He also constructed emergency accommodations. He saw to it that food was brought in from neighboring towns and that the price of corn was cut so that the destitute could afford it.

When after six days the fire was finally controlled, Nero and his advisors were overwhelmed by the extent of the disaster. Only four of Rome's fourteen districts remained intact. The losses in terms of public records, works of art, and historic buildings were staggering. Even the shrine containing the official images of Rome's National Gods was lost.

Nero set out at once to rebuild the city. In the gutted areas the streets had been extremely narrow, with tenements six stories high or more. The emperor now decreed that the streets in the new Rome were to be broad, and houses no more than seventy feet tall. He further decreed that pillared colonnades be constructed on either side of each street and in front of each dwelling place to provide shade and lessen the danger of fire. Numerous courtyards, gardens, and public parks were designed. Row-houses were forbidden. Each dwelling was to be surrounded by land on all four sides. The lower story of each building had to be built of fireproof stone, and no wooden beams were allowed below the second floor. Moreover, every house was supplied with water conduits, and public fountains were provided on every corner.

Despite Nero's humanitarian efforts in behalf of the stricken populace and his conscientious efforts to rebuild the city, the emperor found himself the object of his people's hatred. Long wearied of reports of imperial debaucheries and incompetence, citizens were angered by Nero's plans to construct a lavish new palace for himself. They felt that he was devoting far more attention and lavishing far more expense on the rebuilding of his own private residences than on his plans for the common people. In fact, it began to be rumored that Nero had ordered the city fired so that he would have space to build his gigantic Golden House. It was further whispered that Nero had been seen during the fire, standing on a height overlooking the blazing city, singing a ballad about the burning of Troy, accompanying himself with a lyre (not a fiddle — violins were not then in use). The populace began to express its growing outrage at the dissipated emperor's misrule.

Nero sought to divert public scorn from himself. He found a victim: the Christian community. He had never liked them anyway. Religion was of no interest to him, but he had been mildly concerned during the trial of that fellow Paul two years earlier. This old Jew assured him that his "king" was not of this world, and he had believed him. But had not Paul made a comment about the world being destroyed by fire? Paul's king would come after a fire destroyed the world. Now it was apparent what his plans were, under the syrup of all that disgusting spirituality. The great and mighty Nero was always right when he believed that apparent goodness was only a front for baser motives. The Christians planned to burn Rome and him with it, and then set Paul, or maybe Peter, as king. He saw through this cunning malignity. This old Jew had duped him. Now he was going to get even with Peter and Paul and all their followers. Nobody could treat glorious Caesar this way and get away with it. Besides, there were numerous reports of men throwing torches into homes, saying that they were acting under orders. People believed that he, Nero, had ordered them to burn the city down. But it was all a filthy Christian plot. Those aides of his who said such incidents were the act of looters who wanted to fire the houses of the rich as an excuse to plunder them, such people were trying to pull the wool over his godlike eyes. Maybe they should die too! And so it was probably in the year following the fire, the year when Nero kicked the pregnant Empress Poppaea to death, that he ordered the extermination of the entire Christian population of the empire.

First he ordered all known Christians arrested. Under torture, myriads more were implicated. Tacitus wrote that an "immense multitude" were sent to their deaths. Paul was arrested, probably in Greece, and taken back to the capital and thrown into prison to await execution. From his cell in Rome he planned two letters to his great friend, Timothy of Lystra, bishop of Ephesus. In the last, he exhorted the prelate to "always be steady, endure suffering, do the work of an evangelist, fulfil your ministry. For I am already on the point of being sacrificed; the time of my departure has come. I have fought the good fight, I have finished the race, I have kept the faith. Henceforth there is laid up for me the crown of righteousness, which the Lord, that righteous judge, will award to me on that Day, and not only to me but also to all who have loved his appearing" (2 Timothy 4:5-8).

Some time in the spring of 67 Paul was beheaded. Around the same time Peter, the head of the entire Christian community, was crucified along with his wife. Peter had apparently been in Rome at the time of the fire and had escaped the flames with his wife and invalid daughter. When the imperial wrath fell upon the Christian community, he had been urged to flee for safety, as some of the brethren were convinced that the faith could not be preserved without him. (Peter was then seventy or more. What were they going to do in the event of his death from natural causes?) Peter was thus persuaded to leave Rome. Hiding on the outskirts of the city, he dreamed he saw Jesus, as if the Master were entering the city with a cross-beam strapped to His shoulders, just as Peter had seen Him in Jerusalem many years before. "*Quo vadis?*" asked Peter in Latin. "Where are you going?" The Lord replied that He was going to Rome to be crucified again. When Peter awoke, he realized that it was not God's will for him to flee, that now he was to share literally in his Lord's passion. Doubtless he remembered the words of his risen Lord so many years before: "Truly, truly, I say to you, when you were young, you girded yourself and walked where you would; but when you are old, you will stretch out your hands, and another will gird you and carry you where you do not wish to go." Peter also remembered the words that followed: "Follow me" (John 21:18-19). And he followed.

Doubtless it was from prison that Peter wrote to the Christians in the provinces, warning them that "for a little while you may have to suffer various trials, so that the genuineness of your faith, more precious than gold which though perishable is tested by fire, may redound to praise and glory and honor at the revelation of Jesus Christ" (1 Peter 1:6-7). He told them, ". . .Do not be surprised at the fiery ordeal which comes upon you to prove you, as though something strange were happening to you. But rejoice in so far as you share Christ's sufferings, that you may also rejoice and be glad when his glory is revealed" (1 Peter 4:12-13). Peter went on to say that Christians should understand that the same experience of suffering was required of the brotherhood throughout the world. "And after you have suffered a little while, the God of all grace, who has called you to his eternal glory in Christ, will himself restore, establish, and strengthen you" (1 Peter 5:10). And so, Peter and his wife, Perpetua, were led to the cross, confident that after their sufferings, the Lord for whom they had figuratively as well as literally given their lives would restore them, establish them, and strengthen them in His kingdom beyond the bounds of this earthly life.

And so, throughout the empire, Christians were rounded up and put to death, by crucifixion, by fire, and often in even more cruel ways. In Rome, Nero held mass executions in the rebuilt Circus Maximus and in his gardens, which were located near the present site of the Vatican. As the emperor watched amidst the crowds, Christians were torn to pieces by maddened dogs or attached to crosses, covered with flammable substances, and set on fire to illuminate the night.

Nero declared that his victims were being punished for conspiring to burn Rome and put him off his throne. They were haters of the human race. He circulated stories that they drank blood, committed incest, and did other violent and immoral things. Nero, of course, believed that everyone did these things — as he himself did — but expressed indignation that these people should be such hypocrites as to maintain that they lived purely.

The Christians were hated, mostly because they stayed to themselves and spurned the National Religion and thus risked angering the gods. So great, however, was the extent of Nero's violence and cruelty, that the suffering martyrs gained the sympathy of many who had hithertofore despised them. People began to pity the Christians and to declare publicly, "These poor souls are being sacrificed to one man's brutality rather than to the national interests."[3] Many pagans, seeing the bravery of the sufferers, were led to examine the teachings of Jesus and become Christians.

Nero grew more and more hated, not only because of his wholesale murder of hundreds, even thousands, of members of a controversial religious sect, but also because of his political crimes as well. By now Nero was striking out against everybody, ordering the execution of scores of prominent and influential people against whom he harbored some grudge. Finally, rebellion broke out in the army in January 68. Although this revolt, led by Vindex, governor of Gaul, was crushed, Servius Sulpicius Galba, governor of Nearer Spain, was proclaimed emperor by his troops a short time later. This time the Roman Senate proclaimed Nero deposed in favor of Galba. Abandoned by his own bodyguards, Nero committed suicide on June 9, 68. "What an artist the world is losing!" he boasted as he prepared to drive a sword into his throat. At the last moment, his courage failed, and his death-wound had to be inflicted by his private secretary. So ended the life of the first great persecutor of the Church.

# 5

# 'Coax the beasts on': Ignatius and the martyrs under Trajan

Nero had failed utterly in his attempt to wipe the "pestilential superstition" of Christianity from the face of the earth. The ranks of those killed were more than made up by pagans impressed by the courage and resolution of the martyrs. The reign of Nero did leave an enduring legacy in the history of relations between the Roman state and the Christian Church: a law known as the Neronian Institution that stated, "It is unlawful to be a Christian." Christianity was formally declared a forbidden religion. How was the law to be applied and interpreted? Was everyone suspected of being a Christian to be arrested and executed without a trial, as in the days of Nero? Were Christians to be given an opportunity to renounce their faith to save their lives? Were members of the forbidden sect to be tracked down by the authorities, or were they to be arrested only if they caused trouble? Over the next few decades, there would be wide differences in the way the Neronian Institution was applied by various emperors.

The Church knew comparative peace for a time after Nero's death. After three emperors succeeded Nero and each other in rapid succession, a sixty-year-old soldier of middle-class background, a man named Vespasian, seized power and held on to it. Cut from a completely different mold than Nero and his predecessors, even according to Suetonius (who was generally hostile to all emperors), Vespasian was an unpretentious man who never made any effort to conceal his humble origin. In private life, too, the new emperor was, at least for his culture, respectable. Moderate in his eating and drinking, he was faithful to one woman, his concubine Caenis, with whom he had lived for many years. Although he went along with the official cult of the emperor's "genius," he did not take it seriously. Mindful of the practice whereby emperors were proclaimed gods after their deaths, Vespasian, in his final illness, would comment, "I think I'm becoming a god!"

Although he reduced Palestine to rubble, destroyed Jerusalem and its Temple, and massacred thousands of Jews, Vespasian left the Church in peace. So did his son Titus, who was also respected as a decent and able ruler. During the 70s of the first century, many important Romans became Christians. Up until then, Christianity was thought of as a religion of the lower classes: artisans, menials, slaves, Jews, Asiatics, of the destitute and starving who had no hopes in this world who might be accused of looking for a "pie in the sky" to preserve their sanity. Now the situation was beginning to change, and wealthy, privileged, and aristocratic Romans began to join the Church. Some of the most prominent converts were Titus Flavius Sabinus, his son Flavius Clemens, and his daughter-in-law Domitilla. Titus Flavius Sabinus was Vespasian's brother. Another powerful and influential convert was Marcus Acilius Glabrio, who became consul in A.D. 91.

Still, Christians were a very small minority and still encountered substantial opposition from pagans. The historians Tacitus and Suetonius cherished the simple way of life that characterized the old Roman Republic. They had nothing but contempt for most of the emperors and their decadent and ostentatious way of life, but had nothing good to say about the Christians either. Tacitus, for example, excoriated Christians as "notoriously depraved," and dismissed Christianity as a "deadly superstition."[1]

Why this hostility? As we have seen, part of the reason for the widespread hostility toward Christians was the fact that they were "different." Many of their customs were considered antisocial. For instance, because most meat found in public markets had been sacrificed to the National Gods in heathen slaughterhouse-temples, many Christians refused to buy meat. In communities where Christians were numerous, butchers lost money and blamed their troubles on the "deadly superstition." In addition, Christians would not celebrate the emperor's birthday, because this implied a recognition of his divinity. Many Christians who had the means to do so would not send their children to school, because children were taught about pagan deities. Many Christians refused to be treated in such hospitals as then existed, because those institutions were always consecrated to a pagan god.

One of the favorite pastimes of the masses in the Roman world was going to the "games." Almost all towns of any size had at least one arena, and there, in the vivid words of Victorian historian Philip Schaff, "From sunrise to sunset men and beasts were sacrificed to satisfy a savage curiosity and thirst for blood."[2] When the famous Colosseum in Rome was dedicated by Vespasian, that kindly and moderate man put on a show in which between five thousand and nine thousand animals were killed *each day*. Nor were animals the only victims. To use Schaff's words again, "Painted savages from Britain, blonde Germans from the Rhine and Danube, Negroes from Africa" were brought in to fight the wild beasts or each other. Christians were forbidden by their leaders to attend such shows, not only because they were brutal and disgusting, but because all such "games" were dedicated to some god or goddess.

Moreover, many Christians would not serve in the armed services. Although some Christians felt that it was permissible to serve in the army so long as they were not compelled to butcher civilians, many Church leaders taught that when Christ, in the Garden of Gethsemane, told Peter to put up his sword, He disarmed all soldiers. Consequently, many Christian men refused to serve, even though the penalty for refusing induction was death. "We will pray for the empire, but we will not fight for it," was a comment that enraged many Roman officials.

Not only did Christian leaders forbid incest, premarital sex, adultery, homosexuality, divorce, abortion, infanticide, and other practices that were almost universally condoned among the pagan population, they also encouraged celibacy. One Church Father wrote, "Many may be found among us, of both sexes, who grow old unmarried, full of hope that they are in this way more closely united to God."[3] The Roman government, in order to keep its population stable in the face of a high rate of abortion and infanticide, as well as a naturally low fertility rate, strongly discouraged not only celibacy but childlessness. Caesar Augustus had long ago decreed severe penalties for people who for any reason failed to reproduce.

All told, the life and practices of Christians made them "peculiar" to the Romans. In addition to this, Christianity was lumped together in the minds of many reasonable people with the mystery cults, many of which, as we have seen, were rather sordid affairs. Worse, another Eastern cult, known as Gnosticism, was beginning to incorporate a number of Christian elements. This religion was popularized in Rome by Simon Magus, a native of Palestine, who was challenged at Rome by Peter. Gnosticism was associated with magical watchwords and the possession of divinely conferred secrets upon which entrance into a higher life depended. The Gnostics taught that matter was evil and that the initiate escapes from it to be absorbed in the godhead. God was pure abstraction, a fathomless abyss. From Him emanated "divine potencies," which, in their totality, were taught to constitute the "Pleroma." "Wisdom" disturbed the harmony of the Pleroma and fell into the formless void, which was called the "Hysterema." The Hysterema and the Pleroma united to produce the "Demiurge." Gnostic teachers identified the Demiurge with the "evil god of the Old Testament," claiming that redemption took place through the restoration of the harmony of the Pleroma and the liberating sparks of light from matter, accomplished when the Most Perfect Aeon entered Jesus at baptism and left Him before He went to the cross. Christ, they taught, accomplished His work by teaching Wisdom, which was received by only a select few initiates.

There were a number of Gnostic sects flourishing in the first century, and many of them incorporated different Christian ideas, in distorted form, in their unwholesome rites. Many of them believed in reincarnation. Some proponents of that patently unscriptural doctrine today complain, "Christians believed in reincarnation until the time of Constantine, and then that emperor burned all the writings that dealt with it." The "Christians" who believed in reincarnation, whose works were burned by Constantine, as well as other guardians of orthodoxy, were in fact but Gnostics, not Christians.

Worse, many Gnostics engaged in obscene parodies of the Blessed Sacraments. Some of them actually smeared themselves with semen, and, after raising polluted hands heavenward and shouting "We offer to thee this gift, the body of Christ," actually consumed it. To complete their anti-Mass, they drank menstrual blood.[4]

It is easy to see that these obscene cults could confuse themselves with Christianity in the popular imagination. Many otherwise fair-minded Romans, such as Tacitus, were convinced that Christianity was simply another gross and depraved Oriental cult working to further undermine traditional Roman values of thrift, frugality, hard work, and devotion to the gods of the state.

The second persecution of the Church came about through the Emperor Domitian, who succeeded his brother Titus in A.D. 81. His uncle and cousin were Christians, and he knew very well that the faith was not accurately to be associated with immoral and abominable practices. His reason for persecuting the Church lay simply in the fact that he was fearful, suspicious, and bent on absolute power. Like Nero, to whom he was frequently compared, Domitian lived in such mortal fear of revolution that he did not hesitate to eliminate anyone whom he viewed as a potential threat. He also took the imperial cult very seriously. Sacrificing incense before the emperor's statue was for him an indispensable act of loyalty. Refusal to do so was treason.

We do not know very much about the persecution under Domitian. Clement I, the bishop of Rome, wrote of the "misfortunes and catastrophes" that overwhelmed the Christian communities both at Rome as well as in the provinces.[5] Christians were not Domitian's only victims. Philosophers, intellectuals of all stripes, and leaders of all unauthorized cults were the diverse victims of the emperor's paranoiac wrath. So, too, were the Jews. By then Palestine was a land of utter desolation. Eusebius wrote of cities of the dead, grisly with the innumerable unburied skeletons and of naked, half-starving survivors inhabiting a province "full of indescribable horrors."[6] Vespasian had decreed that Jews, while still not required actually to sacrifice, were now required to support the National Religion with their tax monies. Vespasian and Titus, however, had not enforced the law. Domitian, in 88, decreed that from then on, not only Jews but Christians as well were to pay the tax. Those who refused had their property confiscated by the government and were sent to concentration camps in various penal colonies. Occasionally, dissidents were put to death, but Domitian seems to have been much less intent on a bloodbath than Nero.

The consul Glabrio was killed, however, as well as the emperor's cousin Flavius Clemens. Domitilla, wife of Clemens, was allowed to live, but exiled to a prison colony on the island of Pandataria in the Mediterranean. The charge against these prominent people was that they were "atheists," that is, they refused to reverence the gods of Rome, including the emperor, and were therefore traitors and subversives.

It was during these days that the Apostle Philip, at the age of eighty-seven, was martyred in Hierapolis (in what is now Turkey), and St. John, who was the same age, was exiled from Ephesus to a prison colony on the island of Patmos. There he composed the book that we call the Revelation, or the Apocalypse. Domitian also ordered the arrest of the leaders of the Church at Jerusalem. Just before the destruction of Jerusalem in 70, Bishop Simeon of Jerusalem had advised all his flock to move from Jerusalem to the town of Pella in what is now Jordan. There they were able to survive the subsequent bloodbath. Two years later, Simeon led the Christians back to Jerusalem, or what was left of it. The bishop apparently escaped arrest during the persecution of Domitian, but two of his subordinates were seized and taken to Rome for interrogation. Like all the leaders of the Catholic Church, these men were related to Jesus. Eusebius recounted that they were descendants of Jude, one of the men described in the Gospels as "brother" of the Lord. Domitian himself interviewed them. Domitian asked them, "What about Christ and His kingdom? What is it like? When and where will it appear?"

"It is not of this world or anything on earth," they explained. "It is angelic. It is in heaven, and it will be established at the end of the world, when Christ will come in glory to judge the living and the dead and every man will be rewarded according to his conduct on earth."[7]

Domitian decided that these men were inoffensive crackpots who posed no threat to his power. And so, in A.D. 95, he called off his persecution of Christians. The enforcement of the religious tax on Christians and Jews was not worth the trouble, and, like his father and brother before him, Domitian allowed it to fall into "benign neglect." He allowed those who had been imprisoned to return to their homes. The Apostle John, then ninety-two, was released from captivity at Patmos and allowed to return to Ephesus, where the five years remaining to him were some of the most productive of his life.

Domitian did not have many years remaining to him. As many like-minded rulers before and since learned, or should have, opposition to tyrannical rule was like a mythical monster known as the Hydra. When one head was cut off, the beast grew two more in its place. For every suspected subversive that Domitian killed or imprisoned, two more replaced him. Although he ceased to vent his wrath on Christians, he continued to attack members of the aristocracy until he grew so hated that even his wife supported the palace coup that snuffed out his life on September 18, 96.

Domitian was succeeded by a senator by the name of Nerva. Although he reigned for only two years, he is considered the first of the "Good Emperors," a dynasty that lasted nearly a century. One of the practices that Nerva inaugurated was to appoint his own successor, rather than leave the throne to incompetent relatives, or allow the succession to be fought out by various contenders after his death. This ensured a succession of able, competent administrators. Yet all of these men persecuted the Church.

Nerva's designated successor was a highly respected military commander named Trajan, who had been born in Spain of Italian ancestry on September 18, 53. When Nerva died suddenly of an apparent heart attack in the year 98, Trajan became emperor. One of his first acts was to approach the commander of the Praetorian Guard and offer him his sword. "Take this sword, in order that if I rule well you may use it for me, but, if ill, against me."[8] Well-loved and respected, Trajan was accused of making himself too accessible to the common man. "I behave toward private citizens," he replied, "in the manner in which, as a private citizen, I wanted emperors to behave toward me."[9]

During his reign of nineteen years, Trajan reduced taxes, built new roads and aqueducts, and conquered parts of what are now Romania and Hungary. He established a system of public welfare to aid the poor and care for abandoned children, and revised the penal code in setting limits to the period of time a person could be imprisoned without a trial. Furthermore, he forbade arrest on the grounds of anonymous denunciations, declaring, "It is better to let the guilty go unpunished than to sentence the innocent."[10] Although he was a heavy drinker and a homosexual, these vices were accepted in imperial Rome if practiced in relative moderation. These "minor indiscretions" were overlooked by the public, "because he drank all the wine he wanted and yet remained sober, and in his relations with boys he harmed no one."[11]

Trajan took a hard line against Christians, yet as one might expect of a man renowned as an administrator, his position was clear and methodical. Trajan's reason for upholding, at least to a limited extent, the Neronian Institution, was his fear of private "clubs." Trajan feared the Roman counterparts of such normally innocuous societies as the Masons and Elks because social organizations, begun harmlessly, often became hotbeds of subversion and political unrest. Trajan even rejected a request for a charter for a volunteer fire-fighting organization in the province of Bithynia-Pontus (in what is now Turkey), where his friend, Pliny the Younger, was governor.

Trajan wrote Pliny, "If people assemble for a common purpose, whatever name we give them and for whatever reason, they soon turn into a political club. It is a better policy then to provide the equipment necessary for dealing with fires, and to instruct property owners to make use of it, calling on the help of crowds which collect, if they find it necessary."[12] In other words, the emperor was saying, "It's better to make firefighting the responsibility of the individual homeowner rather than allow volunteer fire departments and run the risk of its getting involved in subversive political activity."

With such an attitude, it is no wonder that Trajan looked suspiciously on unauthorized religions. Through his letters to Pliny, we know exactly what the emperor's policy toward Christians was.

The governor was receiving complaints about Christians from various people in his province. Apparently, the butchers were enraged because their meats were rotting in their stalls as a result of the usual boycott by the large Christian population. Pliny was concerned about his course of action. He had never been present before at a trial of Christians. Should any distinction be made between individuals on grounds of age? Should he pardon anyone who has been a professing Christian but then renounces his belief? Or should any profession of the faith at any time in the past be sufficient to establish guilt? Was it "the mere name of Christian which is punishable," even if the defendant was innocent of any crime, or should prisoners be punished only for the commission of specific crimes?[13] Pliny had no evidence of any crimes, however. He was convinced that the food eaten during Christian rituals was not blood, semen, or the parts of dead bodies, but ordinary bread and wine.

> The sum total of their guilt or error amounted to no more than this: they had met regularly before dawn on a fixed day to chant verse alternately among themselves in honor of Christ as if to a god, and also to bind themselves by oath, not for any criminal purpose, but to abstain from theft, robbery, and adultery, to commit no breach of trust and not to deny a deposit when called upon to restore it. After this ceremony it had been their custom to disperse and reassemble later to take food of an ordinary harmless kind.[14]

Without waiting for a reply from Trajan, Pliny took his own initiative and had arrested everyone accused of ever being a Christian. Pliny asked each prisoner three times if he were a Christian, warning that if the reply were in the affirmative, a capital sentence would result. Pliny sent those Roman citizens who refused to renounce their faith to Rome for trial; the other believers he executed.

Pliny used the following test to determine if a person was a Christian. He displayed statues of the emperor, Jupiter, Juno, and Minerva. The accused were invited to make an offering of wine and incense to Trajan's statue and to repeat a formula "of invocation to the gods." If a defendant was unwilling to do this, it was clear that he was a Christian.

When Trajan wrote, it was to confirm Pliny in his course of action:

> You have followed the right procedure, my dear Pliny, in your examination of the cases of persons charged with being Christians, for it is impossible to lay down a general rule to a fixed formula. These people must not be hunted out; if they are brought before you and the charge against them is proved, they must be punished, but in the case of anyone who denies that he is a Christian, and makes it clear that he is not by offering prayers to our gods, he is to be pardoned as a result of his repentance, however suspect his past conduct may be. But pamphlets circulated anonymously must play no part in any accusation. They create the worst sort of precedent and are quite out of keeping with the spirit of our age.[15]

The policy of Trajan was clear. First, to be a Christian was still a capital crime. The Neronian Institution was upheld. The crime of being a Christian was, however, a special kind of crime, since one had but to regret it to be pardoned. Second, Trajan acknowledged that Christians were innocent of the crimes against morality and public decency with which they had been charged over the years. Thirdly, Christians must not be sought out by the authorities. They were to be apprehended only in response to a complaint. Even so, proper legal denunciations had to be made in accordance with the law. Anonymous accusations were to be rejected. Finally, renunciation of the faith at the time of interrogation was deemed sufficient for acquittal.

This was the policy toward Christians that was in effect for one hundred years. Whenever there was a persecution, the government acted only in response to public complaints. Complaints were, however, numerous.

According to tradition, Clement I, bishop of Rome. was one of the first victims of Trajan's "enlightened" policy. Formally denounced as a Christian, the pope was invited to sacrifice, refused, and was sent to the marble quarries of Crimea (in what is now southern Russia). More than two thousand Christians were sentenced there during the opening years of Trajan's reign. Not only did the Christians refuse to renounce their faith under the rigors of their confinement, but began to convert the other prisoners. The superintendent of the prison camp wrote to Trajan for advice and was evidently told to follow the standard procedure. Clement was again invited to sacrifice. This time, upon his refusal, he was bound and thrown into the Black Sea with an anchor around his neck.[16] Whether Clement was killed alone as an example, or whether some or all of the other Christian prisoners died with him, is not recorded.

Another prominent victim was Simeon, bishop of Jerusalem. At the age of one hundred and twenty, Simeon was one of the oldest men in Palestine, but was still actively in command of the Jewish Christian community when, around the year 107, anti-Christian riots broke out in Jerusalem and formal complaint was lodged with the governor that Simeon was a Christian. So the man who was probably one of the last on earth with vivid memories of Jesus was arrested and taken before the governor Atticus. Atticus had no sympathy for Simeon's great age, and ordered him to sacrifice. When the old man refused, Atticus directed that Simeon be tortured "for days on end." That a man of one hundred and twenty, confined in a dungeon, could survive several days of beatings and floggings amazed everyone. When Simeon still proved obdurate, Atticus ordered him crucified.

Another link to apostolic times was severed around the same year. Ignatius Theophorus, bishop of Antioch, then in his late seventies, was proud of the fact that when he was a child in Palestine, Jesus had held him in His arms. Ignatius became the third bishop of Antioch in the succession from Peter, succeeding Euodius, who had been appointed by the Prince of Apostles himself.

Ignatius was accused of being a Christian while Trajan was in Antioch on his way to do battle with the Iranians on the eastern frontier. The emperor was in a bad mood and not of a mind to tolerate an attitude which to him smacked of disloyalty. When Trajan learned of Ignatius' arrest, he ordered that the eminent bishop be brought to him. He was furious that Ignatius not only refused to sacrifice, but was ordering his flock to follow his example.

"You wicked wretch!" shouted Trajan when Ignatius refused to sacrifice.

The august presence of the godlike emperor held no fear for the feisty old bishop. Without a trace of awe or reverence, Ignatius retorted that Trajan was unfair to call him "wicked," for "all evil spirits have departed from the servants of God." He accused Trajan of being wicked because he worshipped evil spirits. Ignatius, on the other hand, professed to have the Holy Spirit dwelling within him. Everyone present must have cringed at the impertinence of the old man's remarks.

"Don't you think," Trajan asked, "that we have the gods in mind when we ask their assistance in fighting against our enemies?"

"You are wrong when you call demons 'gods,' " replied Ignatius. "There is but one God, who made heaven and earth and all that are in them, and one Jesus Christ, the only begotten Son of God, whose kingdom I hope to enjoy."

Trajan asked Ignatius if he was referring to a man crucified some seventy years before by the procurator of Judaea. Ignatius replied that he was indeed. "Jesus has crucified my sin and destroyed the power of the inventor of it, and has condemned all the deceit and malice of the devil. The devil's power is broken for all those who carry Jesus in their hearts." Trajan, in a rage, condemned Ignatius to be bound and sent to Rome to be devoured by beasts in the Colosseum at the public games.[17]

Ignatius, who thanked God for the privilege of being bound with iron chains like his friend St. Paul, had the opportunity to visit various Christian communities in Asia Minor and to write to others as he was conveyed to Rome. At Smyrna, he was able to talk to his old friend, Bishop Polycarp, who, like him, had studied under the Apostle John.

In his letters, Ignatius urged Christians "with undivided mind" to obey "the bishop and the priests and break one bread, which is the medicine of immortality and the antidote against death, enabling us to live forever in Jesus Christ."[18] Presenting himself as a sacrifice for Christians the world over, Ignatius declared, "I offer up my life as a poor substitute for the cross, which is a stumbling block to those who have no faith, but to us salvation and eternal life."[19] Begging the Christians at Rome not to try to prevent his martyrdom, he bade them praise Jesus that the bishop of Syria had the grace of "being transferred from the rising to the setting sun," referring, on the one hand, to his journey westward to Rome, and, on the other hand, to the setting of his earthly life. "It is good to set, leaving the world for God, and so to rise in Him. . . . Beg only that I may have inward and outward strength, not only in word but in will, that I may be a Christian not merely in name, but in fact." He longed with all his heart "to die for God — if only you do not prevent it."

> Please let me be thrown to the wild beasts; through them I can reach God. I am God's wheat. I am ground by the teeth of wild beasts that I may end as the pure bread of Christ. If anything, coax the beasts on to become my sepulchre, and to leave nothing of my body undevoured, so that, when I am dead, I may be no bother to anyone. I shall really be a disciple of Jesus Christ if and when the world can no longer see so much as my body. . . . If I suf-

fer, I shall be emancipated by Jesus Christ, and in my resurrection shall be free. But now, in chains, I am learning to have no wishes of my own.[20]

Indeed, Ignatius characterized his guards as "ten leopards whom kindness makes even more cruel." Yet, "the wrongs they do make me a better disciple." Even so, "that is not where my justification lies."[21] That is, Ignatius' salvation was not through his patience or any other good works, but through faith in his Lord Jesus Christ.

Ignatius was led to the Colosseum before a howling crowd. There he prayed aloud that there might be an end to persecution. "May mutual love reign among the brethren," were his last words.[22] The wild beasts were released, and within minutes there was nothing left of the proud, courageous, and outspoken old man but a few bones, which the faithful wrapped in linen and sent back to Antioch for veneration.

Under Trajan, the kingdom of Osroene with its capital, Edessa, previously independent, was annexed by Rome and became part of the province of Armenia. Ever since the Apostle Jude Thaddaeus had prayed successfully for the healing of Prince Abgar V shortly after Pentecost and had been given permission to preach in his dominions, Osroene had been a haven for a growing Christian population. Now, the imperial governors were under orders to execute anyone accused of being a Christian. Although Christians still were not to be hunted down, there was no lack of hostile pagans to denounce them to the authorities.

One of the first targets of the pagan faction was Sharbil, who had been a heathen priest before his conversion to Christianity, after which time he had led innumerable souls to "uphold the doctrines taught by the Apostle Thaddaeus and his successor Palut." The brutal Roman governor Licinius summoned Sharbil and asked him how he dared defy the emperor.

Sharbil replied, "Of the King of Kings I am afraid, but at any king of earth I tremble not, nor yet at any threats toward me." He told Licinius to go ahead and kill him, as he would not change his beliefs.

Licinius thought a good flogging might do the trick, but after Sharbil was scourged, he declared to the governor, "You are not aware of the scourging of justice in the world to come. You will cease to exist and your judgments also will pass away, but justice will not pass away."

"You are so intoxicated with this new religion that you do not even seem to realize before whom you are judged and by whom you have been scourged," replied Licinius. He again demanded that Sharbil sacrifice. When the Christian refused, the governor ordered him strung up and his sides ripped up with a metal comb — a common form of torture used by the Romans.

"It is for the sake of Christ, who has caused His light to arise upon the darkness of my mind, that I endure this torture," responded Sharbil. When he still refused to sacrifice, Licinius ordered his victim scourged again. When Sharbil declined a fourth opportunity to offer sacrifice, Licinius ordered him thrown into a dungeon. There Sharbil languished for months. When he was taken once more before the governor, Licinius could see that endless days and nights of confinement had not altered Sharbil's commitment. "I will not play false with my word. I will not again confess idols, which I have renounced, nor will I renounce the King Christ, whom I have confessed."

Further tortures were applied. Sharbil was branded with a hot iron between his eyes and on each side of his face. When he was led again before Licinius, everyone could smell the stench of burnt flesh. Again Sharbil refused to sacrifice, and this time his wounds were torn with metal combs and vinegar was rubbed in. Still, he remained firm. Licinius, now in a white heat of rage, ordered that iron nails be driven into Sharbil's forehead. "Let Christ, whom you have confessed, deliver you from all the tortures which I have inflicted on you and intend further to enact upon you if you do not sacrifice to the emperor!" He had Sharbil burned with red-hot pokers, which so destroyed his already mangled flesh that the ribs showed through the charred skin.

"Neither fire nor sword nor death nor life nor height nor

depth can separate my heart from the love of God, which is our Lord Jesus Christ," murmured Sharbil.

Licinius was not ready to give up. He told his prisoner not to entertain hopes of a speedy death. "I mean to bear with you until you come to your senses and sacrifice to the emperor." It was extremely important that this man, who was Edessa's most articulate Christian spokesman, be made to recant. If Sharbil renounced the faith, most other Christians in the area would be expected to follow suit. Sharbil was made to stand on hot coals until the soles of his feet were burned off. Even so, he continued to mock the pagan gods. "One had intercourse with boys and another fell in love with a maiden who fled for refuge into a tree." In a towering rage at this insult to the gods of Rome, Licinius vowed to make Sharbil sacrifice if it was the last thing he did. "I will bring you to account for your blasphemy against the gods and your audacity in insulting the emperor. I will not leave you alone until you offer incense to him."

Sharbil's charred and maimed body was further tortured with the metal combs, and still he would not yield. Licinius was weary now and wanted to put an end to the case that he now knew he would not win. He gave Sharbil one more opportunity to sacrifice, and, of course, Sharbil refused. Thereupon Licinius ordered the prisoner taken outside the city walls to the place of execution, there to be held in place in a wooden vice, and sawn apart. First Sharbil's torso was sawn in two, from breastbone to private parts. Incredibly he was still alive when they slowly sawed off his head.

The martyr's sister Babai claimed the grisly remains and collected his blood in her skirts, murmuring, "May my spirit be united with your spirit in the presence of Christ, whom you have known and in whom you have believed." She was overheard and denounced to Licinius, who had her arrested and commanded her to sacrifice. When she refused, she too was tortured to death.[23]

Numerous other Christians were denounced, arrested, tortured, and killed in the new province of Armenia under the violently anti-Christian Licinius, who, with his demonic tortures, was far different from Pliny and most other governors who quickly executed their victims if they refused to sacrifice. But even Licinius had to wait for formal accusations before he moved against individual Christians.

Trajan, at sixty-four, died of a stroke during the summer of 117. It is interesting to note that, despite his clear anti-Christian policy, he was so admired and respected, even by Christians, that the legend was born that one of the popes, unwilling that such a brilliant man be lost to heaven, interceded with God so that Trajan was presented with the Christian message in the other world, and, accepting it, was admitted into Paradise!

# 6

# 'Polycarp to the lions!'

Trajan was succeeded by his cousin and hand-picked successor, Aelius Hadrianus, known to history as Hadrian, and best remembered for his immense circular tomb, which is still one of the most familiar sights in Rome. Hadrian, forty-one when he became emperor, was, like his kinsman, born in Spain. He had held a number of high civil and military posts. A tall, elegant man with a full beard, who loved music, poetry, literature, and animals, Hadrian did his best to maintain peace throughout his empire. To do this he strengthened the army and tried to secure the borders. In Britain this involved building a massive wall across the northern limits of the territory occupied by Rome, so as to protect the settlements there from the hostile and unsubjugated Picts of what is now Scotland. In the East, Hadrian decided that the current borders were too hard to defend, and so, in making peace with the Iranians, he ceded them all the land east of the Euphrates River. This included the province of Armenia, where persecution against Christians had been raging.

Although he was an initiate in the Eleusinian Mysteries, Hadrian seems to have been a religious sceptic who lumped Christianity, Judaism, Gnosticism, and the cult of the Egyptian god Serapis all together as superstitious humbug. "There is no ruler of a synagogue, no Samaritan, no presbyter of the Christians who is not an astrologer [and] a soothsayer. They have but one God, who is none."[1]

Hadrian probably persecuted Christians less intensely than any second-century emperor except for Commodus, who reigned much later. In fact, Hadrian decreed severe penalties against people who denounced others falsely as Christians. This policy drastically cut the number of accusations and complaints. There were sporadic incidents, however, such as the one which swept a handful of Roman aristocrats to their death in the summer of 124.

In June 124, a deputy consul name Cerealis journeyed to the village of Gabii, outside of Rome, to investigate complaints against Getulius, a wealthy Roman who was alleged to have opened his home to Christian meetings and who was reputed to be instructing inquirers in the forbidden religion. When Cerealis arrived, he caught Getulius in the act of instructing converts in his home.

"Aren't you aware of the emperor's orders?" asked Cerealis.

Getulius replied with an almost insolent flippancy, "Why should the orders of the emperor be obeyed?"

"Tell me why they should *not* be obeyed?" insisted Cerealis, urging him to sacrifice to the national gods.

Getulius refused. "We must adore God, the Son of God, who is King of Kings and whom all must obey. We must obey Him rather than some worm-breeding mortal."

Ignoring this insult against the majesty and dignity of the emperor, Cerealis asked Getulius what he meant when he insisted that God had a Son, then asked the Christian to "prove to me that the 'Son of God' is in fact God." The two men conferred at length and were joined by Getulius' brother, the tribune Amantius, who was a close friend of Cerealis. That very day Cerealis was persuaded not only to accept baptism, but to remain at Gabii for instruction. Within a few days, the missing civil servant was located at the Christian compound, and, along with Getulius and several other members of the community, was arrested and taken back to Rome for trial.

The judge urged Cerealis to renounce the Christian faith if he wished to live. "If I didn't want to live, I wouldn't be a Christian," replied Cerealis. Urged to sacrifice to Jupiter and Mars or die, Getulius retorted, "My life will not be extinguished, and I rejoice with joy unspeakable to refuse to sacrifice to the gods!"

"Do not despise the commands of the emperors," urged the judge, "but obey the mighty gods."

"I thank my God, the Father Almighty," declared Getulius, "that I am able to offer Him an acceptable sacrifice."

"What sacrifice?" asked the judge.

"The sacrifice of a broken and contrite heart."

Getulius, Cerealis, Amantius, and a man named Primitivus, were sentenced to die and taken to a farm outside of the city to be burned alive. Cerealis, Amantius, and Primitivus were burned to death, but the pile of wood upon which Getulius was bound was wet and would not burn the victim, so the executioners each uprooted one of the fence posts, which were found in abundance on the property, and battered out his brains.[2]

The Christians who suffered most under Hadrian were probably the members of the Jerusalem Church. After the martyrdom of St. Simeon, thirteen bishops succeeded one another in quick succession during the next twenty-eight years. Whether this rapid turnover was due to martyrdoms we do not know. In 135, however, under the leadership of a man named Bar Cochba (which means "Son of the Star"), the Jews of Palestine revolted a second time against Roman rule. Rufus, governor of Palestine, after receiving reinforcements from Rome, suppressed the revolt mercilessly, slaughtering thousands of men, women, and children. And so, for the second time in less than a century, Jerusalem was completely razed. Hadrian renamed the city Aelia Capitolina, after himself, and insulted both Christians and Jews by erecting temples to Jupiter and Venus over the sites of the Temple and of Calvary. Moreover, he forbade all those of Jewish blood to set foot in the area. This included Jewish Christians, too, and though this group set up churches throughout Palestine, Syria, and Mesopotamia, the phenomenon of Jewish Christianity gradually petered out. Gentile Christians were permitted to live in Jerusalem, under the leadership of Bishop Mark.

Hadrian's successor, Antoninus Pius, who became emperor in 138, was a wealthy landowner from what is now France. A tall man of striking appearance, he was renowned as a scholar and orator. According to a contemporary biographer, he was called "Pius" because he was "most merciful by nature and did no harsh deeds in his own times."[3] The Christian community at Smyrna could hardly have agreed with this assessment, for this city was the site of a savage effusion of blood in 155.

Smyrna, today called Izmir by the Turks, was the largest city in Asia Minor. Located on the Hermus River, hard by the Aegean Sea, it was a city renowned for its wealth, its beautiful buildings, and as a center of science and medicine. The large Christian community there had been headed for the last half of that century by Polycarp, who must surely have been one of the last living links with apostolic times. If we take this statement that he had been a Christian eighty-six years to mean that he was a life-long believer, we can assume that Polycarp was the child of Christian parents. He had studied under the Apostle John and been a friend of Ignatius Theophorus.

There was quite a bit of anger directed at Christians at the time. There had been disastrous earthquakes in the lands around the Mediterranean as well as fires in Rome, Antioch, and Carthage. Many pagans blamed these disasters on the wrath of gods made hostile by Christian refusal to sacrifice to them. Philip, governor of Asia, was goaded into action by complaints by not only pagan residents of Smyrna, but by Jews as well. The governor began to arrest individuals accused of professing the Christian faith. Those who affirmed their faith were tortured in an effort to force a recantation. Eusebius recounted that these nameless martyrs were strung up and torn open with metal combs until their internal organs could be seen through the gaping holes in the mangled flesh. Others were forced to lie on beds of spikes. Those who survived these tortures were given another opportunity to sacrifice. When all but a handful refused, they were thrown to the wild beasts in the stadium. The courage and dignity with which these men, women, and children met their end only inflamed the passions of the bloodthirsty mob, which howled for additional Christian blood. When a young man named Germanicus, thrown to the beasts, showed such courage that he coaxed the reluctant animals to attack him, the crowd went wild, chanting, "Death to the atheists! Death to the atheists!" Soon their chant turned to "Death to Polycarp! Death to Polycarp! Death to Polycarp!"

The venerable bishop was reluctantly persuaded to hide in

a farmhouse a few miles away from the city. There he remained for several days with a few companions, engaged in almost constant prayer, day and night, that God would grant peace to the churches throughout the world. One night Polycarp dreamt that his pillow caught fire and burned to ashes. The next morning he told his friends that this dream convinced him that he would be burned to death. As the police intensified their search, Polycarp was moved to still another farm.

One day a farmhand, arrested and examined under torture, revealed Polycarp's hiding place. The Christians concealing the bishop got word of this and were ready to convey him to another hiding place, but the old man refused to go. His capture and death, he insisted, were inevitable and, moreover, "God's will." Early in the morning of February 23 the police stormed the farmhouse and demanded Polycarp. They could not believe their eyes when the bishop appeared voluntarily. He impressed them with his "cheerful and gentle manner" and his "dignified confident bearing," so that they "marveled that so much effort should be made to capture a man like him."

Polycarp insisted that his companions set the table and invite the policemen to eat as much as they pleased in return for one more hour to pray. Everyone present was moved as Polycarp stood with outstretched hands, praying for everyone who had ever come in contact with him, "small and great, famous and obscure, and the whole Catholic Church throughout the world."

When Polycarp finished praying, the police put him on an ass and led him into Smyrna. It was the start of the Jewish feast of Purim in that city, in which the Children of Israel comprised a large minority. There the police chief, whose name was Herod, pulled his carriage alongside Polycarp, who was still mounted, and tried to persuade him to deny Christ to save his life. "What harm is there in saying 'Lord Caesar' and sacrificing, and saving your life?" the chief asked.

"I am not going to do what you advise me," said the old bishop.

When Polycarp resisted repeated attempts at persuasion,

one of the officers knocked him off his beast, causing him to scrape his shin. Thereupon Polycarp was marched to the stadium, where the governor was attending the games during which, in recent days, numerous members of the bishop's flock had been thrown to the lions. As the bishop drew near the stadium, his captors heard distinctly a voice, as if from heaven, saying, "Be strong, Polycarp!"

Already the news had reached the crowd that Polycarp had been arrested, and when the prelate was brought to the stadium in the presence of the governor, the people went wild. Philip, who was in no hurry to kill Polycarp, urged him to deny the charges. "Respect your years. Swear by Caesar's fortune. Change your attitude. Say, 'Away with the atheists!' "

Philip now demanded that Polycarp deny Christ. "Swear, and I will release you. Revile Christ."

Polycarp said to the governor, "Fourscore and six years I have been serving Him and He has done me no wrong. How then can I blaspheme my King who saved me?"

"Swear by the genius of Caesar!" the governor insisted.

"If you suppose that I will swear by the genius of Caesar, as you put it, pretending not to know who I am," said Polycarp, "Hear, plainly, I am a Christian. If you wish to learn the doctrine of Christianity, assign a day and you shall hear."

"Persuade the people," said the governor, indicating that it was they, not he, who were demanding his blood.

"I think it is appropriate to discuss these things with you personally, for we have been taught to render to princes and authorities ordained by God the honor that is due, so long as it does not injure us, but as for these [people], do not consider them the proper persons to whom to make my defense."

"I have wild beasts," threatened Philip, "and I will throw you to them if you don't [change your attitude]."

"Call them," responded Polycarp. "We cannot change our attitude if it means a change from better to worse. It is a noble thing to change from wickedness to righteousness."

"If you [make light of the beasts]," replied Philip, "I will cause you to be burned up by fire, unless you repent."

"You threaten a fire which burns for an hour and after a

little while is quenched," replied Polycarp. "For you do not know the fire of the future judgment and of the eternal punishment which is reserved for the impious. But why do you delay? Do what you will."

Philip the governor was amazed that the old man did not "wilt in alarm" and that he was filled not only with courage, but even with joy. Nonetheless, he instructed a crier to take his place in the middle of the stadium and proclaim three times, "Polycarp has confessed that he is a Christian."

The crowd now went wild. The governor could hear the bishop loudly denounced as a "teacher of Asia," "the father of Christians," "the destroyer of our gods," "the man who teaches us not to sacrifice or even to worship." Soon the crowd took up the chant, "Polycarp to the lions! Polycarp to the lions!"

Philip shouted that he had no more lions available, as the games were almost finished for the day and the supply of the requested animal had been exhausted. "Then burn him alive!" shouted someone. The rest of the crowd began to chant, "Burn him! Burn him! Burn him!"

A group of heathens and Jews gathered a pile of logs from nearby workshops and baths and prepared a pyre for Polycarp. The bishop removed his outer garments, but could not stoop down far enough to remove his shoes. His executioners were about to nail him to a wooden frame above the pyre, but Polycarp insisted, "Leave me as I am. He who enables me to endure the fire will enable me, even if you do not secure me with nails, to remain on the pyre without shrinking." So the executioners obliged him, simply tying the old man's hands behind his back. Polycarp then prayed:

> Father of thy beloved and blessed Son, Jesus Christ, through whom we have received the knowledge of thee, the God of angels and of powers and of the whole creation and of the entire race of the righteous who live in thy presence, I bless thee that thou hast deemed me worthy of this day and hour, that I might receive a portion in the manner of the martyrs, in the cup of Christ, unto resur-

> rection of eternal life, both of soul and of body, in the immortality of the Holy Spirit. Among these may I be received before thee this day, in a rich and acceptable sacrifice, as thou, the faithful and true God, hast beforehand prepared and revealed, and hast fulfilled. Wherefore I praise thee also for everything; I bless thee, I glorify thee, through the eternal high priest, Jesus Christ, thy beloved Son, through whom, with him, in the Holy Spirit, be glory unto thee, both now and for the ages to come. Amen.

The men in charge lit the fire and the flames shot up and enveloped the bishop's body. A Christian who witnessed the execution recounted that the fire took the shape of a vaulted room, like a ship's sail filled with the wind, "and made a wall about the body of the martyr," which looked not like burning flesh, but glowed like gold and silver refined in a furnace." Witnesses smelled not the stench of charred flesh, but a "fragrant odor, like frankincense or some other precious spice." To make sure that Polycarp was dead, the "confector," an official whose duty it was to administer the *coup de grace*, was summoned. He drove his sword through the body, provoking a stream of blood so profuse as to extinguish the smoldering fire.

The Christians at Smyrna wished to claim their bishop's remains. By this time, bodies of martyrs were held in special reverence by the faithful. As the Christian who described the last hours of Polycarp recounted, "To the martyrs, as disciples and imitators of the Lord, we give the love that they deserve for their unsurpassable devotion to their own King and Teacher." Although a number of Jews tried to dissuade him, the officer in charge, after burning the cadaver until no flesh remained, gave the bones to his followers. For them, his relics were "more precious than stones of great price and more splendid than gold." Ever afterwards the Christian community in Smyrna assembled at Polycarp's grave, on the anniversary of his death, "in gladness and joy to celebrate the birthday of his martyrdom, to commemorate those who have already fought and for the training and preparation of those who shall hereafter do the same."[4]

In the account of Polycarp's martyrdom, we can see that, despite the intense hostility of an apparent majority of Smyrneans, the persecution of Christians in that region was limited and selective. Acknowledged Christians were allowed, unmolested, to reclaim Polycarp's remains. The governor of Asia moved against individual believers only at the insistence of his constituents, and these he chose to interrogate and punish as a warning to their co-religionists.

# 7

# 'The blood of the martyrs is the seed of the Church': The massacre by Marcus Aurelius

As the second century passed the halfway point, Christians continued to be the victims of preposterous calumnies. Marcus Cornelius Fronto (c.100-161), a tutor to the young nobleman Marcus Aurelius, who was eventually designated by Antoninus Pius as his successor, was an inplacable foe of Christianity. He maintained that during the Mass young babies were covered with flour, beaten to death, doused with olive oil, and eaten. Other pagans insisted that Christians worshipped a donkey's head. Still others published the preposterous story that during the Mass a dog was tethered to a lampstand, which at the end of the ceremony he was induced to overturn the lampstand and plunge the room into darkness, and signal the beginning of a colossal sexual orgy.

By now Christianity had become sufficiently respected to draw more rational criticism from Roman intellectuals. Galen (c.30-100), an eminent Greek physician and philosopher, criticized both Christianity and Judaism for maintaining that God had created the world out of nothing and for holding that nothing is impossible with God. Writing in behalf of traditional Roman religion, he maintained, "Certain things are impossible by nature and God does not even attempt such things at all." He further insisted that the universe was governed by "unalterable laws according to reason," and that God was merely a part of nature.[1]

Celsus, another Roman physician who wrote around the same time, ridiculed the notion of the Resurrection. "What sort of body, after being entirely corrupted, could return to its original nature and that same condition in which it had been before it was dissolved? As [Christians] have nothing to say in reply, they escape to a more outrageous refuge by saying that 'anything is possible to God.' "[2] Stooping to blasphemous slander, Celsus maintained that Mary was a poor peasant woman who made her living by spinning and had an adulterous affair with a Roman soldier named Panthera, as a result of which she had been divorced from her husband Joseph. Celsus continued to blaspheme Christ by insisting that He had been versed in Egyptian magic and was nothing but a garden-variety carnival magician, of the type "who for a few [coins] make known their sacred lore in the middle of a marketplace and drive demons out of men and blow away diseases and invoke the souls of heroes."[3] As for the Resurrection, according to Celsus, it was the result either of wishful thinking, dreams, hallucinations, or somebody who "wanted to impress the others by telling this fantastic tale, and so by this cock-and-bull story to provide a chance for other beggars."[4]

Not only was the Church threatened by attacks from without, but from dissension within. Various teachers who claimed to be Christian taught distorted doctrines, such as that of Symmachus and the Ebionites, who insisted that Christ was an ordinary man, the son of Joseph and Mary, and held that Christianity was simply a sect of Judaism, insisting that the ceremonial laws of Israel should be kept in their entirety. The Encratites preached compulsory celibacy and adopted the Gnostic ideas that the God of the Old Testament was not the Father of the Lord Jesus. Jehovah had to be evil, the Encratites insisted, because He created sex. Cerdo, who was a contemporary of Galen and Celsus, but insisted that he was a Christian, taught that "the God proclaimed by the Law and the prophets was not the Father of Our Lord Jesus Christ; for the one was known, the other unknown; the one righteous, the other gracious."[5] Marcion of Pontus likewise taught that there was a god greater than the Creator, and denied that the maker of the universe was the Father of Christ.

It is amazing that the Church did not splinter apart amidst the onslaught of these attacks from both within and without. As Philip Schaff, the Swiss Protestant church historian, wrote:

> All Catholic antiquity thought of none but the actual, historical church, and without hesitation applied to this . . . those four predicates for unity, holiness, universality, and apostolicity. . . . The Fathers of our period all saw in the Church . . . a divine, supernatural order of things . . . the continuation of the life of Christ on earth, the temple of the Holy Spirit, the sole repository of the powers of divine life, the possessor and interpreter of the Holy Scriptures, the mother of all the faithful.[6]

The leaders of the Church insisted that all believers must hold strictly to the doctrines delivered by the apostles and not to exchange the yoke and teaching of Jesus for "other doctrines new and strange." Irenaeus (c.120-202), a priest from Asia Minor who later became bishop of Lyon (in what is now France), maintained that the Church preserved and passed on the tradition inherited from the apostles. There were no secret teachings, as many of the teachers of heretical doctrines insisted. The "Apostolic Tradition" had always been taught openly in all the great episcopal sees, all of which could trace the succession of their bishops back to the founding apostles. Tertullian, an aristocratic Roman from Carthage who was a wealthy attorney before his conversion to Christianity in midlife, insisted that Christians must not pick and choose doctrines according to their whims. The Christian's sole authority is the "Apostolic Tradition," interpreted by the leaders in the succession of the apostles.

Probably the first important Christian intellectual who explained Christian doctrines to the pagan world was Justin, a native of Shechem, a town mentioned in the Bible. Born of Greek parents, he received a classical Greek education and, from an early age, looked for the truth among the current systems of philosophy. He first embraced Stoicism, but found that it was not spiritual enough. Then he became a Pythagorean and then a Peripatetic before embracing Platonism, which seemed to present him with an adequate vision of God and the eternal verities. Then one day, in middle age, while teaching philosophy at Ephesus, he was walking in silent contemplation along the seashore when he encountered an elderly man who engaged him in conversation. The man was a Christian and convinced Justin that the only true wisdom comes from God and was taught by the prophets and apostles. Justin came to hold that Christianity was the only true philosophy and that though the Stoics, Platonists, and Pythagoreans may have, through reason, attained an imperfect vision of the Truth, Wisdom was revealed fully only in Christ. Justin thought that any open-minded person would be convinced by the verity of the Christian Gospel by reading the Old Testament, but he also insisted that Christ was foretold through Greek philosophy.

As for the traditional gods and goddesses, however, Justin held that they were nothing but demons.

> In the days of old evil spirits appeared in various guises and defiled women and corrupted boys, and made a show of such horrors that those who did not judge actions by the light of reason were struck with amazement. Such men were seized with dread and failed to understand that they were wicked spirits: instead they called them gods and addressed them all by the titles which each demon bestowed on himself. When Socrates tried to bring these matters to the light and to rescue mankind from those demons by the critical application of sound reasoning, then those very demons used the agency of man who delighted in wickedness to secure his execution for atheism and impiety, alleging that he was introducing novel supernatural powers. They are active against us on just the same lines.[7]

Responding to the charge that Christians were "atheists," Justin replied that it was in fact true that Christians refused to worship the demon-gods, but affirmed that they worshipped "the most true God, the Father of righteousness and moderation and the other virtues, the God who is without a trace of evil," along with "his Son, who came from him and taught us of these things." Justin stated that Christians also adore "the host of other good angels who attend on God and are of god-like nature," as well as "the Spirit of Prophecy."[8] Thus he seems to teach a Quadrinity rather than a Trinity.

In order to refute obscene rumors about the Mass, Justin, in his *Apology* (meaning "explanation"), provides a vivid picture of Christian worship in the second century.

> On the day which is called the Sun's Day there is an assembly of all who live in the towns or the country; and the memoirs of the Apostles or the writings of the prophets are read, as much as time permits. When the reader has finished, the president [i.e., priest] gives a discourse, admonishing us and exhorting us to imitate these excellent examples. Then we all rise together and offer prayers. . . .[9]
>
> At the end of the prayers we embrace each other with a kiss. Then bread is brought to the president of the brethren, and a cup of water and wine: this he takes, and offers praise and glory to the Father of all, through the name of his Son and the Holy Spirit; and he gives thanks at length for our being granted these gifts at his hand. When he has finished the prayers and the thanksgiving, all the people present give their assent with *Amen*, a Hebrew word signifying, 'So be it!' When the president has given thanks and all the people have assented, those whom we call 'deacons' give a portion of the bread over which thanksgiving has been offered, and of the wine and water, to each of those who are present; and they carry them away to those who are absent.
>
> This food is called Eucharist with us, and only those are allowed to partake who believe in the truth of our teaching and have received the washing for the remission of sins and for regeneration; and who live in accordance with the directions of Christ. We do not receive these gifts as ordinary food or ordinary drink. But as Jesus Christ our Saviour was made flesh through the word of God, and took flesh and blood for our salvation; in the same way

the food over which thanksgiving has been offered through the word of prayer which we have from him — the food by which our blood and flesh are nourished through its transformation — is, we are taught, the flesh and blood of Jesus who was made flesh.[10]

The well-to-do who wish to give, give of their own free choice, and each decides the amount of his contribution. This collection is deposited with the president, who gives aid to orphans and widows and all who are in want through sickness or any other cause; he is also the protector of those in prison, of strangers from abroad; in fact, of all who are in need of assistance.[11]

The emperor contemporary with Justin was Marcus Aurelius, who was likewise esteemed as a philosopher. The Roman writer Julius Capitolinus declared that Marcus Aurelius excelled all other emperors in "purity and character." A descendant of the ancient Roman king Numa Pompilius, Marcus Aurelius was born in Rome in April 121, and showed from an early age an intense interest in philosophy. At the age of twelve, he took to sleeping on the floor, and soon afterwards began to wear a Greek-style cloak, such as the philosophers wore. Despite a frail constitution, he excelled in boxing, wrestling, and running. A distinguished attorney, Marcus Aurelius had a successful career as a civil servant and statesman before he was picked as emperor-designate by Antoninus Pius. After he became emperor, the scholarly leader was fond of quoting Plato's maxim, "States flourish if either philosophers are rulers or rulers are philosophers."[12]

The record of the accomplishments of this well-beloved emperor is impressive. According to Julius Capitolinus:

He . . . provided carefully for public expenditures, and he prohibited libels on the part of informers, the mark of infamy being placed on false accusers. Accusation [made solely to swell the budget through fines] he despised. He devised many wise measures dealing with the child wel-

> fare system. He appointed curators from the Senate for many communities, so as to extend senatorial functions more widely. During the time of famine he presented grain from the city to the Italian communities, and he took care of the grain supply in general. He limited gladiatorial spectacles in every way. . . . The streets of the city, too, and the highways, he maintained with greatest care.[13]

One would imagine that this humane prince, who was "a very great influence for moderation in deterring people from evil and urging them to good deeds, generous in rewarding and mild in granting pardon," who "made the bad good and the good very good,"[14] would have looked at least with tolerance upon the Church of Christ. Such was by no means the case. Marcus Aurelius, that quiet, austere philosopher, whose book of meditations is esteemed as a classic still today, was the most bitter persecutor the Church had known since the days of Nero.

Marcus Aurelius was probably prejudiced against Christianity early in life by his tutor Fronto, whose gross libels we have already discussed. The emperor was aware of the valor with which the martyrs faced death, but despised them because their courage, as he saw it, came not as a result of self-control or mastery of the will, but as the result of illogical hopes based on irrational ideas.[15] A further reason for Marcus Aurelius' anti-Christian position was his conservatism. A man who favored reviving old laws rather than inventing new ones, Marcus Aurelius was very much intent on enforcing the National Religion. Despite his involvement in Greek philosophy and his obsession with being logical, he believed that the gods of Rome watched over the state and were offended if not properly venerated. The reign of Marcus Aurelius was marred by almost constant invasions by such Germanic peoples as the Marcomannians, the Hermundurians, the Sarmatians, and the Quadrians, as well as by natural disasters, such as a terrible epidemic of smallpox, which killed between twenty-five and thirty percent of the population of Italy between 165 and 180.

Like many other Romans, Marcus Aurelius seems to have blamed these disasters on those stubborn folk who refused to honor the gods of Rome.

Marcus Aurelius, therefore, strictly enforced the Neronian Institution. Because of the invasions and epidemics, complaints against the Christians were more strident than ever before. In fact, in many cities there were anti-Christian riots as pagans, terrified of the vengeance of their deities, mobbed Christian neighborhoods, looting, pillaging, and killing. The emperor and his officials lent a sympathetic ear to the complaints, conscientiously arresting many Christians and executing those who refused to abjure their faith.

In 165, Justin the philosopher and six other Christians were denounced by a pagan philosopher named Crescens. Examined by Rusticus, prefect of Rome, Justin was commanded to "obey the gods."

"To obey the commandments of our Saviour Jesus Christ is worthy neither of blame nor of condemnation."

"What kind of doctrine do you profess?" asked the prefect.

"I have endeavored to study the doctrines of all faiths and philosophers, but at last I came to adhere to the true doctrines — the doctrines of the Christians — though they do not please those people who hold false opinions."

"You utterly wretched man," snapped the prefect, "are these the doctrines that please you?"

"Yes," replied Justin, "since I adhere to them with the right dogma."

"And just what do you mean by 'the right dogma'?"

"I mean that we worship the God of the Christians, whom we reckon to be One from the beginning, the maker and fashioner of the whole creation, visible and invisible; and the Lord Jesus Christ, the Son of God, who had also been preached beforehand by the prophets as destined to appear among the race of men, the herald of salvation and teacher of good disciples. . . . Moreover, I know that of old the prophets foretold the appearance of the Son of God among men."

Wishing to hear no more theological vagaries, Rusticus asked Justin where he and his companions assembled for worship. "Where each one chooses and can," replied the philosopher. "Do you think that all Christians meet in the same place? Not so, because the God of the Christians is not circumscribed by place, but, invisible, fills heaven and earth, and everywhere is worshipped and glorified by the faithful."

"Get to the point," demanded the prefect. "Tell me where you meet, the place where you collect your followers."

"I live above a man named Martinus, at the Timiotinian Bath," answered Justin, "and during the whole time I have been at Rome — and this is the second time I have lived here — I have never worshipped at any other meeting place except the home of Martinus. I taught the doctrines of truth to whomsoever wished to come to me."

"Are you then a Christian?"

"Yes," said Justin. "I am a Christian."

Rusticus turned to the other people who had been arrested with Justin and inquired if they, too, were Christians. All of them said that they were. Rusticus then asked them if Justin was responsible for their conversion.

"No, I was a Christian all my life, and will always be," replied a man name Hierax. A second man, named Paeon, likewise affirmed that he was reared "in this good confession" by his parents. A third, Euelpistis, admitted that he had studied under Justin, but had been born and raised a Christian. Rusticus asked where Euelpistis' parents were, to which he replied that they lived in the province of Cappadocia (in what is now Turkey). Hierax, in response to a similar question, replied that his parents were dead and that he was a native of Iconium (also in what is now Turkey), but came to Rome after being forced out of his hometown because of his faith. Rusticus then questioned a fourth prisoner, Liberianus, who also affirmed his faith in Christ.

Turning once more to Justin, Rusticus sarcastically asked, "If you are scourged and beheaded, do you really believe that you will ascend into heaven?"

"I hope that if I endure these things, I shall have his gifts. For I know that to all who have lived thus, there abides the divine favor until the completion of the whole world."

"Do you suppose then," asked the prefect, "that you will ascend into heaven to receive some reward?"

"I do not suppose it," replied Justin, "but I know it and am fully persuaded of it."

"Let us now come to the matter at hand," said Rusticus. "I want all of you to sacrifice to the gods of Rome."

"No right-thinking person falls away from piety to impiety," protested the philosopher.

"Unless you obey, you shall be mercilessly punished," threatened Rusticus.

"Even when we have been punished, through prayer we can be saved through our Lord Jesus Christ, our Saviour," declared Justin. "He guaranteed salvation for us and will give us confidence when we appear before his fearful and universal judgment seat."

The other Christians declared, almost in unison, "Do what you want with us, but we are Christians and will not sacrifice to idols."

"Let those who have refused to sacrifice to the gods and yield to the command of the emperor be scourged and led away to suffer the punishment of decapitation, according to the laws," said Rusticus, pronouncing sentence.[16]

And so Justin and his companions laid down their lives for the faith. The remains of their bodies were recovered by other Christians and buried. Ever after that, the Christian philosopher has been known as St. Justin Martyr.

Another courageous man who laid down his life during this period was Concord, son of the priest Cordianus. Concord had just been consecrated a subdeacon in Rome by Bishop Pius I. Both Concord and his father were very devout, spending long hours in prayer, fasting frequently, and giving much of their income to the poor. In 175, Marcus Aurelius, going to war against the Marcomannians — a tribe which lived in what is now Czechoslovakia — ordered all citizens of the empire to sacrifice to the gods for his success. The gentle emperor, when informed that there was substantial non-compliance by Christians, was driven to a white heat of rage and instructed his officials to investigate complaints against Christians more thoroughly than ever. As arrests and executions multiplied, Concord asked his father to arrange for him to be sent out of Rome to a safer place. "Son," objected Cordianus, "it is better to stay here so that we might both be crowned together."

Concord was nevertheless assigned to Spoleto, where he worked as subdeacon to the priest Eutyches. There the young man, as time went on, became renowned for his holiness as well as his charismatic gifts. Word of a number of miraculous healings reached the ears of Torquatus, governor of Umbria, who had Concord arrested.

"What is your name?" the subdeacon was asked.

"I am a Christian."

"I asked about you, and not about your Christ!" shouted the governor.

"I have said that I am a Christian and Christ I confess."

"Sacrifice to the immortal gods and I will be like a father to you and will obtain the emperor's favor, and he will exalt you to a priest of the gods [of Rome]."

Concord, not without some sarcasm, retorted, "You listen to me. Sacrifice to the Lord Jesus Christ, and you will escape eternal misery."

The governor ordered the impertinent young man beaten and thrown into prison. Presently Eutyches appeared with Anthimus, the local bishop, who happened to be an old friend of Torquatus. The governor explained that he did not want to hurt the boy, but if he was going to be as blatantly contemptuous of the National Religion as he had been at his hearing, there was no way of saving him. To Anthimus he granted permission to take Concord to his home to try to talk some sense into him.

The bishop, who had no intention of trying to talk the young man out of his resolution, ordained him a priest. A few days later Torquatus sent for Concord. He asked the young man what he had decided.

"Christ is my salvation," responded Concord, "to whom I offer the daily sacrifice of praise."

Torquatus ordered Concord tortured in hope that he could be forced into sacrificing. But as he was scourged, Concord murmured, "Glory be to Thee, Lord Jesus Christ!"

Torquatus put Concord back in prison, manacled with irons on his hands and neck. For three days Concord sang the angelic hymn, "Glory to God in the highest and peace to men of goodwill." At length Torquatus sent two officers to Concord's cell with a small image of Jupiter. "Hear what the governor has ordered," they announced. "Sacrifice to Jupiter or lose your head."

The single-minded young priest spat at the statue and cried, "Glory be to Thee, Lord Jesus Christ!" Instantly he was beheaded.[17]

The most famous victim of Marcus Aurelius was a wealthy Roman lady named Cecelia. French Church historian Henri Daniel-Rops pieced together the story of her life from fragmentary accounts. We do not know Cecelia's given name. Cecelia was her second name — the name of her clan, which was one of the most distinguished in Rome. She was a descendant of Marcus Licinius Crassus, the statesman and financier who, with Julius Caesar and Gnaeus Pompey Magnus, formed the First Triumvirate which controlled the Roman world for a few years in the middle of the first century B.C. Cecelia's parents were evidently pagan, but Cecelia, unknown to them and perhaps instructed by a servant, had been a secret Christian since childhood. She had memorized the Gospels and under the gold-embroidered gowns she wore a hair shirt.

When she was twelve or thirteen (the normal age at which aristocratic Roman girls were married) her family affianced her to an affable young man named Valerian, who was also from an old family, and Valerian lived in an imposing mansion on the Tiber. On her wedding evening Cecelia confided to Valerian that she was a Christian and would not marry him unless he became a Christian, too. She presented such a convincing argument, or he loved her so deeply, that he went immediately to the bishop, who obligingly baptized him. And so Cecelia and Valerian were married.

Not long afterwards, Valerian's brother Tiburtius came to visit the couple and was astonished by the testimony of Cecelia and Valerian. That very evening Tiburtius was persuaded to accept Christ.

Cecelia and Valerian converted their mansion into a house church and led many people to Christ. Cecelia became renowned for her powers of persuasion. Many a hardened heart was melted by the words that God lent her. The couple put their private underground cemetery at the disposal of the members of their house church. Unfortunately, the burial space was soon in great demand, as probably more than 800 Christians were put to death in Rome during the last five years of the reign of Marcus Aurelius. At length, Valerian and Tiburtius were denounced, arrested, and beheaded. Their composure was such that one of the soldiers who guarded them during their last hours was converted, professed Christ openly, and was flogged to death on the spot.

Cecelia lived on as a widow, still hosting services in her home. It was only a matter of time until she too was denounced as a Christian. When called upon to deny her faith, she declared, "We will never deny the most blessed name that we know. We cannot. That is impossible. Rather than living in misery by rejecting our Lord, we prefer to die and achieve supreme liberty. This truth, which we proclaim, is torturing you — you who are toiling so hard to make us lie." She turned to the image to which she was asked to sacrifice and jeered, "Are these the gods that you worship? Or are they blocks of wood and pieces of stone?"

The prefect sentenced Cecelia to be scalded to death in her own home. His police locked her in her bathroom and heated it as hot as they could. After twenty-four hours Cecelia was still alive, probably because the bathroom could not be heated to a lethal intensity. When this fact was reported to the prefect, he sentenced Cecelia to decapitation. A brutal, incompetent executioner aimed three blows with his axe, which failed to sever her head and left her slowly bleeding to death. Still conscious, Cecelia was able to speak to her friends and comfort them while the life gradually drained from her mutilated body.[18] Her tomb quickly became the object of intense veneration. In 1599 the grave beneath the plaque bearing the inscription "St. Cecelia" was opened, and in it was found the skeleton of a woman who had been partially decapitated. Since around that time St. Cecelia has been known as the patroness of musicians, probably because her *Acts* speak of her singing to God at her wedding.

During the spring of 177, a gruesome pogrom was enacted against the Christians of Lugdunum in Gaul (now Lyon, France). The native people were probably suspicious of the Christians not only because of their religion, but also because most of them were foreigners, recent immigrants from Asia Minor. In May a mob of heathens ran amok in the Christian neighborhood, looting, firing and smashing, and dragging suspected Christians from their houses to kick, pommel, and stone. The Roman magistrates took action not against the aggressors, but against their victims, moving them from the streets where they lay bruised and bleeding to the city jail. Then the decision was made to imprison all the Christians who lived throughout the region, and so, during the next twenty-four hours authorities imprisoned dozens of Christians from Lyon and the nearby town of Vienne. The names of forty-eight of these believers have been recorded, but there were probably many more whose names have been forgotten. When the local magistrates were satisfied that they had captured all known Christians in the district, the prisoners were taken from prison to the forum, where, after a public examination, all but ten confessed that they were Christians. All the prisoners (including those who had protested their innocence) were remanded to the prison to await the arrival of the governor of Narbonensis.

When the governor arrived and began the trials at the public forum, a prominent attorney by the name of Vettius Epagathus argued in defense of the Christians, attempting to prove that none of the defendants were guilty of godless or irreverent behavior, but he was shouted down by the pagans. The governor asked Vettius if he were a Christian, and when he answered in the affirmative, he was arrested too.

Several pagans who were servants of the family in which the Church met in Lyon were called as witnesses. Under torture, they had agreed to charge the Christians with incest and cannibalism, and (in the words of the author of the letter which was later circulated to describe the catastrophe) "things we ought never to speak about, or even believe that such things ever happened among human beings." The pagans, hearing the testimony, went wild in a pandemonium of bestial rage.

The governor selected four prisoners to torture in hopes of extracting damaging confessions. One was Sanctus, a deacon from Vienna; the second was Maturus, a recent convert; the third, Attalus, was a native of Pergamum in Asia Minor who only recently had moved to Lyon; and the fourth was a little slave girl named Blandina, who seemed so weak and frail that her mistress feared that she would quickly break down. None of the four, however, broke down.

The torturers first directed their attention to little Blandina, but after subjecting the girl to a gruesome assortment of public tortures from morning to night, failed to break her resolution to confess her Lord. Sanctus refused to tell his name, race, birthplace, or even whether he was slave or free. To every question he replied, "I am a Christian." To make him talk, to the delight of the half-barbarous crowd, the governor directed that he be stripped naked and red-hot copper plates be pressed against the intimate parts of his body. Even when the stinking smoke from his burning flesh wafted gruesomely throughout the forum, Sanctus refused to yield. "I am a Christian," he repeated. Attalus and Maturus likewise refused to deny Christ.

The governor next interrogated a woman who had initially denied that she was a Christian. He hoped that this prisoner, whose name was Biblis, could be forced, out of fear of torture, to accuse Christians of indecent and inhuman practices. "How could people eat children who do not think it lawful to taste the blood even of irrational beasts?" she declared. Thereupon Biblis confessed that she was in fact a Christian, and was sent back to jail.

In the filthy, teeming pitch-black dungeon the Christians languished, packed together without food, light, or fresh air. Constantly the guards would select one of their number to torture in hopes of extracting a renunciation of Christ. Although dozens of prisoners began to die of starvation or torture, none renounced their faith. Interestingly enough, most of those who perished in prison were the younger prisoners, who had never experienced persecution before. One of those who survived days of confinement and torture was the bishop of Lyon, Pothinus, who was in his nineties and extremely weak and sick.

When Pothinus was taken to the forum for interrogation, the crowd shouted and jeered at him "as if he were Christ Himself." When the governor asked the prelate, "Who is the Christian's god?" Pothinus replied cryptically, "If you are worthy, you shall know." The governor, who thought the answer impertinent, ordered the torturers to teach the old man some respect. Pothinus, beaten and kicked senseless, was flung back into his prison cell, where he expired two days later.

An annual festival known as the Augustalia was now at hand, and the governor decided that the public games should be enlivened by the public torture of the surviving prisoners. The howling crowds were puzzled because the prisoners, taken from the dungeon to the stadium, looked so calm and happy. Moreover, they smelled an exquisite aroma emanating from the prisoners (a fragrance sometimes called "the odor of sanctity"), and wondered how the prisoners had been able to douse themselves with perfume.

Maturus and Sanctus were tortured first. They were put through the "gauntlet." That is, they were forced to run between two rows of soldiers who flogged them with whips. The two men were then exposed to wild beasts (of unspecified breed and number), which mauled them but did not kill them. The victims were then fastened to iron chairs which were heated red hot until the men nearly suffocated in the smoke from their burning flesh. The crowd roared and cheered as the prisoners burned to death. Maturus was silent, but Sanctus kept repeating over and over the only words he had uttered publicly since his arrest, "I am a Christian."

After the two men burned to death, Blandina, her body mangled from her previous tortures, was crucified and exposed as food for the beasts. When the animals refused to touch her, she was taken down and returned to prison. After Attalus was paraded around the stadium with a placard around his neck reading, "This is Attalus the Christian," the governor decided to expose no more Christians that day.

Shortly thereafter the governor, who had sent to the emperor for instructions, received a message from Marcus Aurelius, who ordered him to reexamine all the prisoners. Of those who still persisted in their confession of Christ, the Roman citizens were to be decapitated and the rest were to be fed to the beasts.

While the Christians were being reexamined in the forum, a well-known physician named Alexander appeared. Like most of the victims, he was a native of Asia Minor but he had been a Christian in secret. The governor thought Alexander seemed to be encouraging the Christians by his gestures and ordered the doctor's arrest. "Who are you?" demanded the governor." "A Christian," was all that Alexander said. Instantly he was sentenced to be thrown to the beasts.

When all the surviving prisoners had been interrogated and none of them had denied Christ, the governor sentenced them all to death. Over a period of several days, at least four dozen men and women perished in the arena through various spectacular forms of torture concocted to delight the crowds. The governor ignored the Roman citizenship of several prisoners so that he could please the crowds in making their death as gruesome as possible. Attalus, Alexander, Blandina, and a fifteen-year-old boy named Ponticus were the last to die. Alexander and Attalus were exposed to wild beasts. Alexander prayed silently and uttered not so much as a groan, as he was torn to bits by the lions and bears. Attalus, who survived the mauling, was fastened to the iron chair and roasted alive. As the smoke rose from his burning body, he called out in a strong voice to the spectators, "This thing which you are doing is devouring men, but we do not devour men or do any other wicked thing!" When asked what name God had, he answered, "God hasn't a name, as a man has."

On June 2 only Blandina and Ponticus remained. The crowd bellowed its glee as the teen-age boy was subjected to a spectacular series of tortures and then died. Blandina was flogged again and then placed in the iron chair. Her cheerful demeanor enraged her torturers and she was removed while she was still alive and suspended in a basket within reach of a maddened bull. She remained conscious, praying aloud, after seemingly endless gorings. When she finally expired, the crowd was subdued. Everyone agreed that they had never seen a woman suffer so much or so long.

The corpses were taken to the city dump to be eaten by dogs. A contingent of soldiers was dispatched to guard this grisly collection of decaying cadavers, left festering for days in the prison cells in which they had died; charred remains of victims who died in the iron chair; and a ghastly assortment of heads, torsos, and limbs of those who had been hacked to pieces and disemboweled by gladiators for the delight of the crowds. The governor ordered that the bodies be refused burial. For six days the heathens of Lyon crowded the dump to view the ghastly spectacle. Many laughed and jeered and hooted at the dead. Some shouted, "Where is their God? What did they get for their religion, which they chose rather than life?" Finally the bodies were burned to ashes and dumped into the Rhone River. "Now, let's see if they'll rise again!" railed the pagans.[19]

Eusebius recounted that the massacre at Lyon was just an example of what was going on in all the provinces of the empire during the latter part of the reign of Marcus Aurelius, during which "countless martyrs came to their glory." Many victims were not killed outright, but sentenced to a slow death in the mines. Normally the sentence was ten years, but few who were sent to the mines ever returned. Most of the Italian Christians who were sentenced to this punishment were dispatched to the lead mines in Sardinia. Here, as in mines elsewhere in the empire, both male and female prisoners were crippled by having the joint of one foot destroyed with the thrust of a red-hot knife. One eye was cut out and a number was branded on the forehead. All males under thirty were castrated. Prisoners were manacled together in pairs, with iron rings soldered around the ankles and linked together with a six-inch chain, as well as a tight chain around the waist, which was in turn attached by a third chain to the ankle chain in such a way that the prisoner was unable to stand erect. After being mutilated, chained, and branded, the prisoners were flogged, handed a pick and shovel, and sent to work in the mine. Usually two-thirds of each new contingent of prisoners died within twenty-four hours. As for the others, in the words of a modern writer:

> Henceforth, they neither shaved, washed, cut their hair or finger and toenails, were not supplied with more clothes, got one meal of bread and water per day, worked four five-hour shifts, had a daily assigned workload, and slept on the ground in their own filth. . . . The guards were Roman mercenaries, mainly Asiatics, who spoke no Latin, no Greek, no Aramaic, no Gaulish, no German or any language known in the Empire. Communication between masters and slaves was one way, and only by blows.[20]

In the midst of this massacre, a rather interesting event, attested to by both Christian and pagan historians, took place in the presence of Marcus Aurelius, who was deploying his forces for battle with the Samaritans. His men had run out of water and were parched with thirst. Suddenly, in sight of the enemy, a number of soldiers in the Melitene Legion knelt on the ground and began to pray to the Christian God. According to Eusebius, "The enemy were astonished at the sight, but the record goes on to say that something more astonishing followed a moment later: a thunderbolt drove the enemy to flight and destruction, while rain fell on the army which had called on the Almighty, reviving it when the entire force was on the point of perishing from thirst."[21] While it is not known whether the emperor retaliated against the soldiers who had revealed their Christian affiliation, the incident, if accurately reported, did nothing to ameliorate his hostility to the Church. Marcus Aurelius continued to enforce the Neronian Institution until his death on March 17, 180, at fifty-nine, after a long illness in what is now Vienna, Austria. His last words were, "Go to the rising sun, for my sun is setting."

The mechanism for persecution remained intact for several months after his death. Governors continued to respond to pagan complaints by rounding up Christians and sentencing them to death. One of the best documented martyrdoms took place in Carthage in July 180, four months after the death of Marcus Aurelius. It was then that twelve Christians from Scili or Scillis, a village in Numidia, which was part of the province of Africa, were brought before Governor Publius Vigellius Saturninus. The leader of the group was a man named Speratus.

"You can win the favor of our lord the emperor if you return to your senses."

"We have never done any evil," replied Speratus. "We have never spoken ill of anyone, but when we are ill-treated we give thanks. Moreover, we obey the laws of our emperor."

"We too are religious," said Saturninus, "and our religion is simple. We swear by the genius of our lord the emperor and pray for his welfare, as you ought to do too."

"If you will listen, I can tell you the mystery of simplicity," offered Speratus.

"I will not listen to you if you start to speak evil of our sacred rites. Rather, you must swear by the genius of our lord the emperor."

Speratus continued, "I know nothing of the empire of this world, but I serve that God whom no man has seen or can see with the eyes of the body. I have committed no theft, but if I have bought anything I have paid the tax, because I know my Lord, the King of kings and Emperor of all the nations."

"Cease to be of this mind," the governor urged.

"It is wrong," added Speratus, "to murder and to speak false witness."

"Don't be a party to this folly," Saturninus urged.

A Christian named Cittinus broke in and said, "We have no one to fear except our Lord God, who is in heaven."

A woman named Donata added, "Honor to Caesar as Caesar, but fear to God."

"I am a Christian," said another, named Vestia.

"What I am, that I wish to be," affirmed Secunda, another Christian.

Calmly Saturninus went on. He asked Speratus if he persisted in being a Christian. He once again declared his faith and was joined in his confession by the others, who all affirmed that they were Christians.

"Do you want time to consider?" asked the governor.

"In a matter so straightforward, there is no considering," replied Speratus.

Saturninus asked Speratus what was contained in the box that had been confiscated at his arrest and which had been brought into the judgment hall. Speratus answered that the chest contained the books and epistles of Paul, "a just man."

"Have a delay of thirty days and consider the matter, all of you," urged the governor.

All twelve prisoners once again affirmed that they were Christians and would never change their minds. Thereupon Saturninus read out the decree: "Speratus, Nartzalus, Cittinus, Donata, Vestia, Secunda, and the rest having confessed that they lived according to the Christian rite, since after opportunity was offered them of returning to the custom of the Romans they have obstinately persisted, it is determined that they be put to the sword."

"Thanks be to God!" shouted Speratus. "Today we are martyrs in heaven, thank God!" affirmed Nartzalus.

The governor then ordered the herald to declare: "Speratus, Nartzalus, Cittinus, Veturius, Felix, Aquilinus, Laetantius, Januaria, Generosa, Vestia, Donata, and Secunda, I have ordered to be executed."

All declaring, "Thanks be to God," the "Scillitan Martyrs" were led out and beheaded.[22]

Under Commodus, who succeeded his father as emperor, the persecutions halted. In contrast to his serenely intellectual and morally impeccable father, Commodus was an irresponsible ruler universally detested as a drunken, murderous lecher. Roman historian Aelius Lampridius stated that from his earliest boyhood Commodus was "base, shameless, cruel, lecherous, defiled of mouth, too, and debauched, already adept at those arts which do not accord with the position of an emperor. . . ." He slept, like Caligula, with his own sister, and "used to order his concubines . . . to be debauched [by other men] before his own eyes, and he was not free from the disgrace of submitting sexually to young men, being defiled in every part of his body, even his mouth, with both sexes." Commodus loved to wear women's clothing, and incongruously, play at being a gladiator, appearing in the arena hundreds of times during his twelve-year reign. A brutal, stupid alcoholic with a vacant expresson and dyed hair, he seemed an unlikely champion of the Church.[23] One of his concubines, Marcia, however, was a Christian and was able to prevail upon him to show clemency toward her co-religionists.

Early in his reign Commodus sent for Eleutherius, bishop of Rome. The pope, who must never have expected to leave his audience a free man, was astounded when the emperor promised to end the persecution and asked him to give him a list of all the Christians who had been sent to the mines, so that he might free those who survived. From the bishops throughout Italy, Eleutherius assembled the names of all the Christians sent to the mines. Commodus was as good as his word. Those still alive were freed.

By the last part of the second century, according to Philip Schaff, there were 700,000 Christians in the empire. A constant stream of converts had more than replaced those who had perished. However, as members of a forbidden religion, Christians could not have public houses of worship. The Romans, because of their dread of the shades of the dead, left undisturbed their growing network of underground cemeteries, now called catacombs. Christians, to be sure, were not the only group to use catacombs. Mithraists, Jews, and some pagans also had underground cemeteries. Excavated by *fossores*, or gravediggers (who held a special honored status in the Church), the Christian cemeteries had existed not only in and around Rome, but in other parts of Italy, and in Sicily, Africa, and Asia Minor since the first centuries. They consisted of long narrow galleries in the bowels of the earth, carved in the hills outside urban areas. The dead were usually buried in two or more tiers. Small compartments were cut like shelves in the walls and rectangular chambers were fashioned for families or distinguished martyrs. The ceilings were sometimes flat, sometimes arched. The chapels, which appeared at intervals in the narrow passageways, were ideal for funeral services and private devotion, but not for public worship. Most of the walls, especially in the chapels, were plastered over, and decorated with religious symbols, such as the *orans* — a figure with hands outstretched in prayer — or such figures of the Resurrection as Daniel in the lions' den and Jonah and the whale. Christ was usually shown beardless, as the Good Shepherd, or as Orpheus, the mythic animal-tamer (to show Christ's function as a tamer of men), or as a philosopher carrying a scroll.

It is uncertain whether the Church ever met in the catacombs for worship in times of persecution. Only twenty to thirty people could fit, crammed like sardines, in the tiny chapels. It is certain that many Christians fled thither in time of trouble. All cemeteries were protected by law from desecration, and even at the height of Marcus Aurelius' persecution, Christians were allowed to bury their dead there. Government troops seldom would venture to search the tombs in making arrests.

People were attracted to the Church not only by the teaching of a good and loving God, by the hope of a life after death, or by the requirements for a righteous life, but also by the conduct of the believers. "See how they love each other," was the reaction of many outsiders. Christian charity was especially noticeable during the smallpox epidemic. While many pagans abandoned sick members of their family and fled, Christians tended not only to their own sick but to the stricken pagans as well. This and other acts of love and concern won the sympathy of many pagans.

Another thing that left awestruck those who had any association with believers was the occurrence of the miracles that were still taking place at the end of the second century. This is documented by Irenaeus, bishop of Lyon. A Greek, born in Ionia, Asia Minor, around 120, he studied under Polycarp. His education included not only sacred subjects but also the writings of Plato, Homer, and other Greek authors. At an early age Irenaeus went to Lyon, where he was ordained by

Pothinus. He was on a mission in Rome in 177 when the terrible massacre occurred there, and he was appointed as successor to Pothinus. Under Irenaeus, the Church in Lyon revived through an influx of converts. Lyon, in the latter part of the second century, was the site of many supernatural manifestations.

Irenaeus, for example, recounted how on several occasions, when the entire community met together and "besought God with much fasting and supplication" subsequent to the death of an individual, "the spirit of the dead man has returned and his life has been granted to the prayers of God's people. . . ." Irenaeus moreover recounted that in his diocese there were exorcists who "really and truly" drove out demons. Furthermore:

> Some have foreknowledge of the future, visions, and prophetic utterances; others, by the laying-on of hands, heal the sick and restore them to health; and before now, as I said, dead men have actually been raised and have remained with us for many years. In fact, it is impossible to enumerate the gifts which throughout the world the Church has received from and in the name of Jesus Christ crucified under Pontius Pilate.[24]

As the second century drew to a close, the Church was stronger than ever. Wrote Tertullian, "We appeared only yesterday, and we now fill your cities, your homes, your squares . . . the councils, the tribunals, . . . the palace, the Senate, and the Forum. We have left you nothing save your temples. Should we secede from you, you would be terrified by your own loneliness."[25] Go on, he challenged the Roman world, "Rack us, torture us, grind us to powder. Our numbers increase in proportion as you mow us down. The blood of Christians is the seed of the Church."[26]

# 8

# 'I cannot call myself anything else than what I am': The martyrdom of Perpetua

For now, there was no more racking, grinding, or torturing, for, in the words of Eusebius, "Through the grace of God the churches throughout the world enjoyed peace and the word of salvation was leading every soul from every race of man to the devout worship of the God of the universe, so that now at Rome many who were distinguished for wealth and family turned with all their household and relatives unto their salvation."[1] A number of high officials were now openly professing Christians, including Prosenes, secretary of the Treasury.

Commodus continued to govern badly. He squandered his nation's revenue on his personal amusements and showed no interest in affairs of state, except to accuse and execute prominent Romans whom he viewed as a personal threat. Finally, on December 31, 192, he was assassinated. For several months the ship of state foundered as one emperor succeeded another in a series of coups, until power at last was consolidated in the hands of a military man named Septimius Severus.

Severus, who was forty-eight years old when he seized power, was a Roman aristocrat born and raised in the province of Africa (now Tunisia and Algeria). He grew up speaking Punic, and as an adult spoke Latin with an African accent. Having studied at Athens, he occupied important civil posts in Spain and Sardinia before becoming governor of Africa, and later, military commander in Syria. A small, handsome man with a long beard and curly grey hair, Severus, in marked contrast to Commodus, was sparing and abstemious: he seldom ate meat and drank little wine. Although he was a conscientious administrator and was respected as emperor, British historian Edward Gibbon characterized him as a "haughty and inflexible man," who "considered the Roman Empire his personal property" and caused the decline of Roman civilization by increasing the army's power at the Senate's expense.[2]

Following a pattern that had begun with Marcus Aurelius and would continue for many years, a pattern in which it was often the "bad" emperors who left the Church alone and the conscientious ones who persecuted it, Severus regarded Christianity with a jaundiced eye. This phenomenon is not difficult to explain. It was the efficient, conscientious emperors who were most concerned with preserving the Roman way of life, including the national religion. It was the incompetent ones who did not care. In America, many would expect a "good" president, among other things, to maintain "law and order," and would look askance at national leaders who were "soft on crime." For the Roman establishment, Christianity was a force of disorder, a crime, a factor as destructive to its state as communism, Nazism, or the Ku Klux Klan. Just as conscientious presidents in America would not (at least in recent times) allow the Ku Klux Klan to run rampant, conscientious Roman leaders were unwilling to permit the spread of the Church. A good emperor ran a "tight ship" and strictly enforced the laws — including those against Christianity. The emperors who tolerated Christianity generally did not do so out of any conviction or sympathy for Christian teaching, but because they were too weak or too lazy to enforce the laws. If they did not oppress the Church, it was not because they were religious, but because religion, in all of its forms, was of little concern to them.

Severus held a traditional religious viewpoint. He believed in astrology and did nothing of importance without consulting fortune-tellers, soothsayers, and mediums, and was inclined to fear the wrath of evil spirits if the Old Religion was not maintained. Yet he decided not to take action against the Church at once. He allowed Prosenes to continue as secretary of the Treasury, took no action against the many Christian senators, and even employed a Christian physician for a time.

After nine years as emperor, Severus decided to stop the spread of the New Religion. In 202 he issued an edict forbidding both Christians and Jews to make converts. From then on it was a capital crime to make or to become a convert; to accept baptism or circumcision was punishable by death. People who had become Christians or Jews before the promulgation of the edict were left in peace, unless they were caught in the act of making converts. An early victim was Irenaeus. Arrested in Lyon in June for making converts, the eighty-two-year-old bishop was placed between a cross and a statue of the emperor and told to choose between the two. Irenaeus of course chose the cross.

For the first time in a century, the Roman government was actively searching for Christians, albeit only converts and their instructors. One of the most poignant accounts of martyrdom concerns a young African lady, Vibia Perpetua, who kept a diary in prison, which account was preserved and integrated into the *Acts* of her martyrdom, which many believe were written by none other than Tertullian. Perpetua was a young married woman of twenty-two, from an aristocratic family. One of her brothers was a Christian, but the rest of her family remained pagans. Perpetua and four other catechumens (Revocatus, Saturninus, Secundulus, and a slave girl, Felicitas) were arrested in Carthage. When Saturus, the man who had been instructing them, learned of the arrests, he turned himself in.

In jail, awaiting trial, Perpetua was visited by her frantic father, who tried desperately to persuade her to abandon her faith. Pointing to a pitcher in her cell, Perpetua asked him, "Would you say this vessel was a pitcher or something else?"

"Well, of course it's a pitcher."

"Can it be called by any other name than what it is?" she asked.

"No."

"Well, neither can I call myself anything else than what I am — a Christian."

In a paroxysm of grief, Perpetua's father "flung himself on me as if he would tear my eyes out," she wrote. Nevertheless, his tears and entreaties failed to weaken her resolve.

Since Christians baptized before the edict went into effect

were undisturbed, members of Perpetua's congregation were allowed to visit her, and, in view of the danger of execution, she and the other catechumens were baptized. A few days later Perpetua was taken to a cell where she "had never felt such darkness before." Two of the deacons in her congregation bribed the jailers to allow her and the other Christians to have a few hours a day "in the pleasanter part of the prison." Perpetua was even allowed to keep her newborn son, whom she was nursing. After a while, "The dungeon became to me, as it were, a palace, so that I preferred being there to being elsewhere."

Perpetua had mystical gifts, and when her brother, a Christian, came to see her in prison, he pressed her to pray to God for a vision which would reveal whether her imprisonment would end in death or freedom. Perpetua wrote in her diary, "I, who knew that I was privileged to converse with the Lord, whose kindnesses I had found to be so great, boldly promised him and said, 'Tomorrow I will tell you.' " When her brother left, Perpetua prayed and was graced with a vision.

> I saw a golden ladder of marvelous height, reaching up even to heaven, and very narrow, so that persons could only ascend it one by one; and on the sides of the ladder were fixed every kind of iron weapon. There were . . . swords, lances, hooks, daggers; so that if anyone went up carelessly, or not looking upwards, he would be torn to pieces, and his flesh would cleave to the iron weapons. And under the ladder itself was crouching a dragon of wonderful size, who lay in wait for those who ascended, and frightened them in the ascent. And Saturus went up first . . . attained the top . . . and turned towards me and said to me, 'Perpetua, I am waiting for you, but be careful that the dragon does not bite you.' And I said, 'In the Name of the Lord Jesus Christ, he shall not hurt me.' And from under the ladder itself, as if in fear of me [the dragon] slowly lifted up his head; and as I trod on the first step, I trod upon his head. And I went up, and I saw an immense extent of garden, and in the midst of the garden a

> white-haired man sitting in the dress of a shepherd. [He was] of a large stature, [and sat] milking sheep. Standing around were many thousands of [people in white robes]. He raised his head and looked upon me and said to me, 'Thou art welcome, daughter.' And he called me, and from the cheese as he was milking he gave me as it were a little cake, and I received it with folded hands, and I ate it and all who stood around said, 'Amen.' And at the sound of their voices I was awakened, still tasting a sweetness which I cannot describe.

When Perpetua's brother returned the next day, she related the vision to him, and they both agreed that it meant that Perpetua's ordeal would end in death, and so "we ceased henceforth to have any hope in this world."

Perpetua's pagan father was still unreconciled. On his next visit he fell on his knees and kissed her hands and beseeched her to "have pity on my grey hairs," reminding her that she had always been his favorite child, whom he preferred to all her brothers. Begging her not to "deliver me up to the scorn of men," he bade her have pity on her brothers, her mother, and her aunt, and, especially on her son, "who will not be able to live after you." Sobbing, he went on, "Don't bring us all to destruction, for none of us will be able to speak in freedom if you suffer anything."

Perpetua told him, "On that scaffold, whatever God wills shall happen. You should know that we are not placed in our own power, but in that of God."

We hear nothing of Perpetua's husband. Nowhere is he mentioned in the *Acts*. Did he abandon her as soon as she became a Christian? Had he died — perhaps as a martyr? Was he perhaps one of the men who had been arrested with her? This is a question to which we have no answer.

Finally the time came for the trial. One day, as Perpetua was eating, guards entered her cell and escorted her to the city hall, where she, with the others, was to be interrogated. During the trial Perpetua placed her son in her father's arms. When it was her turn to be interrogated, the old man ran up to her with the baby in his arms. "Have pity on your son!" he shouted.

The procurator Hilarianus, who was presiding, said to Perpetua, "Spare the grey hairs on your father, spare the infancy of your son, offer sacrifice for the well-being of the emperors."

"I will not do so," answered Perpetua.

"Are you a Christian?" asked Hilarianus.

"I am a Christian."

At this point Perpetua's father went berserk and had to be removed forcibly from the courtroom. Thereupon Hilarianus sentenced Perpetua and her comrades to be thrown to the wild beasts. The prisoners showed no signs of terror or dismay, but, returned "cheerfully" to their dungeon to await execution.

Perpetua asked the deacon Pomponius to get her baby back from her father, who had taken him home with him. The old man refused to yield his grandson, but Perpetua was able to rest easy at the knowledge that "even as God willed it, the child no longer desired the breast."

A few days later, when the prisoners, now all crowded into the same cell, were praying, a "word" came to Perpetua and she named the name "Dinocrates." She was amazed that the name had come into her mind, as Dinocrates was a long-dead brother about whom she had not so much as thought of for years. Now she was "grieved as I remembered his misfortune." "This Dinocrates," she noted in her diary, had "died miserably" at the age of seven, "his face so eaten out with cancer that his death caused repugnance to all men."

Immediately she "began earnestly to make supplication and to cry with groaning to the Lord." That very night she was shown a vision in which she saw Dinocrates in "a gloomy place," "parched and very thirsty, with a filthy countenance." His face was horribly disfigured, the way it had been when he died.

> Between him and me there was a large interval, so that neither of us could approach to the other. And, moreover, where Dinocrates was, there was a pool full of water, having its brink higher than was the stature of the boy,

> and Dinocrates raised himself up as if to drink. And I was grieved that, although the pool held water, still on account of the height of its brink, he could not drink. And I was aroused and knew that my brother was in suffering. But I trusted that my prayer would bring help to his suffering, and I prayed for him every day until we passed over into the prison of the camp [outside the stadium].

In the prison camp Perpetua continued to pray day and night for Dinocrates, "groaning and weeping that he might be granted to me." Finally, she had another vision.

> I saw that the place which I had formally observed to be in gloom was now bright, and Dinocrates, with a clean body was finding refreshment. [His face was now healed] and that pool which I had seen before I saw now with its margin lowered even to the boy's navel. And one drew water from the pool incessantly, and upon its brink was a goblet filled with water, and Dinocrates drew near and began to drink from it and the goblet did not fail. And when he was satisfied, he went away from the water to play joyously, after the manner of children, and I awoke.

Perpetua was happy now, convinced that through her prayers Dinocrates, who had never heard of Christ in his lifetime, had been "translated from the place of punishment."

Members of the Christian community continued to visit the prisons. So did Perpetua's father, who made a final heartbreaking appeal to Perpetua. Tearing out his beard and throwing himself on the ground on his face, he began "to utter such words as might move all creation."

The night before the prisoners were to be executed, Perpetua had nother vision.

> I gazed upon an immense assembly in astonishment. And because I knew that I was given to the wild beasts, I marvelled that the wild beasts were not let loose upon me. Then there came forth against me a certain Egyp-

tian, horrible in appearance, with his backers, to fight me. And there came to me, as my helpers and encouragers, handsome youths; and I was stripped and became a man. Then my helpers began to rub me with oil, as is the custom for contest; and I beheld the Egyptian on the other hand rolling in the dust. And a certain man came forth, of wondrous height, so that he even overtopped the top of the amphitheatre . . . and he carried a rod, as if he were a trainer of gladiators, and a green branch, upon which were apples of gold. And he called for silence and said, 'This Egyptian, if he should overcome this woman, shall kill her with the sword; and if she shall conquer him, she shall receive this branch.' Then he departed. And we drew near to one another, and began to deal out blows. He sought to lay hold of my feet, while I struck at his face with my heels; and I was lifted up into the air, and began thus to thrust at him as if spurning the earth. But when I saw that there was some delay, I joined my hands so as to twine my fingers with one another; and I took hold upon his head and he fell on his face, and I trod on his head. And the people began to shout, and my backers to exult. And I drew near to the trainer and took the branch, and he kissed me and said to me, 'Daughter, peace be with you,' and I began to go glorious to [the gate of victors].

This vision Perpetua interpreted as a message that she was to fight against the devil.

Saturus, the man who had been instructing Perpetua, also had a vision that evening. He told her about it.

We had suffered and we were gone forth from the flesh and were beginning to be borne by four angels into the east, and their hands touched us not. And we floated . . . as if ascending a gentle slope. And being set free, we at length saw the first boundless light, and I said, 'Perpetua (for she was at my side), this is what the Lord promised to us. We have received the promise.' And while we were borne by those same four angels, there appeared to us a vast space which was like a pleasure-garden, having rose-trees and every kind of flower. And the height of the trees was after the measure of the cypress, and their leaves were flowering incessantly. Moreover, there in the pleasure-garden four other angels appeared, brighter than the previous ones, who, when they saw us, gave us honor and said to the rest of the angels, 'Here they are! Here they are!' with admiration. And those four angels who bore us, being greatly afraid, put us down, and we passed over on foot the space of a furlong in a broad path. There we found Jocundus and Saturninus and Artaxius, who had suffered the same persecution and were burnt alive, and Quintus, who, also himself a martyr, had departed in prison. And we asked where the rest were. And the angels said to us, 'Come first, enter and greet your Lord.'

And we came near to a palace, the walls of which were such as if they were built of light, and before the gate of the palace stood four angels, who clothed those who entered with white robes. And being clothed, we entered and saw the boundless light and heard the united voice of some who said without ceasing, 'Holy! Holy! Holy!' And in the midst of the palace we saw as it were a hoary man sitting, having snow-white hair and with a youthful countenance, and his feet we saw not. On his right hand and on his left were four and twenty elders, and behind them a great many others were standing. We entered with great wonder and stood before the throne and the four angels raised us up and we kissed Him and He passed His hand over our faces. And the rest of the elders said to us, 'Let us stand,' and we stood and made peace. And the elders said to us, 'Go and enjoy.' And I said, 'Perpetua, you have what you wish.' And she said to me, 'Thanks be to God, that joyous as I was in the flesh, I am now more joyous here.'

Saturus saw Optatus the bishop and Aspasius the priest, who had been rebuked because they let their congregations assemble "as if returning from the circus" and for "contending about factitious matters." He also "began to recognize many brethren and . . . martyrs" and was "nourished with an indescribable odor, which satisfied us."

Felicitas, the slave girl, was heartbroken that she was not to die with her friends. She was eight months pregnant, and the law forbade the execution of women with child. So she prayed that she might be delivered. Immediately she entered into labor. One of the jailers scoffed, "If you're in such pain now, what are you going to do when you're thrown to the beasts, which you despised when you refused to sacrifice?"

"Now it is I alone who suffer," she said. "Then there will be Another in me who will suffer for me, because I am about to suffer for Him." She gave birth to a daughter, whom she gave to her sister to rear.

That night the prisoners were given a last supper. The jailers were dumbfounded that, far from showing signs of fear or depression, the Christians were laughing and joking. Some of the jailers made fun of them. "Note our faces diligently," warned Saturus, "so that you may recognize them on the Day of Judgment." On the other hand, one jailer, named Pudens, was so impressed by the Christians that he told Saturus privately that he accepted Christ as his Savior.

On the morning of the scheduled execution, the Christians were marched into the stadium. Secundulus had already died in prison, so the martyrs were five: Saturus, Revocatus, Saturninus, Felicitas, and Perpetua. Everyone noted their "joyous and brilliant countenances." Normally the condemned men were forced to don the clothing of the priests of Saturn and the women the garb of the priestesses of Ceres. It was Felicitas who voiced a strong objection. They had forfeited their lives because they refused to serve the pagan deities and had no intention of allowing themselves to go into eternity masquerading as such objectionable beings. The authorities allowed the prisoners to have their wish. While Perpetua and Felicitas chanted psalms, the male prisoners turned to the procurator Hilarianus, who sat in the stands, and declared, "You are judging us, but remember, one day God will judge you."

The prisoners were run through the gauntlet, then Saturus

and Revocatus were tied to a scaffold as a wild boar was let loose on them. The terrified animal, however, instead of charging the prisoners, turned on its keeper and injured him so badly that he died the next day. A bear was then released, but it too refused to touch the prisoners. The two men were unbound and returned to the prison to await further tortures.

Perpetua and Felicitas were now led into the arena. They were forced to appear naked, but this was too much for the crowd, which was moved to a kind of pity at the sight of "a young woman of delicate frame and another with breasts still drooping from her recent childbirth." The women were ordered back and allowed to dress. Now they were led back into the arena, where "a very fierce cow" was let loose on them. The animal first charged Perpetua, tossed her on its horns, and threw her to the ground. In this dreadful moment Perpetua's chief thought was her modesty. Seeing that her dress was ripped open, she gathered the torn folds of her garment and drew them around her middle. She tied up her disheveled hair. In those days, loose and flowing hair was a symbol of grief and mourning, and Perpetua declared, "It is not becoming for a martyr to suffer with disheveled hair, lest she appear to be mourning in her glory." While she was arranging herself, Felicitas was being attacked by the maddened cow. When the animal left the girl, Perpetua went over to her and helped her to her feet. Both women, bruised and bloody, were allowed to leave the arena and return to prison and the other Christians. There Perpetua fainted. When she regained her senses, she kept asking when she was going to be led out to the cow. She could not be persuaded that she had already faced the animal until Rusticus, another prisoner, called her attention to her cuts and bruises and her torn clothing. Her brother — the one who was a Christian — was there and she told him, "Stand fast in the faith and love one another, all of you, and don't be grieved at my sufferings."

It was now time for Saturus to be led out to face a leopard, which he expected to kill him with one bite. This did not prove to be the case, and Saturus was led back to prison, bloody but alive. He took a ring from his finger and bathed it in his blood and gave it to Pudens, the jailer who had recently professed Christ. "Farewell," he said. "Remember my faith. Don't let these things disturb you, but confirm you."

Now it was time for all the prisoners, mangled and bloodied by the animals, to be dispatched by gladiators. The five were marched out into the arena. Before the men, far more savage then any of the beasts they encountered, set upon them, the martyrs embraced and kissed each other. All were quickly killed except Perpetua. The gladiator assigned to end her life was nervous and missed her heart, but caused her to scream in pain. He was trembling so violently that he could barely hold his sword, so Perpetua laid hold of his weapon and guided it to her throat. As the crowd dispersed to their homes after witnessing the hideous spectacle, many were heard to exclaim, "They probably couldn't have killed that woman at all unless she herself had done it. It's clear that the impure spirits feared her."

Perpetua was typical of the Christians of North Africa, who were well-known for their asceticism and their uncompromising attitude toward life. Their guiding light was the "stern" Tertullian, the jurist-turned-priest who has already been quoted several times. A prolific adulterer in his youth who had "drained the cup of lust to the dregs," Tertullian did a 180-degree turnabout after his conversion, and insisted on a life-style rigorously strict. He strongly opposed churchmen who urged converts to go into hiding. To do so, argued Tertullian, was the equivalent of apostasy. When Perpetua wrote that her dungeon had become a palace and that she preferred being there to being anywhere else, she was echoing Tertullian, who, in his *Address to the Martyrs*, declared:

> For if we reflect that the world is more really a prison, we shall see that you have gone out of a prison rather than into one . . . Wherefore, O Blessed, you may regard yourselves as having been translated from a prison [i.e. the world] to a place of safety. It is full of darkness, but you yourselves are light; it has bonds, but God has made you free. Unpleasant exhalations are there, but you are an

> odor of sweetness. The judge is daily looked for, but you shall judge the judges themselves. Sadness may be there, for him who sighs for the world's enjoyments. . . . The Christian, outside the prison, has renounced the world, but in the prison he has renounced a prison too. It is of no consequence where you are in the world, you who are not of it. And if you have lost some of the world's sweets, it is the way of business to suffer present loss, that after [death] the gains may be the larger.[3]

Tertullian held that no one could be considered a good Christian who attended public amusements of any kind — not only the repulsive gladiatorial games, but any sort of athletic event whatever, or even the theater. He later went so far as to insist that the Church had no authority to forgive murder, immorality, or the renunciation of the faith. Eventually he broke with the bishops of Rome and associated himself with a sect called the Montanists, which taught the imminent return of Christ and encouraged emotional services and manifestations of "spiritual gifts."

Although the Christians of Carthage were unusually strict and uncompromising, Christians throughout the empire responded with bravery to Severus' edict. In the city of Alexandria, Egypt, for instance, "untold numbers" of converts were executed. It was during the persecution by Severus that there came into prominence a Church leader no less dedicated to his faith than Tertullian, possibly even more ascetic than the Carthaginian sage, but nonetheless of a far more irenic and amiable disposition.

Origen Adamantius was the eldest of the seven sons of Leonidas, a Church leader who was imprisoned for the crime of proselytization. Origen, although only in his teens, longed to be a martyr, and his mother had to hide his clothing to keep him from surrendering to the authorities as an instructor of converts. Imprisoned in his house by his mother, Origen nevertheless managed to send a letter to his father urging him not to compromise his faith.

Leonidas was in fact beheaded, his property was confiscated, and his widow and children were plunged into desperate straits. It was only through a wealthy lady who took Origen into her home that he was able to finish his studies. Before he was eighteen, Origen became the principal of the Christian Catechetical School of Alexandria. Despite the fact that conversion to Christianity was a capital offense, he was besieged by pagans who wanted to become Christians. Over a period of several years, Origen instructed hundreds of converts. He had an enthusiasm for Christ that was contagious. Pagans said of him that "his manner of life was as his doctrine, and his doctrine was as his life."[4] Surviving on a near starvation diet, he slept on the floor, and but for a few hours in twenty-four devoted several hours in the day to strenuous manual labor and most of the night to the study of the Scriptures. He kept literally Christ's injunction about not keeping more than one coat or one pair of shoes. He also took literally — with what Eusebius calls "absurd literalism" — the Savior's words that "there are eunuchs who have made themselves eunuchs for the sake of the kingdom of heaven" (Matthew 19:12).

A number of Origen's students were arrested and killed. Those who were Roman citizens were beheaded; the others were burnt alive. One of Origen's most promising pupils was a beautiful girl named Potamiaena, whose chastity and virginity were beyond reproach. She and her mother were seized and subjected to tortures "too terrible to speak of." The magistrate Aquila ordered that Potamiaena be subjected to "several tortures upon her entire body." When she still refused to renounce her faith, he threatened to hand her over to the gladiators to be gang-raped. On second thought, he decided that it would save a lot of trouble to have her taken away and executed immediately. The officer assigned to lead her to her execution was named Basilides. As the crowd pressed forward and shouted obscenities at Potamiaena, Basilides drove them back and protected the unfortunate girl from insult. Potamiaena thanked him for his kindness and promised, when she was in heaven, to "ask the Lord for him" to repay him for all he had done for her. She was killed by having boiling pitch poured over her, little by little, from her toes to the crown of her head. The record is silent as to the fate of her mother.

Not long afterwards, Basilides was asked by his fellow soldiers to take some sort of an oath, not at all related to religion. Basilides refused, saying that he would not swear under any circumstances, since he was a Christian. His comrades laughed, thinking at first that he was joking, but when he insisted that he was serious, they took him to their superior officer, who put him in jail. A group of Christians visited Basilides in prison and asked him why he had converted, to which the soldier replied that three days after her martyrdom, Potamiaena had appeared to him in a dream and put a wreath around his head. "I have prayed for you to the Lord," she had said, "and have obtained what I asked. Soon I will take you with me." When they heard this, the Christians baptized Basilides, who was beheaded the next day.[5]

Origen, despite the risk to his life, did not hesitate to visit the martyrs in prison, encouraging them to stand fast. He frequently managed to attend their trials and executions. Although the authorities in Alexandria were confining their arrest to converts at the time, Origen was once nearly stoned to death by crowds of angry pagans. Eventually, when it was clear that the authorities were about to devote their attention to those who disseminated Christian doctrine, Origin's friends insisted that he go into hiding, persuading him that he was too valuable an asset to the Church to be lost at so young an age. And thus the celebrated catechist spent several years "underground."

In February 211, Septimius Severus died at York, England, after a long "grave" illness, his last words being, "I have been everything and gained nothing."[6] He was succeeded by his sons, Geta and Caracalla. Caracalla lost no time in killing his brother and gaining a reputation as a bloodstained tyrant. As in the case of Commodus, although Caracalla was a cruel incompetent who cared nothing about religion, he never bothered to enforce his father's decree, and so the Church knew peace for a time and Origen and others who had gone into hiding were able to return to their homes.

# 9

# 'Terror was universal': The persecution by Decius

The fortunes of the faith did not change substantially after the assassination of Caracalla in 217 or during the brief reign of his successor Macrinus, who was succeeded in 218 by a dissolute young man named Antoninus, who proved to be one of the most hated and despised of all Roman rulers. Antoninus, who was called Elagabalus, was the son of Julia Soaemia, daughter of Septimius Severus' sister-in-law Julia Maesa. Soaemia claimed that Antoninus was the illegitimate son of Caracalla, but it was widely believed that Soaemia was so debauched that even she did not know the identity of the father. A native of Emesa, Syria, Antoninus was a high priest of the sun god Elagabalus, from whom he took his title — and worshipped a black stone which represented the phallus of the deity. Elagabalus was as disgusting as the divinity he served. Even after he attained to the highest power, he practiced human sacrifice, choosing young boys from all over Italy to be tortured to death and sliced open so that he and his magicians could predict the future from their entrails.[1] The bisexual emperor, who had seven wives and was described as "constantly in heat," loved to wear women's apparel and recruited boys from all over the empire to serve his lusts, and, on the other hand, made it his practice to sleep with a different harlot every night. When not engaged in the pleasures of the bedchamber, Elagabalus lay on his golden coverlets, guzzling "swimming pools full" of wine and gorging himself on peacocks' tongues, flamingo brains, parrots' heads, sows' udders, and mullets' intestines.

Elagabalus identified himself with his god and erected a temple to himself, the Elagabalum, on the Palatine Hill. He said he planned to erect images of the Roman gods, as well as of Jesus, whom he recognized as a subordinate deity. This was so that "the priesthood of Elagabalus should possess the secret of all religions." Indeed, Elagabalus expected that his cult would replace the old Roman religion and be adopted by everyone in the empire.[2]

During his four-year reign, Elagabalus did not harm the Church, but had he lived long enough, he surely would have tried to force Christian leaders to submit to his cultic amalgamation, and persecution would have broken out anew. Elagabalus was more engrossed in his own dissipations than in promoting a new religion. Then, on March 11, 222, the army revolted and Elagabalus and his mother were hacked to pieces as they pleaded for mercy in the public lavatory whither they had fled.

The new emperor, Elagabalus' adopted son, was the fourteen-year-old Alexander Severus, who was almost the exact opposite of his predecessor. Described as a happy, mild, gentle soul, Alexander declared he did not want to let a single day go by without doing some act of goodness.[3] Both he and his mother, Julia Mammaea, were attracted to Christianity. The empress-mother, whom Eusebius characterizes as "one of the most religious and high principled of women," asked for a conference with Origen. When they met at Antioch, Origen talked to Julia Mammaea "for some time, revealing to her many things, to the glory of the Lord and of the virtue of the divine message."[4]

Alexander, for his part, ordered engraved on all public buildings the famous saying of Jesus, "Treat others as you would like others to treat you." He executed Elagabalus' "ministers of debauchery" and tried his best to stamp out the "hellish crime" of homosexuality and to promote chastity and continence among his people. He even forbade men and women to use the public baths at the same time. In contrast to previous emperors, Alexander refused to allow himself to be worshipped as a god, and even insisted that his subjects call him by his first name. "Chaste and regular" in his private life and frugal in his eating and drinking, he declared that "the majesty of the empire consists in virtue, not in the ostentation of riches."[5] According to the historian Lampridius:

> As soon as there was opportunity — that is, if he had not spent the night with his wife — he performed his devotions in the early morning hours in his oratory, in which he had statues of the divine princes and also a select number of the best men and more holy spirits, among whom he had . . . Christ, Abraham, Orpheus, and others similar, as well as statues of his ancestors.[6]

Thus, like Elagabalus, Alexander Severus favored a kind of religious syncretism in which Jesus would be integrated into an all-embracing religious potpourri. Alexander came up squarely on the side of the Church, however, when there was a dispute between a Christian house-church and the Guild of Tavern Keepers over a tract of land. When the dispute was appealed to the emperor, Alexander ruled in favor of the Christians. This decision was extremely important, in that Alexander recognized the Christian Church as a legal entity with the right to bring suit in a court of law. At long last, Christianity was recognized as an authorized religion within the Roman Empire.

This state of affairs was short-lived. Although a man of maximum moral rectitude, Alexander was a weak and fumbling ruler, and in 235 was overthrown and killed by a general named Maximin Thrax. Of Gothic ancestry, Maximan Thrax was born a peasant in what is now Bulgaria. Beginning life as a shepherd, Thrax could neither read nor write, but working his way up through the ranks of the army, he distinguished himself for his toughness and ferocity. Sixty-two when he became emperor, Maximin Thrax was physically a genuine giant standing eight feet tall, with fingers so thick that he could wear his wife's bracelet as a finger ring.[7] With the aid of emetics and the vomitorium, the emperor ate up to forty pounds of meat a day and was every bit as voracious a tippler as Elagabalus. When enraged, as was frequently the case, the new emperor was wont to bang his massive head against the wall, and, to relieve his tensions, he enjoyed knocking out horses' teeth or shattering their hooves with a kick from one of his immense and powerful legs. Thrax, who never sat foot in Rome, was bitterly hostile to the Church. Some said that his hatred arose because he attributed a severe earthquake to the ire of neglected gods. Others felt that his antipathy to the Church was simply a reaction to his predecessor's favorable attitude. Moreover, at a time when Thrax needed troops to consolidate his power, he resented the fact that most Christian men chose to be conscientious objectors. Furthermore, in desperate need of money, the emperor imagined that the Church had vast resources that he could confiscate.

Maximin Thrax withdrew official recognition of Christianity as a legal religion and decreed the arrest of all Christian clergy and the confiscation of all Church property. In September 235, two of the most prominent Christian leaders in Italy were arrested. One was Pontian, bishop of Rome, a former slave who had become a Christian in his teens, and, in 230, at sixty-two, had succeeded to the pontificate. The other was Hippolytus, who for many years had been Pontian's archenemy. He had clashed with Pontian's predecessor Callistus over the Roman bishop's policy of readmitting into the fellowship of the Church penitents, who after baptism had been guilty of apostasy, murder, or immorality. Like Tertullian, Hippolytus felt that, although God might forgive such sins, the Church had no authority to pardon mortal sin after baptism. Hippolytus had disagreed so sharply with Callistus that when the pope died, he allowed his own followers to proclaim him bishop of Rome. The pope in those days was chosen in a general election by the adult male and female Christians of Rome, and although the majority opted for Urban I, Hippolytus and his followers insisted that he, and not Urban, was the legitimate bishop.

Thrax did not care about such distinctions of Church policy, and had both men arrested along with scores of other priests and deacons. A day after his arrest, realizing that he was doomed, Pontian abdicated in favor of a man named Anterus. Then, in October, he was shipped to the Sardinian mines, where Hippolytus was already a prisoner. Eventually the two leaders, maimed and mutilated, met and were reconciled. Then, in January 236, the two were separated by the soldiers from the file of prisoners, knocked to the ground, thrashed, and then stabbed to death with a sword thrust through the jugular vein. As the blood spurted out, dogs pawed at the faces and necks of the dying men, lapping up their blood. When the guards were satisfied that Pontian and Hippolytus were dead, their bodies were loaded onto a flat board and dumped into a sewer.[8]

Fortunately, Thrax was too preoccupied fighting his rivals to bring the full weight of imperial authority against the Church. In the few months following Thrax's assassination in 238, several men succeeded each other as emperor in quick succession. Gordian III, who emerged victorious, never bothered the Church. During the six years he was emperor he was too busy trying to consolidate his power to worry about religious matters. In 244, while campaigning on the eastern frontier against Iran, Gordian, who was only in his early twenties, was assassinated by a general named Philip.

Philip, called the Arab, was born in Galilee and grew up in a predominantly Christian area, and while never himself a Christian, he was, like Alexander Severus, sympathetic to the faith, and cultivated the friendship of Origen. A kind and gentle man tormented by a guilty conscience over his murder of his predecessor, the Arab was said to have sought the counsel of Church leaders, and even toyed with the idea of baptism.

It had now been more than three decades since a full-scale attack had been launched on the Church. Between Septimius Severus and Philip the Arab, the only persecution had been the short-lived campaign of Maximin Thrax. Now, by the middle of the third century, Christians comprised perhaps ten percent of the population of the major cities and towns. In more rural areas, the faith took hold more slowly, hence the expression "pagan" (which comes from *paganus*, which, in Latin, means "rustic") for those who continued to worship the old gods. The austere Tertullian, who had died in his bed perhaps in his ninth decade, probably around the year 240, was too much of a hard-line perfectionist ever to reconcile himself with the mainstream of the Church. Challenging the pagan world, he declared, "What will you do with all the thousands of men and women, folk of both sexes, of all ages and every class, who will offer themselves to you? How many stakes and swords will you need?" Tertullian had pointed out that at least one person in ten in every city would have to be slain if the Christian faith were to be eradicated. Among the condemned, the persecutors would recognize some of their family or friends. "You will never destroy our sect," the old priest had cried. "Mark this well: when you think you are striking it down, you are, in reality, strengthening it. The public will become restive at the sight of so much courage. It will long to know its origin. And once a man has recognized the truth, he is ours!"[9]

Like Tertullian, Origen, who was still alive in the reign of the Arab, seems to have lived without the expectation of another persecution. A man whose brilliance was respected by Christians and pagans alike, he had been ordained a priest in middle age, and after a quarrel with the bishop of Alexandria, had gone to live in Caesarea, Palestine, where he opened a catechetical school. Because he wanted to know the answer to all mysteries, Origen loved to speculate, and some of his ideas, such as the preexistence of souls, the possibility of universal salvation, and the advisability of praying even for the salvation of the devil, had subsequently been ruled unacceptable. Unlike Tertullian, Origen was never disobedient to the teachings of the Church as they were set forth in his day. It was only after Origen's death that some of his ideas were condemned. In his time, no one questioned Origen's holiness or his faithfulness to the Church of Jesus Christ. Origen observed that in the last few decades, "only a few, now and then — so few that they may easily be numbered" — had died for the faith, "while God has always prevented a war of extermination against the whole body of Christians, since it is His pleasure that they should remain."[10]

Of a somewhat different opinion was one of the most remarkable of the younger leaders, the new bishop of Carthage, Thascius Ciprianus, or Cyprian. A celebrated Professor of Rhetoric, Cyprian had been converted to Christianity in 246, in his mid-forties. Such an eminent and enabled a man was he that almost immediately he was ordained to the priesthood and two years later was elevated to the episcopal throne of

Carthage. "So much sanctity and grace beamed from his face that it confounded the minds of the beholders," wrote a contemporary.[11] Despite the peace that prevailed when he assumed his episcopal duties, Cyprian warned his faithful of the possibility of renewed persecution. He spoke frequently of martyrdom, calling it "the end of sins, the limit of dangers, the guide of salvation, the teacher of patience, the home of life," urging his flock to an uncompromising devotion to the Lord that would not hesitate to accept martyrdom, if that became necessary. "What interest have you in this commerce of life and nature, if the amplitude of heaven is awaiting you?"[12]

Cyprian held before his flock graphic pictures of the bliss of heaven, if one was faithful, or, on the other hand, the torments of hell reserved for the unbelieving and apostate. The bishop warned his hearers of "a horrible place . . . with an awful murmuring and groaning of souls bewailing, and with flames belching forth through the horrid darkness of thick night . . . always breathing out the raging fires of a smoking furnace, while the confined mass of flames is restrained or relaxed for the various degrees of punishment." Relying, at least partly, on images from Greek mythology, Cyprian vividly described the torment of the damned:

> Some, for example, are bowed down by an intolerable load, some are hurried by merciless force over the abrupt descent of a precipitous path, and the heavy weight of clanking chains bends over them in its bondage. Some there are also, whom a wheel is closely turning, and an unwearied dizziness tormenting; and others whom, bound to one another, whom tenacious closeness, body clinging to body, compresses, so that both fire is devouring and the load of iron is weighing down, and the uproar of many is torturing.

In contrast, Cyprian described heaven in pastoral images:

> In the verdant fields the luxuriant earth clothes itself with tender grass, and is pastured with the scent of flowers;

> where the groves are carried up to the lofty hill-top, and where the tree clothes with a thicker foliage whatever spot the canopy, expanded by its curving branches, may have shaded. There is no excess of cold or of heat, nor is it needed that in autumn the fields should rest, or again in the young spring that the fruitful earth should bring forth. All things are of one season: fruits are borne of a continued summer . . . A joyous repose possesses the people, a calm house shelters them, where a gushing fountain in the midst issues from the bosom of a broken hollow, and flows in sinuous mazes by a course deep-sounding, at intervals to be divided among the sources of rivers springing from it. . . .[13]

The war of extermination that God had thus far prevented was now close at hand, and both Origen and Cyprian would live to see it burst like a storm over their heads. The empire had fallen on evil days. The frontiers were now constantly under attack by the seemingly innumerable Germanic tribes pressing southwest from eastern and central Europe. Decimated not only by sickness and war, but also a falling birthrate, the population of the empire was declining. Children not destroyed in their mother's wombs were frequently abandoned in the fields to be eaten by roving packs of dogs, while in the cities unwanted babies were frequently thrown alive into the sewers. Many pagans continued to feel that the invasions, the epidemics, as well as the severe economic troubles of the days were the result of the displeasure of neglected gods, but the Emperor Philip paid little attention to such complaints, but his star was setting. During the summer of 249, Philip was, however, like all his predecessors of the previous thirty years, the victim of a bloody revolution. A general named Decius proclaimed himself emperor, and in September 249, engaged Philip in battle near Verona, Italy. Philip and his son were defeated and slain, and Decius assumed the supreme power.

Gaius Messius Quintus Trajanus Decius was then in his late fifties. As in the case of Trajan and Marcus Aurelius, even his victims had to admit that Decius was a man of highest personal integrity. Of Roman aristocratic lineage, Decius was born in the town of Sirmium on the Danube River, in what is now Yugoslavia. A thin man with a serious face, tight lips, and a long, narrow face, noted for his austere self-discipline, Decius had held a number of important posts during a distinguished and irreproachable career. Unlike most of his immediate predecessors, Decius adhered strictly to the Roman National Religion and sincerely agreed with those who blamed recent troubles on the neglect of the old gods. Now that the empire faced a serious threat from a powerful German tribe known as the Ostrogoths, Decius felt that it was imperative that all his subjects return to the Old Religion. The old gods must have the allegiance of every citizen, even if it meant that the emperor would have to kill over a million people to enforce compliance. According to Origen, Decius resolutely determined to wipe out "the very name of Christ everywhere."[14]

Decius decreed that throughout the empire, even in remote villages, soldiers were to seize everyone suspected of being a Christian. Rich, poor, young, old, male, and female were to be interviewed by local commissions composed of imperial officials and prominent pagans from their community. Suspects were to be taken to a temple and invited to sacrifice to the gods. Those who did so were to be freed after being issued a certificate testifying to their compliance. The procedure was standardized throughout the empire. Copies of some of these certificates have been preserved. Typical is this one from Egypt, dated June 25, 250:

> Presented to the Commission for Sacrifices in the village of Alexander Island, by Aurelius Diogenes, the son of Sabatus, of the village of Alexander Island, about seventy-two years of age, with a scar on the right eyebrow.
>
> I have at other times always offered to the gods as well as also now in your presence, and according to the regulations, have offered, sacrificed, and partaken of the sacrificial meal, and I pray you to attest to this. Farewell. I, Aurelius Diogenes, have presented this.[15]

But even before Decius' edict was published, violence broke out against the Christians in the city of Alexandria. Founded by Alexander the Great, this "Second City of the Empire" was renowned as a center of learning and famed for its lighthouse (considered one of the "Seven Wonders of the World"), its medical school, and for the largest library in the world. Alexandria was also a major industrial center. Its population of more than a million was made up of Egyptians, Greeks, Romans, Copts, Nubians, Syrians, Phoenicians, and Spaniards, and these ethnic groups were forever rioting and fighting. There had been a large Jewish population for many centuries, but, during the reign of Trajan, it had been almost completely exterminated during a riot. Now, late in 249, in the beginning of the reign of Decius, a similar program was directed at the large Christian community.

For a year, a heathen prophet had been stirring up popular feeling against the Christians, blaming them for all the current problems. Finally, the prophet, whose name has not come down to us, gathered a mob of savage thugs who stormed into the Christian quarter of the city. They first seized an old man named Metras and ordered him to blaspheme Christ. When he refused, they beat him with sticks and clubs, put out his eyes with sharp reeds, and stoned him to death in a public square. The next victim was a recent convert named Quinta. She was dragged into a pagan temple and commanded to sacrifice. When she refused, she was tied up and attached to a horse and dragged through the cobblestoned streets of the city, with a howling mob following, cursing her, kicking her, and beating her. When they reached the same square where Metras had perished, they stoned her to death, too.

The mob now went crazy in an orgy of blood, rampaging through the Christian quarter, plundering, looting, murdering, and robbing Christian homes of anything considered valuable, and burning everything else in huge bonfires. Despite these outrages, there was no resistance on the part of the Christians, nor was there a capitulation. The bishop of Alexandria, who escaped with his life because he stayed at home — the last place the mob expected him to be — wrote that he knew of only one victim who denied his Lord. The others watched serenely as their houses and possessions were fired, refusing to fight back as they were beaten, tortured, and killed.

The mob went after a "wonderful old lady" named Apollonia, who was one of the pillars of the Christian community at Alexandria. She was renowned for her great holiness as well as for her lifelong virginity. (There were no convents of nuns as such in those days, but it was common for men and women to vow themselves to celibacy, dedicating their lives to the service of the Church.) Several ruffians slugged Apollonia mercilessly in the face until all her teeth were knocked out. The mob erected a pyre in the same square where Metras and Quinta had been stoned, and threatened to burn the old woman alive unless she renounced Christ. With the orange flames crackling angrily in front of her, Apollonia seemed to waver. "Take your hands off me and give me a little time to think it over," she asked. But as soon as the men who were holding her released their grip, the old lady straightaway leaped into the flames and was burned to ashes.[16] Because of the nature of her tortures, St. Apollonia has long been involved as the patroness of those afflicted with dental problems. When Apollonia was dead, the mob attacked another Church leader, named Serapion, in his home. Cruelly beaten, he was thrown headfirst from his window to his death.

The carnage went on for days. "There was no street, nor public road, nor lane open to us by day or night," recalled Bishop Dionysius. "For always and everywhere all of them cried out that if anyone would not repeat their impious words, he should immediately be dragged away and burned." Dionysius continued, recounting that for a long time the terror remained intense, until, finally, the rioters began to fight among themselves, and "turned their cruelty towards each other."[17]

When news of Decius' edict reached Alexandria, "terror was universal" there as it was throughout the empire, as violence against Christians was systematized and legitimized. Hundreds of thousands of people were now confronted with the choice of apostasy or death. Cyprian recalled the horrible sight and smell of "bodies hissing on red-hot plates" in Carthage,[18] and blood flowing in such profusion as to seem capable of "subduing the flames of hell with its . . . gore."[19] Many Christians stood fast, as "the limbs, beaten and torn as they were, overcame the hooks that bent and tore them. The scourge, often repeated with all its rage, could not conquer invincible faith, even though the membrane which enclosed the entrails was broken and it was no longer the limbs but the wounds of the servants of God that were tortured."[20] Cyprian continued: "Although the hook, springing forth from the stiffening ribs, is put back again into the wound, and with the repeated strokes of the whip the returning lash is drawn away with the rent portions of the flesh, still [the Christian] stands immovable, the stronger for his sufferings, revolving only this in his mind: that in the brutality of the executioners, Christ Himself is suffering."[21]

Many Christians were sentenced to the salt and metal mines, where they endured the same hideous brutality that had been visited upon the victims of Marcus Aurelius and Maximin Thrax. French historian Daniel-Rops wrote movingly of those victims: "One dares not think of their life in those suffocating caverns, of those wretched folk penned together like beasts, eating, sleeping, satisfying their natural needs in disgusting promiscuity. They had but one certainty, that they would never leave this Gehenna alive."[22]

As might have been expected, there were a number of Christians who, in the face of torture and death, capitulated. Dionysius of Alexandria wrote that some sacrificed out of fear of death, others out of dread of losing their jobs. Still others were badgered into sacrificing by relatives and friends.

> As their names were called, they approached the impure and impious sacrifices. Some of them were pale and trembled as if they were not about to sacrifice, but to be themselves sacrifices and offerings to the idols; so that they were jeered by the multitude who stood around, as it was plain to everyone that they were afraid either to die or to sacrifice. But some advanced to the altar more readily, declaring boldly that they had never been Christians.[23]

Many Christians saved themselves by purchasing from sympathetic magistrates certificates declaring that they had made sacrifice when in fact they had not. Church leaders strongly condemned this practice as simply another form of apostasy and capitulation.

Cyprian encouraged his followers to go into hiding. "Our Lord commanded us in times of persecution to yield and to fly. He taught this and he practiced it himself. For since the martyr's crown comes by the grace of God and cannot be gained before the appointed hour, he who retires for a time and remains true to Christ does not deny his faith but only abides his time."[24] So most of the Christians in and around Carthage followed the example of their bishop and went into hiding. Many fled into the desert. Some were never heard from again. Others remained there for the rest of their lives. In Egypt, a man named Paul, then twenty-three, took refuge in a remote cave near Thebes, and found so much peace there that he remained a holy hermit at that spot for another ninety years until his death at the age of one hundred and thirteen.

On the other hand, Bishop Fabian forbade the faithful at Rome to flee. Fabian had succeeded Anterus, who had been martyred by Maximin Thrax late in 235, only a month after succeeding Pontian. When the congregations at Rome had met to elect a successor to Anterus, few noticed Fabian, a simple country pastor in Rome on a visit, until, as Eusebius recorded, "suddenly a dove, flying down, lighted on his head, resembling the descent of the Holy Spirit on the Saviour in the form of a dove. Thereupon the people, as if moved by one Divine Spirit, with all eagerness and unanimity cried out that he was worthy, and, without delay took him and placed him upon the episcopal seat."[25] On January 20, 250, after refusing to sacrifice, Fabian was arrested and put to death. The rest of the clergy of Rome were either butchered or sentenced to the mines. Because of the virtual extermination of the Christian community in and around Rome, there was no bishop of Rome for months.

Similar scenes of bloodshed were played out elsewhere. Bishops Babylas of Antioch, Denis of Paris, and Saturninus of Toulouse were slaughtered along with most of their clergy.

The aged Bishop Alexander of Jerusalem, who had ruled his See for more than forty years and had been tortured during the persecution of Septimius, was arrested and taken to Caesarea for trial. After his "honorable and illustrious confession" at the tribunal of the governor, the old man was thrown into a dungeon, where he died within a few days.[26]

Origen, now sixty-five, was arrested in Caesarea. The agents of Decius recognized him as the most eminent spokesman for Christianity alive. It was to their advantage not to kill immediately this priest who had led thousands to Christ, but to keep him alive as long as possible under torture, in hopes of forcing him to renounce Christ and by his example encourage his followers to do likewise. For over a year Origen was confined in chains in a pitch-black cell, daily subjected to excruciating tortures. For days on end he was fixed in a device which pulled his legs apart until his joints were ripped to pieces. Origen endured his tortures without complaint. Yet he was not to attain the crown of martyrdom he had sought since he was a boy, for he was still languishing in prison when Decius died and the persecution was suspended. Released from prison a broken man, Origen died three years later at the age of sixty-nine, without regaining his health.

Clergy and intellectuals were by no means the only Christians to suffer. Throughout the empire, large numbers of ordinary folk refused to yield either to the temptation of phony certificates or to the threat of torture, and went to their deaths as witnesses for Christ. A poignant incident was recorded in Sicily, where Quintianus, the governor, fell in love with Agatha, a beautiful, talented girl from a wealthy family. Unbeknownst to Quintianus, Agatha was not only a Christian, but had taken a vow of celibacy. When she learned that the governor wanted to make her his bride, she fled her parents' home in Catania and went into hiding. Discovered and brought back to the governor, she declared that she was a Christian. After a month's imprisonment, Agatha was brought again before Quintianus, who asked if she had changed her mind. Replying in the negative, Agatha declared, "The service of Jesus Christ is the highest nobility and the truest freedom." Quintianus ordered the poor girl broken on the rack. When she still refused to reject Christ, the governor, in a rage, gave orders that Agatha's breasts be torn off. After this shameful act of mutilation, the savaged girl was thrown back into prison, where, denied all medical aid, she died four days later.[27] Because of the manner in which she was tortured, St. Agatha, in Christian art, is usually portrayed carrying her severed breasts on a dish.

Alexandria was the site of numerous scenes of courage in the face of torture and death. A soldier named Besas, a pagan, watched with horror as three Christians were brought to trial. The first, an aged man named Julian, so crippled that he could neither walk nor stand, was brought before the magistrate supported by two other prisoners and refused to sacrifice. While one of the other men capitulated, the third prisoner, whose name was Cronion, was one with his friend Julian in refusing to sacrifice. The two Christians were tied to the backs of camels and paraded about the city, savagely whipped all the while. Finally, to the delight of the howling crowd, the men were plunged into a pit of quicklime. Besas, who witnessed the trial as well as the execution, expressed his disgust and outrage and was arrested. Boldly proclaiming himself a convert to Christianity, he was instantly beheaded.

Bishop Dionysius recounted a typical day in the life of a magistrate in Alexandria during the reign of Decius. First, a Libyan named Macar was led to the dock. Despite the determined efforts of the judge to make him deny his faith, Macar held firm and was sentenced to burn alive. Next a group of six was led before the bench. The judge committed two of them, Epimachus and Alexander, to a dungeon to allow an opportunity for reconsideration. (There they were flogged daily and scraped with metal combs. After weeks of torture, they were buried alive in quicklime). Three of the women the judge ordered beheaded at once. The first was Atha, the second Mercuria, "a dignified old lady," and the third was Dionysia, "the mother of a large family." A fourth woman, Ammonarion, "a respectable young woman," was committed to the dungeon, where after days of "the most savage and prolonged torture," she died.

Next, four Egyptians were led into the courtroom. Three of them, Hero, Ater, and Isidore, were adults, but one, Dioscoros, was only fifteen years old. The judge tried first to talk the boy out of his commitment to Christ. When the expected "feeble resistance" proved to be unshakable, the judge ordered Dioscoros tortured. Part of his torment was watching his three friends torn limb from limb and burned alive before his eyes. Dioscoros, however, "behaved so splendidly in public and gave such wise answers when questioned in private, that he astonished the judge, who let him go, saying that in view of his youth, he would allow him to come to his senses."

The judge used different tactics with the next prisoner, an Egyptian by the name of Nemesion. Although he had been arrested for being a Christian, Nemesion was now accused of being a bandit as well as a Christian. He denied the former charge but confessed the latter, and, refusing to sacrifice, was flogged without mercy and then burned alive.

The next prisoner, after being harangued by the judge, seemed on the point of sacrificing, but several soldiers in attendance — Ammon, Zeus, Ptolemy, and Ingenuus — as well as another prisoner, an old man named Theophilus (who had not yet had his turn before the judge) were seen to gesture toward the prisoner in such a way as to encourage him to keep the faith. When everyone stared at the soldiers in amazement, all four went up to the judge and proclaimed themselves Christians. Along with the two prisoners, they were instantly sentenced to death.[28]

In many villages, especially in Egypt and North Africa, Christians, without even the opportunity to sacrifice, were "torn to pieces" by heathen mobs. Sometimes entire congregations, numbering in the hundreds, were buried alive together in quicklime. There were also incidents similar to that which befell Ischyrion, who was in government service in Alexandria. His employer, evidently suspicious, ordered him to sacrifice at his place of work. When Ischyrion refused, the employer seized a sharp pole and impaled him.[29]

Across the Mediterranean, in Pamphylia in Asia Minor, Nestor, bishop of the small town of Magida, ordered his flock to flee, but remained at home, calmly awaiting arrest. The imperial soldiers found Nestor at prayer and took him into custody. The bishop was amazed that everyone rose as a sign of respect to him when he entered the courtroom.

"God pardon you, why have you done this?" asked Nestor.

"Because your way of life is deserving of respect," he was told.

Nestor was taken into a room where stools were placed for the magistrates and lawyers and the only chair was offered to the bishop. "Sir, are you aware of the order of the emperor?" the head judge asked.

"I know the command of the Almighty, not that of the emperor," replied the bishop.

"Nestor, don't give us trouble. Don't force us to judge you."

"I obey the commands of the heavenly king."

"You're crazy!" protested the judge.

When Nestor continued his uncompromising line to the point of insult, characterizing the gods of Rome as devils, and insisting that the judges were themselves insane to sacrifice to them, the chief magistrate reluctantly announced that there was no recourse except to send Nestor to the governor. "Beware of torture," he said.

Signing the cross on his brow, Nestor declared, "Why threaten me with torture? The only torments I dread are those of my God. Be well-assured, in torture, or out of torture, Him shall I confess."

Nestor was taken to Pollio, governor of Pamphylia, at Perga. Like the officials of his hometown, Pollio was kind and courteous in urging the bishop to sacrifice. Nestor was unmoved. "Torment me as you see fit, with chains, wild beasts, or sword, as long as there is any breath in my body I will confess the name of my Lord Jesus Christ."

Pollio ordered Nestor tortured. As his sides were torn with iron hooks, Nestor chanted Psalm 34: "I will bless the Lord at all times; his praise shall continually be in my mouth. My soul makes its boast in the Lord; let the afflicted hear and be glad. O magnify the Lord with me, and let us exalt his name together! I sought the Lord, and he answered me, and delivered me from all my fears. . . ."

"Aren't you ashamed to put your faith in a mere man, and a short-lived one at that?" Nestor was asked.

"Let that be my confusion, and that also for all who call on the name of the Lord Jesus," answered Nestor.

"What, then, is your final choice," asked Pollio, "to be with us, or with your Christ?"

"With my Christ have I ever been, with Him am I now, and with Him shall I ever be."

"Nestor," said Pollio, "you have rejected the immortal gods to follow the Crucified One, so I will not be so wanting in devotion to this God of yours as to condemn you to any other death. I sentence you to be crucified on the wood."

Nailed to the cross, Nestor exhorted the crowds and bade them kneel and pray to God through Jesus Christ. They all knelt, and when he said his final amen, he gave up his spirit.[30]

One of the most notable martyrs in the eastern provinces was a soldier named Polyeuctus. At the time of the promulgation of Decius' decree, Polyeuctus was a pagan, but he had a close friend named Nearchus who was a Christian. When he learned of the decree, Nearchus went to see Polyeuctus and told him that as of the next day their friendship was ended. Alarmed, Polyeuctus said that this was impossible. What had he done? As far as he was concerned, only death could end their friendship. "You're right," said Nearchus. "We are about to be separated by death." He showed Polyeuctus the edict.

Much to Nearchus' surprise, his friend related a recent dream in which Christ had appeared to him and removed the soldier's uniform and replaced it with a gorgeous silk robe, linking it at the shoulder with a golden brooch. Christ had then mounted him on a winged horse. Nearchus was able to interpret Polyeuctus' dream in such a way that his friend not only believed in Christ, but longed to die for Him as well.

Polyeuctus was arrested first and refused to give up his faith, despite torture. In an attempt to convince the soldier to sacrifice, the authorities called off the torture and promised him promotion if only he would return to the worship of the old gods. When Polyeuctus remained adamant, the guards resumed the torture, beating him furiously with iron rods.

When the wife of Polyeuctus learned of his arrest, she brought their young son and wept so loudly that she could be heard throughout the prison. She begged him to sacrifice for the sake of the child, warning him that if he were executed, their property would be confiscated and his entire family would never be free of suspicion. Polyeuctus refused to give in, and urged his wife to accept Christ.

Convinced that there was no way of persuading the soldier to renounce his faith, the judge pronounced capital sentence. Giving thanks, Polyeuctus was led out to be beheaded, dying a "glorious death" after announcing to Nearchus, who had not yet been arrested and who had followed him to the place of execution, that they would soon meet in heaven.[31]

In Smyrna, Bishop Eudaemon complied with the authorities and sacrificed, as did most of his flock. One man who refused to follow the crowd was the priest Pionius. Arrested while celebrating Mass on February 23, 251 (the feast day of St. Polycarp), he was taken before the local high priest and urged to sacrifice.

"I am a Christian," Pionius declared.

"Who do you worship?" asked the priest, whose name was Polemon.

"I worship the Almighty God who made heaven and earth, all things in heaven and earth, and us men, as well, and who gives to all men liberally, as they need, whom we know through Christ, His Word."

"Sacrifice, then, only to the emperor, if you do not want to sacrifice to the gods of Rome."

"I cannot sacrifice to any man," replied Pionius. "I am a Christian."

"What is your name?" asked the pagan priest.

"Pionius."

"Are you a Christian?"

"Certainly I am."

"To which sect do you belong?"

"I belong to the Catholic Church. There is no other with Christ."

Polemon examined the other Christians who had been arrested along with Pionius. When one of them, Asclepiades, replied that he worshipped Jesus Christ, Polemon asked, "What? Is that another God?" The prisoner answered, "No. He is the same God of whom the others spoke."

Pionius and the other prisoners were taken to a dungeon, followed by a jeering crowd. The following day Polemon tried physically to force the prisoners to sacrifice. He ordered garlands, such as were worn by those who were performing the customary sacrifices, thrust onto the heads of Pionius and his comrades. When the Christians tore the wreaths off, Polemon, his patience exhausted, delivered them to Quintilianus, governor of Asia, who sentenced them to be racked and torn with iron hooks, and finally to be nailed to posts and burned alive.[32]

Decius, as far as his duties allowed, took an active part in the massacres. Whenever, during his campaigns, he entered towns and villages where there were large numbers of Christians, he ordered all suspected of professing Christ arrested, personally supervising the trials and executions of those who refused to sacrifice. Many Christians were tortured to death beneath his gaze. In Babylon, Decius ordered the arrest of Bishop Polychronius, along with three priests and two deacons. Decius personally ordered all six men to sacrifice to the gods of Rome.

Polychronius answered, "We offer ourselves in the Lord Jesus Christ, and will not bow to idols made with hands." Decius promptly ordered the men imprisoned. A few days later, the Church leaders were led once again into the presence of the emperor. "So, you are the sacrilegious Polychronius, who refuses to keep the commandments of the gods of the emperor!" roared Decius. When Polychronius did not reply, the emperor turned to the other clergy and snarled, "Your chief is silent."

One of the priests, Parmenias, disdainfully replied, "Our chief will not defile his mouth. He keeps the command of Our Lord, 'Cast not your pearls before swine.' Do you think it seemly that what has once been purified should be defiled with dung?"

"So, we're dung, are we?" bellowed the enraged emperor, who forthwith ordered the prisoners' tongues cut out before their execution. Before Parmenias was mutilated, he turned to Polychronius to ask the bishop to pray for him. When it was Polychronius' turn, the emperor once again bade him sacrifice to the gods. Polychronius again was silent. Decius was now beside himself with rage. "Smash in his mouth!" he screamed. Speechless and mangled, Polychronius, on the ground, raised his eyes to heaven, spread out his hands in silent prayer, and died.[33]

During the spring of 251, Decius spent most of his time in eastern Europe fighting the Ostrogoths, those "screaming, skin-clad" warriors led by Cniva. The emperor had won several battles and even issued coins commemorating his victories. Then, in June, he was pursuing Cniva's retreating army in expectation of striking a final blow, when he was ambushed in a swamp where the Danube empties into the Black Sea. As the Roman troops slogged through the mud, the Goths sent a rain of javelins hurtling upon them. Decius saw one of his sons killed before his eyes. "The loss of one soldier is not important for the Roman state," he shouted to his men. "Let no man mourn the emperor's son!" Along with thousands of his troops, Decius perished in the marsh, and his body was never found.[34]

# 10

# 'Don't you know that there are many gods?': Valerian tries to save the empire

When the death of Decius was announced, Gaius Vibius Trebonianus Gallus was proclaimed emperor. Scion of an ancient aristocratic family from Perugia, Italy, Gallus had served Decius loyally as governor of Moesia (part of modern Yugoslavia). He adopted the same policy toward the Church as his predecessor. According to Christian writer Hermammon Dionysius, Gallus did not recognize "the wickedness of Decius nor consider what destroyed him, but stumbled on the same stone, though it lay before his eyes."[1] What Hermammon meant was that Gallus, refusing to accept the fact that Decius' downfall was a result of his ban of the worship of the One True God, continued the dead emperor's mistake by attempting to keep his religious policies in force. Had he chosen to avail himself of the "holy men who were praying to God to grant . . . peace and health" to the nation, events, Hermammon thought might have turned out differently.

As events proved, Gallus had more pressing matters to consider than the suppression of Christianity. The Ostrogoths were rampaging through eastern Europe, and then, in the first year of the new reign, a natural disaster of almost unprecedented gravity occurred. Dionysius of Alexandria said that the pestilence was the greatest disaster that had ever befallen the empire.[2] According to medical historians, the disease was measles, to which the Romans had no resistance. Cyprian described the constant, violent, exhausting diarrhea, and intense fever "contracted in the very marrow of the bones," the continual vomiting, and the ulcers that broke out in the throat. Sometimes gangrene putrefied the extremities, and many of those who survived the infection were left blind, deaf, or crippled.[3] By the end of the year, five thousand people were dying each day in the vicinity of Rome alone. Fully half the population of Alexandria was wiped out. The population of the entire empire was decimated, and commerce and agriculture almost came to a halt.

As in the case of the smallpox epidemic a century earlier, Christians behaved heroically. Whereas non-Christians tended to flee the sick and dump even close family members still alive into the streets, Christians tended their sick, even at the risk of their lives. Many heathens, abandoned by their own families, were ministered to by Christians. Dionysius wrote of how the Christians of his diocese "raised the bodies [of the dead] to their bosom . . . closed their eyes and mouths, carried them on their shoulders, and laid them out." They "embraced them, washed them and wrapped them in graveclothes." Many Christians lost their lives in the epidemic, including many priests and deacons. But the heathens noted with amazement that Christians, when taken ill, accepted their pains cheerfully, and, on the point of death, told (as it was) survivors, "Your humble servant bids you good-bye." Pagans typically reacted with bitterness toward sickness and death. Characteristic of the time is the pagan epitaph, "I lift up my hands against the God who took me at the age of twenty, even though I had done nothing wrong." That anyone could accept death — especially premature death — with joy and tranquility amazed the pagans.

After Gallus had reigned for two troubled years, his officers staged a revolution. The emperor sent a request for help to his most loyal commander, Valerian, but before the general could move his troops from the Upper Rhine into Italy, Gallus had been overthrown and killed. Valerian put down the rebels and proclaimed himself emperor. Publius Licinius Valerianus, who was in his early sixties, was, like Gallus, a Roman aristocrat. Gibbon wrote of the man who had served as a consul and senator as well as military commander: "His noble birth, his mild but unblemished manner, his learning, prudence, and experience were revered by the Senate and people, and if mankind had been left at liberty to choose a master, their choice would most assuredly have fallen on Valerian."[4]

By the time Valerian took power, however, conditions

throughout the empire were atrocious. The measles epidemic aggravated a sharp decline in population, and commerce was paralyzed not only by the pandemic but also by continued devastation by the Ostrogoths. Historians have written of the "almost satanic violence" unleashed upon eastern Europe and Asia Minor by the Ostrogoths, who, like a swarm of locusts, destroyed everything in their path, threatening the very existence of civilized life in eastern Europe. Within the ruined towns and cities, total anarchy reigned. Roman citizens who survived the massacre began to prey upon each other and rob and loot the homes of fellow countrymen.[5] Trade and communication were disrupted and poverty and starvation were everywhere.

Even Christians tended to regard the situation with extreme pessimism. Cyprian, for example, wrote of the old age of the world, which "does not abide in that strength in which it formerly stood." He pointed out that in winter there was no longer sufficient rainfall to nourish the seeds and summers were too cool to ensure a good harvest. Even the natural resources of earth, such as marble and precious metals, seemed depleted. "The husbandman is failing in the fields, the sailor at sea, the soldier in camp. . . ." Owing to malnutrition, "We see grey hairs in boys — the hair falls out before it begins to grow, and life does not cease in old age, but it begins with old age. . . . Whatever is now born degenerates with the old age of the world itself; so that no one ought to wonder that everything begins to fail in the world, when the whole world is in the process of failing."[6]

To make matters worse for Christians, dissension broke out within the Church. Valerian at first did not enforce the anti-Christian legislature of his predecessor, but with the easing of the persecution, the question arose as to what action should be taken by the Church against Christians who had sacrificed to the gods of Rome. Although thousands had preferred their integrity to life, the number of compromisers was embarrassingly large. One priest by the name of Novatian argued that the Church had no right to readmit those who had denied their faith. The visible Church, he argued, should be a communion of saints, and saints only. When Bishop Stephen of Rome insisted that the "lapsed" could be readmitted after a long period of penances, Novatian and his followers formed their own sect, which they called the Puritans,* which gained a considerable following.

Stephen then clashed with Cyprian over the issue of rebaptizing the lapsed. Although Cyprian agreed with the pope that the lapsed could be readmitted to Communion, he insisted that they should be rebaptized. Moreover, Cyprian contended that baptism administered by sectarian priests, such as those of the Puritans, was invalid. Stephen insisted that rebaptism was not necessary and that baptism, even if administered by a heretic or sectarian, or even an unbeliever, was valid, so long as it was performed in the name of the Blessed Trinity. Stephen, who was an abrupt and tactless man, made his point most undiplomatically, calling Cyprian a "false Christ, a false prophet, and a deceitful worker." The outraged bishop of Carthage summoned a council of bishops. The seventy-one prelates who met in Carthage supported Cyprian and asserted the right to set their own policy in matters of Church discipline. When two bishops from the conference went to Rome to confer with Stephen, the pope refused to see them, and, furthermore, publicly forbade the faithful of Rome to accommodate the African bishops, show them the smallest hospitality, receive them into their homes, or even wish them "Godspeed." When Cyprian learned of Stephen's behavior, he denounced him as "perverse, obstinate, and contumacious." The bishop of Caesarea, Fermilian, furiously denounced the pope's insolence and declared that by his sin, Stephen had excommunicated himself. Cyprian summoned another council, and this time eighty-seven bishops from Africa and the Middle East declared that Stephen had no right to the title "Bishop of Bishops," and asserted that no one bishop, even the bishop of Rome, had a right to dictate to the rest of Christendom in matters of discipline.[7]

---

*The "Puritans" of the third century had absolutely no relation to seventeenth-century Calvinist Christians.

Cyprian argued for Church unity through diversity. "As there are many rays of the sun, but one light, and many branches of the tree, but one . . . root, and since from one spring flow many streams . . . the unity [of the Church] is preserved in its source."[8] Firmilian pointed out that from the beginning practices in matters of liturgy and ecclesiastical discipline had been diverse. "All things are not observed alike [in Rome] which are observed in Jerusalem, just as in very many other provinces also many things are varied because of the difference of places and names, yet on this account there is no departure at all from the peace and unity of the Catholic Church."[9]

Before a formal split developed between Rome and the bishops of Africa, Valerian stepped in and united the Church by instituting another persecution. Valerian, for three years, had shown himself "wonderfully friendly and gentle to the people of God." His daughter-in-law, Salonina, was alleged to be a Christian, and, through her influence, a number of Christians were appointed to high positions within the government so that Hermammon was led to observe that the palace was virtually "a church of God."

Several things transpired to change Valerian's attitude. There was a falling-out with his son and daughter-in-law. More important was the growing influence of Macrian, the president of the Egyptian Magicians' Guild. Macrian detested Christianity, insisting that the very presence of Christians at court was frustrating the work of the gods he worshipped. As Valerian fell under Macrian's spell, he began to participate in the "devilish rites" of the Egyptian mystery cult. Like Elagabalus, Valerian adopted the practice of human sacrifice, tearing the internal organs from living babies.[10] The higher he rose in the court of Valerian, the more Macrian thirsted for Christian blood. He argued that the dwindling finances of the empire could be supplemented by the confiscation of Christian property, and accordingly he pressed the emperor to exterminate the Christians and take their assets.

Of equal importance in the reversal of Valerian's policy was the king of Persia. Earlier in the century, the land of Iran was ruled by an ethnic group named the Parthians and called Parthia. In 224, under Ardashir, the ethnic group known as the Persians took over and renamed the country after themselves. Since 241, the king had been Shapur I. In 256 he attacked the Roman Empire, invading Syria and Asia Minor. In order to enlist the support of the numerous Christians and Jews there, Shapur proclaimed a policy of religious toleration. As a result, resistance to his incursions in the Middle East was less than Valerian would have liked. This, combined with family tensions and his cultic involvement, led Valerian to inaugurate a new anti-Christian policy. The aging emperor, who was once considered a friend of the Church, now made no secret of the fact that he considered Christians traitors and subversives.

In 257, Valerian issued an edict forbidding all Christian worship. Unlike his predecessors, Valerian even went so far as to forbid gatherings in cemeteries. Members of the clergy were arrested and ordered to sacrifice. Those who refused were first removed from their flocks to a place of exile. The emperor hoped that deprived of its leaders the Church would wither and die. When it did not, Valerian ordered the immediate execution of all exiled clergy. Wealthy Christian laymen were killed and their property confiscated. All Church property, including catacombs, was seized by the state. Women who owned property were allowed to live, but their possessions were confiscated, and they were banished. Slaves and freed men employed in the palace were sentenced to hard labor.

Bishop Stephen was killed in 257. His successor, Xystus, or Sixtus II, succeeded in mollifying somewhat the ruffled feelings of the African bishops.

On August 6, 258, Sixtus was in the catacomb of Callistus, seated upon his episcopal throne preaching to a congregation assembled there, when a detachment of troops burst in. The faithful drew themselves up in a body surrounding the old bishop, declaring to the soldiers that they were all ready to die. Sixtus and four of his deacons, however, begged the worshippers not to sacrifice their lives and surrendered themselves to the troops. The five men were arrested and taken to the

Mamertine prison. The next day they were condemned to die and marched back to the catacomb. En route, Laurence, one of the three deacons still at large, but as yet unidentified by the government, met Sixtus on the way and sobbed, "My father, where are you going without your son?" Turning to Laurence, the bishop declared, "Don't weep, my son. After three days you shall follow me." The soldiers ordered Sixtus to sit on his throne, and beheaded him there. The four deacons were dispatched moments later.[11]

By August 9, all the remaining deacons had been killed except for Laurence, who was arrested that day. The authorities were still unable to locate the extensive "treasure" that Valerian and Macrian insisted that Church leaders had cached away. Laurence was now ordered to produce it. He promised to appear within twenty-four hours with "the treasure of the Church." The next day he appeared not with the expected gold, silver, and jewels, but with a collection of beggars and invalids. "Here," he said, "is the treasure of the Church."

In hopes of making Laurence disclose the location of the non-existent "treasure," the deacon was broiled over a slow fire on a gridiron. When the fire was made ready, Laurence was stripped and laid on the iron bars. To those who stood by as he was tortured, his face seemed to be that of an angel. He showed no sign of suffering as the stench from his burning flesh nauseated his torturers. After a time, with a playful smile, the deacon said, "Turn me, for I am fully roasted on one side."[12] Shortly thereafter, the deacon died under his torture.

Not only priests, bishops, and deacons, but lower orders of clergy (acolytes, exorcists, lectors, and doorkeepers) were rounded up and killed. An acolyte named Tharsicius, still undiscovered, was on his way to take the Blessed Sacrament to the clergy in prison. Laymen, it will be recalled, were not subject to arrest. Tharsicius had not yet been identified as a member of the clergy. As he made his way to the Mamertine Prison, he was stopped by a gang of thugs, who demanded to know what he was carrying so reverently. When the acolyte refused to answer, he was set upon by the toughs. Before he was knocked to the ground, he swallowed the hosts that he was carrying, so as to prevent desecration. When the hoodlums were unable to find anything of value on his person, they literally tore Tharsicius to pieces.[13]

Antioch was the scene of a touching incident. A priest named Sapricius was arrested. He and a layman named Nicephorus had once been friends, but had quarreled and, for years after that, had not spoken to one another. Learning of Sapricius' arrest, Nicephorus decided that it was time to seek reconciliation. Intercepting Sapricius as he was being led by soldiers to his execution, Nicephorus fell at the feet of the priest, beseeching him, "Martyr of Jesus Christ, forgive me my offense." Sapricius was silent. Nicephorus reiterated his request, but the priest would not even look at him.

The soldiers who had custody of Sapricius laughed at Nicephorus and said, "You're the biggest fool we've ever seen. Why are you so intent on seeking the forgiveness of a condemned criminal?" Undaunted, Nicephorus followed his archenemy to the spot where the execution was to take place. Directed to kneel at the block, Sapricius suddenly lost his nerve and cried, "Stop! Don't kill me! I'll do what you want. I will sacrifice."

"Brother, what are you doing?" cried Nicephorus. "Do not renounce Jesus Christ, our good master. Do not forfeit a crown you have already gained by tortures and suffering."

Despite Nicephorus' entreaties, Sapricius renounced his faith. Then, weeping, Nicephorus declared to the soldiers, "I am a Christian and believe in Jesus Christ, whom this wretched man has renounced. See, I am ready to die here in his place."

The soldiers arrested Nicephorus and kept him in custody until they were able to obtain instructions from the governor of Syria, who told them to go ahead and execute him even though he was not a clergyman, and so Nicephorus was beheaded. Despite the heroic action of his erstwhile enemy, the stubborn Sapricius refused either to forgive Nicephorus or reaffirm his faith.[14] It was men like Sapricius, who seemed to court death, who led one sympathetic governor to exclaim, "Unhappy men, if you are weary of your lives, is it so difficult to find ropes and precipices?"[15]

Cyprian had been exiled in August 257 to the town of Curubis on the North African coast. The next summer he was returned to Carthage for execution, where he was kept under house arrest until the time for his final sentencing by the governor of Africa. On a hot August day in 258, he was escorted to the governor's headquarters. When he arrived he was drenched with sweat because of his long walk in the stifling heat. An officer named Tesserarius, a Christian who had compromised his faith to keep job and life, offered the bishop the opportunity to change his clothing. "We apply medicines to annoyances which probably will no longer exist tomorrow," protested Cyprian.

The interview with the governor lasted but a moment. After the governor asked the prisoner's name and the bishop repeated it, Cyprian was sentenced to death. As he was led to "a peaceful little dell lying between thickly wooded slopes," a place known as the Field of Sextius, an immense crowd accompanied the popular bishop, shouting, "We want to die with him! We are for Thascius Ciprianius!" Pagans were impressed by his bearing as the bishop "walked along, radiant and serene, murmuring his prayers." Not a hostile shout was raised against him. When Cyprian reached the Sestian Field, where people were perched in nearby trees to watch, he removed his cloak, knelt, and prayed. Then he removed his dalmatic and stood in his tunic, awaiting the executioner. When the soldier arrived whose duty it was to amputate his head, Cyprian greeted him courteously and asked the friends who had accompanied him to give the executioner twenty-five gold pieces. Then, kneeling again, he blindfolded himself, bade one of his friends to bind his hands, and "like a man stooping to drink," stretched out his neck. The executioner was trembling so badly that he could barely hold his sword. Cyprian told him, "Hurry up and get it over with." The faithful spread cloths and towels on the ground in front of the headless corpse, "so that his precious blood should not disappear into the sand." The faithful took Cyprian's remains, in a torchlight procession, singing hymns, to a private cemetery, where the remains were buried without any interference by the governor.[16]

In Carthage, authorities were conservative in their attack on the Church, limiting themselves to the execution of Cyprian and a few other Church leaders. In other parts of Africa, the entire Christian population of some towns was the object of mob violence, as in the time of Decius. Hundreds of Christians were dragged from their homes and burned at the stake. In many places magistrates sentenced to the mines anyone caught in the act of Christian worship. Police searched catacombs, and on at least one occasion sealed up alive in one of the subterranean cemeteries a group of twenty or thirty Christians found worshipping there.

Persecution was especially severe in the Province of Tarraconensis, which is now eastern Spain, where the governor, Aemelianus, was fanatically anti-Christian. Early in 259, Bishop Fructuosus of Tarragona was awakened by the long-expected midnight knock. The soldiers who arrested him were, however, courteous enough to allow him to dress before they took him away. Along with his deacons Augurius and Eulogius and a number of other Church leaders, Fructuosus was imprisoned. During the days he spent awaiting trial, the bishop spent nearly all his waking hours in prayer.

On January 21, Fructuosus and his deacons were taken before Aemelianus. "Have you heard the orders of the emperor?" they were asked.

Fructuosus replied, "I do not know what the orders are. I am a Christian."

"The emperor has ordered that the gods be worshipped."

Fructuosus replied, "I worship one God, who made heaven and earth, the sea, and all that is in them."

"Don't you know that there are many gods?" asked the governor.

"No, I do not."

"Then soon you will!" snapped Aemelianus, adding, "Who will be heard, who will be feared, who will be adored, if the gods and the countenance of the emperor are despised?"

When the deacon Augurius also affirmed his belief in one "Almighty God," the governor turned on Eulogius and asked him, "Is it not true that you worship Fructuosus?"

"Certainly not. I worship the same God as he does."

Turning back to Fructuosus, Aemelianus asked, "Are you a bishop?"

"I am."

"You *were* one," snarled the governor, who thereupon sentenced the three men to be burned alive in the amphitheater. When the Church leaders were led into the arena, however, their presence was greeted by widespread groans, since Fructuosus was beloved of Christians and pagans alike. A pagan came out of the stands to give the bishop a drink of water, but Fructuosus declined it, saying that he was fasting and intended to break his fast only when he was with the blessed in heaven.

A Christian layman named Augustulus begged Fructuosus to allow him to untie his shoes, but the bishop insisted that he could take off his own shoes. Another Christian, named Felix, seized the prelate's right hand and begged him, "Pray for me when you stand in the presence of Christ."

"I will remember the whole Catholic Church," he said gravely, extending his hands from east to west. "A pastor will not be lacking to you, nor will the love and promises of the Lord fail, now or hereafter. What you see is the infirmity of one hour."

Fructuosus, Augurius, and Eulogius were tied to separate stakes. When the ropes binding their hands were burned through, the dying men fell to their knees, extending their blackening arms in the fire in the form of the cross. That night the faithful came and poured wine over the charred and smouldering remains, and divided up the pieces for veneration by Christians in various cities.[17]

By June 260, Valerian had slaughtered the majority of Christian clergy in his dominions. While waging a campaign against Shapur of Persia in what is now Iraq, the occult powers whom he served deserted him. His army decimated by sickness and starvation, Valerian decided to talk peace with the king. When he offered Shapur a large sum of money to retreat, the Persian king scornfully refused and insisted on a personal conference. Accompanied by a handful of aides, Valerian met

Shapur in the town of Duro-Europos. Despite assurances of safe conduct, the Persian king seized Valerian, taking him prisoner. The Roman army surrendered and Shapur marched on to Antioch, where he slaughtered thousands of citizens. Although the elderly emperor groveled in the dirt on his knees, begging Shapur for his release, he was kept a slave for the rest of his life. Loaded with chains but still clad in the purple robes of royalty, Valerian was exhibited to jeering Persian crowds. Whenever Shapur wished to mount his horse, he forced Valerian to kneel down so that he could put his foot upon the neck of the vanquished Roman. When, after several years, Valerian was finally put to death, his skin was dyed pink, stuffed, and placed as a trophy of victory in a Persian temple.

Publius Licinius Egnatius Gallienus was in his early forties when news reached him of his father's capture. Since he was already co-emperor, there was no need for any formal confirmation of his authority. He received the news of Valerian's misfortune with delight. "I knew that my father was mortal, and since he has acted as becomes a brave man, I am satisfied."[18] It was said of Gallienus that he was "born for his belly and his pleasures," and that he "wasted his days and nights in wine and debauchery." He took six or seven baths a day and drank only from golden cups.[19] Gibbon wrote that he was master of several "curious but useless sciences, a ready orator and elegant poet, a skillful gardener, an excellent cook, and a most contemptible prince."[20] Like many of the more irresponsible emperors, Gallienus left the Church in peace. Influenced, no doubt, by his Christian wife, Salonina, the emperor issued an edict proclaiming a policy of toleration toward the Church. Christians were now free to worship publicly, and all confiscated property, including the cemeteries, was restored.

Conditions in the empire were steadily deteriorating, and Gallienus' policy of toleration was in force only in the parts of the empire where he maintained control, and they were not many. A year before Valerian's capture, a general named Marcus Cassianus Postumus seized control of Gaul and made it an independent nation. The violently anti-Christian Macrian now controlled Egypt and parts of North Africa, where he continued to slaughter Christians. In the East, Shapur was finally defeated by Odenathus, who, in turn, set up the independent kingdom of Palmyra. According to Gibbon, Gallienus, indifferent and bumbling, met "the repeated intelligence [reports] of invasions, defeats, and rebellions . . . with a careless smile."[21] There were in his short reign of eight years no fewer than nineteen revolts. Finally, in 268, Gallienus' calvary commander, Aureolus, revolted. While the emperor was besieging Aureolus at Milan, his chief-of-staff, Claudius, staged a second coup. Claudius and his men informed Gallienus that his camp was being attacked by the troops of Aureolus. The emperor armed himself and leaped on his horse, expecting his soldiers to follow. None of them did. A few hundred yards down the road, Gallienus was surrounded by a band of conspirators who impaled him with their spears.

Under Claudius II, called Gothicus because he won important victories over the Goths, and his successor Aurelian, no further efforts were taken to ban Christianity, and once again the faithful were unmolested in areas under imperial control. It was, however, only the calm before the storm. One of the most savage campaigns of genocide since the beginning of the world was about to occur.

# 11

# Son of the dragon: The great persecution

In 295, the Roman Empire was ruled by a council of four generals. The president of this junta was Gaius Aurelius Valerius Diocletianus, known to history as Diocletian. The son of former slaves, he was born in Salona, Dalmatia, in what is now Yugoslavia. Diocletian, now about fifty years of age, had, through hard work and superior ability, worked his way up through the ranks of the army as a career soldier until he was in position to seize power upon the mysterious death of Emperor Numerian on November 17, 284. Diocletian was a tall, thin man with a long nose and thin lips — dour, humorless, efficient, cold, methodical. Having attained to the highest power, he decided that the empire was too big for any one man to administer alone with any degree of success. So, in 285 he named his friend, the general Marcus Aurelius Valerius Maximianus, or Maximian, as associate emperor. Diocletian was to handle the administrative affairs of the empire and Maximian the military.

After several years passed, Diocletian concluded that still more talent was needed in the running of the empire, so he devised what he called a tetrarchy, or rule by four men. He chose two other generals to act as assistant emperors. By 295, then, there were two senior emperors, Diocletian and Maximian, styled *Augustus*, and two junior emperors, Constantius and Galerius, styled *Caesar*. Diocletian, who continued as president of the tetrarchy, seldom visited Rome, but resided in the city of Nicomedia (now Izmit, Turkey) on the Sea of Marmara, close to the Dardanelles — the strait where the waters of the Black Sea meet those of the Aegean Sea. Diocletian governed directly the area of the empire which now comprises the nations of Turkey, Egypt, Syria, Iraq, Israel, Lebanon, and Jordan. His assistant Galerius, whose headquarters were at

Sirmium (now Sremska Mitrovica, Yugoslavia), had responsibility for the area which included the modern countries of Greece, Yugoslavia, and Rumania. The territories that are now Switzerland, Italy, Sicily, Libya, Tunisia, Algeria, and Morocco, were the responsibility of Maximian, who resided at Milan. Maximian's *Caesar* Constantius resided in what is now France, and had authority over that area as well as Spain, Portugal, and England.

It is hard to know for sure what these generals were really like, because their reigns are best documented by Christian historians who had every reason to want to grind an axe against three of them, and every reason to speak kindly of the fourth. Even his most determined enemies were unable to dig up much scum concerning the private life of Diocletian. The worst they could say about him personally was that he was power-mad. Moreover, Christian historians of the time were unanimous in admitting that the holocaust that would shortly ensue was not Diocletian's idea.

Maximian, like Diocletian, in 295 was in his early fifties, and like his colleague he was from a peasant background. A native of Sirmium, he had entered the army at an early age. Gibbon wrote elegantly of him: "Ignorant of letters, careless of the law, the rusticity of his manners still betrayed in the most elevated fortune the meanness of his extraction."[1] In other words, Maximian was a crude, illiterate ignoramus, who allowed his lowly background to demean him even when he had attained the highest power. Maximian was, however, a good soldier, and this is why Diocletian chose him. What most revolted Christian historians was Maximian's bisexuality. Lucius Caelius Firmianus Lactantius (c. 240-320), a pagan scholar converted late in life to Christianity, decried "that pestilential wretch" for his "hateful and abominable" practice of "debauching males" as well as for his heterosexual "enormities." "Wherever he journeyed," the fourth-century historian recorded, "virgins were suddenly torn from the presence of their parents" to be violated by the "flagitious" Augustus.[2]

Galerius, whose full name was Gaius Galerius Valerius

Maximianus, was also a crude, cruel, ignorant man. Born around 242 in what is now Sofia, Bulgaria, Galerius was also from the lower class. Lactantius recorded that Galerius' mother was born beyond the frontiers of the empire and that the entire family had but a veneer of civilization. Deprived of any formal education, and barely able to read or write, the future emperor worked as a herdsman and farmhand before he entered the army, where, as a ferocious fighter and brilliant general, he distinguished himself. As Caesar he won several resounding victories over the Persians. Galerius was an immense man, notorious for his stupendous obesity. Lactantius wrote of his "horrible bulk of corpulency," and Eusebius characterized him as "an enormous lump of flabby fat." Galerius, who liked to refer to himself as "Son of the Dragon," was a rough, crude, foul-mouthed, hard-drinking, angry man, so prone to violent rages that nearly everyone was at least a little afraid of him.[3]

On the other hand, Lactantius recorded that Constantius was "a prince unlike the others, and worthy to have had the sole government of the empire."[4] The historian had good reason to say that, because it was Constantius' son who came to champion the Christian Church. Aurelius Valerius Constantius, called "Chlorus," or "The Pale One," was evidently cut from a somewhat different cloth than his colleagues. Although, like them, a career soldier, he was apparently of a higher class and better educated. Born around 245 in what is now Yugoslavia, Constantius was reputedly a distant relative of Emperor Claudius II. Mild-mannered, intelligent, friendly, and approachable, he served as governor of Dalmatia before becoming a member of the tetrarchy.

For a period of twenty years, the tetrarchy worked well and brought order to the chaotic affairs of the empire. Gibbon recounted that "the suspicious jealousy of power found not any place among them, and the singular happiness of their union has been compared to a chorus of music, whose harmony was regulated and maintained by the skillful hand of the first artist."[5] While his three soldierly colleagues held in check the barbarian advances in the territories assigned to them, Diocletian instituted reforms which temporarily strengthened the government of the effete and decadent nation. Reducing the power of the Senate to the extent of turning that law-making body into a mere cipher, Diocletian assumed absolute power for himself and his colleagues. He reorganized the provinces into twelve "dioceses," and increased the government bureaucracy so that the administration of the state hinged more on the application of rules and regulations than on personalities. Concerned about the laxity of morals, the emperor tried to encourage the old Roman Republican virtues, proclaiming laws obligating children to take care of their aged parents and parents to provide adequately for their minor children. Diocletian furthermore instituted laws intended to strengthen the ties of marriage and to discourage unnatural practices. Wherever it was deemed possible, he forbade the use of torture. He reorganized the army, imposed a property tax and an income tax, wage and price controls, as well as a penalty of death for violation.

To emphasize the absolute nature of his power, the former peasant "took on airs." He took to wearing a crown — a circlet set with pearls — becoming the first emperor to affect such an honor since the mad Caligula. He directed his colleagues to array themselves in silk and cloth of gold, and load their persons with precious stones. The emperors surrounded their persons with virtual armies of bodyguards and attendants, giving the command that no one was to approach them save on bended knee with forehead touching the ground, groveling to kiss the hem of the imperial robes. Diocletian, on coinage minted during his reign, styled himself as "Lord and God," and commanded that he be addressed as "Most Holy Lord of the Universe." Although he proclaimed himself an incarnation of Jupiter and Maximian an incarnation of Hercules, Diocletian, unlike some earlier emperors, was no egomaniac. He had no illusions about his phony divinity. It was as a means of consolidating his power that he arrogated such honors to himself and his colleagues. Diocletian felt that the future of Rome could be assured only as a police state run by a committee invested with absolute power. In order to gain the respect of the ignorant and contemptible masses, Diocletian reasoned, the emperors had to distance themselves and assume, like the rulers of Persia and China, the dignity of gods before an abject and groveling people. This was the only way to keep order and to command the people's respect.

It was only inevitable that a man like Diocletian, concerned as he was about order and a return to the ancient Roman way of life, should have eventually shown hostility to Christianity. What is extraordinary is that it took him so many years to do it. Diocletian adhered to the traditional pagan beliefs and had an attitude to Christianity similar to that of Decius and Marcus Aurelius. "The immortal gods have, by their providence," wrote Diocletian, "arranged and established what is right. Many wise and good men are agreed that this should be maintained unaltered. They ought not be opposed. No new religion must presume to censure the old, since it is the greatest of crimes to overturn what has been once established by our ancestors and what has supremacy in the state."[6]

There were several reasons why Diocletian did not move against the Church immediately after he seized power. In the quarter century since the fall of Valerian, the Church had grown to the extent that it now comprised perhaps a quarter of the population of the empire. No longer did Christians meet in private homes, but were now constructing large public houses of worship. Many high officials were openly practicing Christians. Even members of the imperial court professed the faith. Lucianus, the chief chamberlain in the imperial palace at Nicomedia in the 280s and 290s of the third century, was one of the most fervent and outspoken believers in the imperial service. He wrote to Theonas, bishop of Alexandria, discussing possible strategies for leading the emperor to Christ. Theonas urged Lucianus to introduce the Gospel only gradually to his boss. First, he should let Diocletian see that he was conversant in pagan literature. Let Lucianus spend some time talking with Diocletian about the emperor's favorite works. Then, gradually, Lucianus might introduce some new quotations. If the emperor liked them, then the chamberlain might let him know that they were from the Christian Scriptures. Then, gradually,

Diocletian might be led to remark on their superiority. Finally, Lucianus might mention Christ to the emperor in private conversation. As things worked out, neither Lucianus nor any other Christian made any headway with the staunchly pagan dictator, but it was a different story with his wife and daughter. By the mid-290s the Empress Priscilla and her daughter Valeria, who was now the wife of Galerius, while probably not baptized, were openly sympathetic to Christianity.

That Diocletian hesitated to undertake a campaign against the Christians was doubtless, first, because of the influence of his wife and daughter; second, because Christianity had been tolerated officially for many years; third, because one Roman in four was now either a baptized Christian or sympathetic to the Church; and fourth, because persecution in the past had served only to strengthen the Church. Diocletian was, however, under constant pressure from the "Son of the Dragon" to take action against the Christians. While Constantius was tolerant of all religions and Maximian could not have cared less, Galerius was a fanatical devotee of the old gods. His old mother, who was born a "barbarian," was said to have been a pagan priestess heavily involved in witchcraft and the occult and to have influenced her son to detest the Church with an insane hatred. Galerius complained that whenever there were public ceremonies involving sacrifice and divination, the Christians present would invariably make the sign of the cross to protect themselves against demons, which he insisted kept the old gods from presenting themselves.

For now the only action Diocletian authorized was a crackdown against the numerous Christians who refused military service on the grounds of their faith. The penalty for conscientious objection had always been death, but it had seldom been enforced. From now on, it was to be. One of the most notable victims of this policy was a young man known to history as St. Maximilian.

The son of an officer named Fabius Victor, Maximilian was twenty-one when he was called to report for duty before Cassius Dio, governor of Africa, in the city of Theveste, Numidia, a territory under the authority of the Emperor Maximian. "Why do you ask my name?" replied the young man to the governor. "I cannot be a soldier, for I am a Christian."

Dio ordered Maximilian to be given his medical examination. "I cannot be a soldier. I cannot do evil. I am a Christian," Maximilian repeatedly insisted. An assistant measured the inductee and announced his height as five feet and ten inches. The governor now ordered Maximilian branded, which was the procedure followed with all conscripts, who, having passed their physical, were stamped on the hand with a red-hot iron bearing the initial of the current emperor. It was also customary for the inductee to be issued a medallion with the emperor's picture on it to be worn around the neck.

Maximilian refused to be branded and kept insisting, "I cannot be a soldier."

"Be a soldier or die!" roared the governor.

"I cannot be a soldier! Cut off my head! I cannot be a soldier of this world. I must serve only under my God."

"Who has given you these ideas?"

"My soul and He who has called me."

The governor asked the boy's father to persuade Maximilian. "He has a mind of his own," insisted Fabius Victor, who, unbeknownst to Dio, had recently become a Christian. "He knows what he is doing."

"You must be a soldier and accept the seal," the governor said.

"I will not accept it. I already have the seal of Christ, my God."

"I will send you straight to your Christ," the governor threatened.

"Do it immediately," urged Maximilian. "It will be my glory!"

"Mark him," ordered Dio. When the assistants took hold of him, Maximilian fought back and shouted, "I will not receive the seal of the world. If you put it around my neck, I will break it, for I put no value on it. I am a Christian. I cannot carry a leaden seal around my neck, for I already carry the sacred seal of Christ!"

When Dio pointed out that there were many Christians in

the army, Maximilian said, "They do not do what is right. As far as I am concerned, I am a Christian and cannot do evil."

"Do those who fight in our armies do evil therefore?" asked the governor.

"You know what they do," said the youth, cryptically.

When it became clear to Dio that no amount of threat or persuasion would change the resolution of the young man, he ordered that Maximilian's name be deleted from the register. Turning to him, he declared, "Since with disloyal spirit you have refused military service, you will be punished as an example to others. Maximilian, who has been found guilty of insubordination by not accepting military service, will be punished by the sword."

"Thanks be to God!" declared the condemned man.

At the place of execution, Maximilian turned to a group of Christians who were there to encourage him. Smiling, he said, "My dearest brothers, hasten with all your strength and desire to gain the vision of God and to merit a similar crown." Then, turning to his father, he asked him to give his new uniform to the executioner as a gift. After Maximilian was beheaded, Fabius Victor returned home, not dismayed or grieved, but full of joy, thanking the Lord for the privilege of having been given such a son.[7]

In time, Galerius prevailed upon Diocletian to require that all soldiers sacrifice. In those territories under the direct jurisdiction of Diocletian, those who refused to do so were demoted if they were officers, or expelled from the army if they were enlisted men. Constantius ignored the order, but Galerius and Maximian decreed death as the punishment for noncompliance.

It was early August 298 when, on the occasion of the birthday of the Emperor Maximian, all the soldiers stationed in the Province of Morocco (Mauretania Tingitana) were ordered to take part in the sacrifices. When he learned of this order, Marcellus, a career officer in the Trajan Legion at Tangiers (then called Tingis), instead of offering sacrifice, threw down his military belt and declared publicly, "I am a soldier of Jesus Christ." Removing the insignia of his rank as a centurion, Marcellus shouted, "If to be a soldier means sacrificing to gods and emperors, behold, I cast away my staff and belt and do not wish to serve." Placed under arrest, Marcellus was sent to Agricolanus, vicar of the prefects of the Praetorian guard, who conducted his trial on October 30. Agricolanus began by reading the official report of Marcellus' offense: "This soldier, throwing away his military belt, declared himself a Christian and uttered many blasphemies against the gods and against Caesar. . . ." He turned to Marcellus and asked, "Did you say the words reported by the prefect in this letter?"

"I did."

"You serve as an ordinary centurion?" asked Agricolanus.

"I do."

"What madness was it that made you refuse the military oath and speak in such a way?"

"Among those who fear the Lord, there is no madness."

"Did you say all those things which were mentioned in this report?" asked the vicar.

"I did."

"Did you throw away your weapons?"

"I did. It is not right for a Christian who serves in the army of the Lord Christ to serve also in worldly armies."

Agricolanus announced that Marcellus must be punished according to martial law. He announced, "Marcellus, who served as an ordinary centurian, publicly refused to take the oath; said it was foul and has uttered other words full of madness referred to in the report of the prefect. We order that he be executed by the sword." As Marcellus was led away to his execution, he looked back at the vicar and bade him, "May God be gracious to you."

When the centurion had been executed, the secretary of the tribunal turned to the vicar and and told him that his sentence was unjust. Agricolanus immediately ordered the imprisonment of the secretary, whose name was Cassianus. At his trial on December 3, Cassianus declared himself a Christian and was sentenced to death, probably for contempt of court.[8]

The purge of the army proceeded sporadically for several

years, with Diocletian strongly urging demotion and expulsion, and discouraging bloodshed except in flagrant cases. One such case involved the centurion Sebastian, who was a commander in the Praetorian prefect, a military division concerned with the emperor's safety. A native of what is now Narbonne, France, Sebastian had been reared in Milan, and had served for many years and been highly decorated. Diocletian had no inkling that Sebastian was a Christian until one day when he learned, to his dismay and horror, that the centurion had not only professed the faith for years, but had been actively encouraging the men under his command to accept Christ and not to sacrifice. "After going through so much, soldiers, are you now going to withdraw from the fight and lay aside your crown?" he asked when some of the Christian soldiers talked of complying with the imperial order to sacrifice.

When Diocletian received this report about Sebastian, he was beside himself. This officer was urging disloyalty to troops upon whom the emperor's safety depended. Sebastian confirmed that he was indeed a Christian, but tried to reason with Diocletian, insisting that Christians posed no threat to the security of the state. "Why, I pray for you every day, and for the prosperity of Rome. The only difference is that I pray to the God of heaven, because I believe that no assistance can be obtained from gods made out of stone." Diocletian insisted that anyone unwilling to sacrifice to the gods of Rome was a traitor. Diocletian insisted that Sebastian sacrifice. The centurion refused and Diocletian ordered him taken into a field and shot to death by archers. His body was to be left unburied, to be eaten by birds and dogs.

Sebastian was placed on a mark and made the target for archers. After he was left for dead, bleeding and bristling with arrows, Castula, a Christian woman, arrived after the execution squad had left. She had intended to retrieve his body for a decent burial, but noticed that there were still signs of life. Since Sebastian was evidently a small man, the robust Castula picked him up and carried him to her house, where she nursed him until he was well on his way toward convalescence.

As soon as he was able to hobble about, Sebastian did not

take advantage of his status of being officially dead to escape to another city and assume another identity. On the contrary, he decided to risk his life in another attempt to convert Diocletian. Returning to the palace, he managed to present himself to the emperor. Again, stressing his loyalty and the patriotism of Christians, Sebastian insisted, "Your priests speak false when they say that we Christians are adversaries of the state. We never cease to pray for your majesty's welfare and for that of the state."

Diocletian refused to listen, and summoning his bodyguards, ordered them to take Sebastian to one of the palace courtyards, pound his brains out with clubs, and then throw his corpse into a sewer. That night a Christian named Lucina recovered Sebastian's body and buried it in her own garden.[9] St. Sebastian has long survived in the memory of the Church. Although in reality he was probably an older man, he is normally depicted as a handsome youth, bound to a stake, his body pierced by arrows. Events like these tended to draw Diocletian from the side of moderation to that of Galerius, who insisted more than ever on a wholesale massacre of Christians. Diocletian stressed to his *Caesar* that the elimination of so numerous a people would involve bloodshed on a scale almost unprecedented in history. Yet, as a firm believer that Rome's prosperity depended on universal adherence to the National Religion, he felt increasingly uneasy as he realized how many officials at court and in the highest echelons of government were members of this disloyal association. Even his wife and daughter seemed to be seduced by this madness.

During the winter of 302-303, Galerius and Valeria stayed with Diocletian at the palace of Nicomedia. During that time the two men conferred on strategies on combating the growing menace of Christianity. Galerius insisted once again that all Christians should be exterminated. Diocletian once more pointed out that the implementation of this final solution would involve the deaths of ten or fifteen million people. Galerius insisted that the slaughter was necessary. Finally, on February 23, 303, Diocletian decided to take action.

That morning, at dawn, members of the Praetorian guard

and officers of the treasury approached the Church of Nicomedia, a tall structure which stood on a hill in view of the royal palace. They forced the gates open and, according to Lactantius, "searched everywhere for an image of the Divinity. The books of the Holy Scriptures were found, and they were committed to the flames; the utensils and furniture of the Church were abandoned to pillage; all was rapine, confusion, tumult." Galerius insisted that Diocletian give orders to burn the church, but the senior emperor refused to fire the structure for fear that the conflagration might spread to neighboring buildings. So he directed that the Praetorian Guards demolish the house of worship. And so the soldiers went to work with axes, and, within a few hours, had leveled the lofty edifice to the ground.[10]

The following day Diocletian issued a decree in which he directed: 1) all Christian houses of worship were to be demolished; 2) all those found holding Christian services of worship were to be executed; 3) all Christian books were to be confiscated and burned; 4) all Christian property was to be confiscated; 5) all Christians who were free men were to be deprived of all public employment; 6) Christian slaves would lose the right of ever becoming free; and 7) Christians were henceforth to be denied the right of being plaintiffs in any legal action, while, at the same time, they were still to be liable to lawsuits.

In Nicomedia, Rome, and in all the provinces, the emperor's orders were carried out. The moderate Constantius tried to do as little as possible in implementing the orders. Although disgusted by the decree, Constantius demolished a number of churches, but tried, wherever possible, to avoid executions.

In parts of the empire controlled by Diocletian, Maximian, and Galerius, Scriptures were burned on an unprecedented scale. An official report of the seizure of a house of worship in what is now Algeria is an example of activities repeated in every city and town and country village through the empire.

When the troops arrived at the church, Bishop Paul was ordered by Felix, the local high priest of the National Religion, to "bring out the Scriptures of your law, and everything else you have got here. . ." When Paul replied that the lectors kept the Scriptures in their homes, Felix insisted that the lectors be summoned.

"You know who they are," the bishop said to the pagan priest.

"We do not know them," responded Felix.

"Your staff know them. . . ."

"Leaving aside the question of the lectors, whom my staff will identify," said Felix, "surrender what you have here." Paul sat down, along with three priests, five deacons, and seven subdeacons. He was shown the inventory of the objects which had been seized by the soldiers. This consisted of two golden chalices, six silver chalices, six silver dishes, one silver bowl, seven silver lamps, two torches, seven short bronze candlesticks with their lips, eleven bronze lamps with their chains, eighty-two women's tunics for use at baptism, thirty-eight veils to cover women's heads in worship, sixteen men's tunics for baptism, thirteen pairs of men's slippers, forty-seven pairs of women's slippers, and eighteen pairs of clogs. Insisting that some vast treasure remained to be discovered, Felix insisted that the clergy tell him where the rest of their valuables were cached. One subdeacon produced a silver case and a silver candlestick which he found behind a jug.

"You would have been a dead man if you had not managed to find those!" menaced Felix. "Now bring out all the Scriptures that you have." When one of the subdeacons produced but a single volume, the high priest shouted, "Why do you bring out a single book? Bring out all the Scriptures you have!"

The subdeacons replied that they had no more. The lectors kept the Scriptures, they said. When ordered to identify the lectors, the subdeacons replied, "We are not informers. Here we stand. Command us to be executed."

"Put them under arrest," ordered Felix.

The lectors' homes were searched after their identities had been ascertained from members of the staff of Felix. One lector was a tailor, the other a schoolteacher. Two books were found in the teacher's home. The tailor was not at home, but his wife, to save him, surrendered six copies of Sacred Writ. When the authorities were satisfied that they had confiscated all copies of Scripture, Paul and his clergy were forced to watch as the Bibles were burned.[11]

Not all Roman officials were as unyielding as Felix, and not all clergy were as compliant as Bishop Paul. A Christian named Felix, who was bishop of the African city of Thibiuca, insisted, "It is better for me to be burned than the divine Scriptures." Anulinus, the kindly governor of Africa who attempted to save him, suggested, "Why don't you give up some spare and useless books?" Bishop Felix refused to cooperate even in this, and so he was sent for trial to Italy. When the prefect there tried to persuade the bishop to make some token concession, Felix insisted, "I have the books, but I am not going to give them up," and so he perished.

At this point, bloodshed occurred only when Christians refused to yield copies of Scripture, when they were caught worshipping, or when they engaged in some act of defiance, such as that of Euethius, a Christian who tore up a copy of the imperial edict posted in the public square at Nicomedia, and was tortured to death. Although bishops urged the faithful not to provoke the authorities deliberately, they insisted that the faithful were neither to yield copies of the Bible nor cease to worship together. Thus, large numbers of lives were lost from the start of the persecution.

For example, at Abithinae, in Africa, police burst in on forty-nine persons at worship in a private home. Among the prisoners were the four young children of the priest, Saturninus. Anulinus, the same magistrate who had tried vainly to spare Bishop Felix, attempted to terrify the children into renouncing their faith. "I will cut off your hair, your nose, and your ears," he threatened. The children, like their parents, stood steadfast. Hilarion, the youngest, replied, "Do as you please. I am a Christian." As he was sent off to prison and death with the others, he declared, "Thanks be to God!"[12]

Although Diocletian made certain that Christian worshippers in his domains were given a trial and a chance to renounce their faith, Galerius, on the other hand, gave orders that whenever Christians were found at worship, they were to be slaughtered with the sword, or, better, sealed in the house where they were meeting to be burned alive when it was set ablaze by the police.

Speaking of fire, in March 303, shortly after the promulgation of the fatal edict, there occurred two fires of suspicious origin right within the imperial palace at Nicomedia. Galerius blamed the arson on Christians unhappy with imperial policy. Christians, in turn, insisted that the fires were set by order of Galerius, who wanted to use the incidents to accuse the Church of treasonous activity and terrify Diocletian into decreeing the general extermination of all believers.

Still, Diocletian was cautious. Later in the year he ordered the arrest of all clergy, who were tortured in an attempt to make them renounce their faith. Those who refused to sacrifice were killed. Eusebius recorded how each was put to death through a series of creative tortures, some flogged unmercifully with the whip, others broken on the rack or scraped to death with iron stones.[13]

At last Galerius got his way. Early in 304, Diocletian published an edict directing that all Christians of all ages and both sexes were to sacrifice to the gods or die. Diocletian did not exempt his closest advisors or members of his family. Priscilla and Valeria were given the choice of sacrifice or death, and sacrificed. On the other hand, three high-ranking civilian aides to Diocletian — Dorotheus, Gorgonius, and Peter — declared themselves Christians and refused to sacrifice. Peter was taken to a public square, stripped naked, bound, and hoisted onto a scaffold where his whole body was torn almost to pieces with loaded whips until, nearly unconscious, he was dragged before an improvised altar and physically forced to sacrifice. When he became aware of what had been done to him, Peter loudly insisted that he had been forced against his will and had no intention of betraying his faith. To soften his resistance, vinegar mixed with salt was poured on his wounds. When he still refused to sacrifice, Peter was chained to a lighted brazier and slowly roasted alive. Dorotheus and Gorgonius, after similar tortures, were strangled.

These murders signaled a fury of violence which was unleashed upon the nation. After Anthimus, bishop of Nicomedia, was beheaded, execution squads went into action. In the realms of Diocletian, the process was orderly. Lists were compiled of the residents of every town and village, and everyone was given an appointment with the local authorities to declare his allegiance to the emperor and the gods of Rome by sacrificing. Maximian pursued the same policy, but Constantius neglected to publish the edict or authorize his governors to hunt down Christians. Galerius simply resorted to wholesale massacre. Eusebius recounted that entire congregations of Christians were butchered at once. Some were sealed and burned alive in their house of worship, some hacked to death, others tied up, weighted, and dumped into rivers.[14] Throughout the empire, except in the territories of Constantius, prisons, built for murderers and bandits, were now so overcrowded with "bishops, presbyters, deacons, readers, and exorcists . . . so that room was no longer left for those condemned for crimes."[15]

Soon civil strife was superimposed upon the state-sanctioned butchery to plunge the empire, which, for two decades had begun to show signs of revitalization, into a nightmare of bloody pandemonium. On December 13, 304, Diocletian, then fifty-nine, suffered what was apparently a serious stroke, leaving him incapacitated both physically and mentally. By spring, although he was able to walk about, Diocletian was still, according to Lactantius, "disordered in his judgment, being at times insane and at other times of sound mind."[16]

Galerius now bullied not only the ailing Diocletian, but also Maximian (who was in excellent health) to resign in May 305. Galerius now assumed the presidency of the tetrarchy. Maximian's place as *Augustus* was taken by his former assistant, Constantius, who, now about sixty, was ailing. Galerius appointed a general named Severus to be Constantius' *Caesar,* and his own nephew, Maximinus Daza, to be his assistant. Diocletian, who was alert enough to deplore Galerius' choices, was aghast at the appointment of Severus. "He is nothing but a habitual drunkard, who turns night into day and day into night," he objected. He was especially appalled at Galerius' choice of Daza, a man in his thirties who was crude, uneducated, and totally without experience in administration. "You do not propose men fit for the charge of public affairs," he exclaimed, bursting into the tears that came so frequently now. "You will soon know more when you have taken supreme power. I have labored long and done all I could to keep the Empire together during my office. If things go wrong now, the fault will be all yours!"[17] Thus Diocletian retired into the shadows of history, to his village at Salona, where he spent his last years tending cabbages in his garden.

Chaos now ensued. Maximian was unhappy about being forced to retire and soon supported his son Maxentius in his attempt to seize power from Severus. During the summer of 306, Constantius died and his son Constantine proclaimed himself emperor in his place. Maximian reclaimed the title of *Augustus*, and Galerius, refusing to recognize either him or Maxentius, appointed another general, Licinius, as the assistant emperor in the West. In February 307, Severus, realizing that his position was hopeless, committed suicide, and Maxentius firmly consolidated his power in Italy. Licinius exercised control only in Illyricum (part of what is now Yugoslavia). Galerius still controlled most of Eastern Europe, and his nephew Daza dominated Asia Minor, Egypt, and Syria — the territories formerly controlled by Diocletian. Maximian had nowhere to exercise his power, but sought actively to unseat Constantine as the *Augustus* of the West. Now, instead of a coalition of four men governing the empire, six generals, all hostile to each other, except for Galerius and Daza, were engaged in a civil war that would ravage the country for a decade. Constantine continued the tolerant policy of his father in western Europe. Maxentius, once in power, proved himself one of those dissipated leaders who left the Church in peace for a time out of sheer indolence, and Licinius, too, showed no great predisposition to carry on the virulent anti-Christian policies of the previous year. Galerius and Daza, however, pursued their policy of extermination with diabolical ferocity.

# 12

# 'The most shameful, brutal, and inhuman of all spectacles': Persecution in the West

Nobody knows for sure how many Christians lost their lives in the years between 304 and 311. Gibbon estimated that "only" two thousand people lost their lives. Will Durant reckoned still fewer — about eighteen hundred. Others estimate ten thousand; still others one hundred thousand; some as many as seven million. Ancient writers simply spoke of "immense multitudes." Certainly the martyrs whose names have been recorded are but the tip of a macabre iceberg. Eusebius, in fact, recorded that during the years of the Great Persecution, in the major cities and towns of southern Egypt, between ten and one hundred Christians were executed a day.[1] If just ten people were killed each day over that seven-year period in a single urban center, the death toll would be twenty-five thousand, just for that one city. Inasmuch as there were at least six major cities in that area, this would imply that more one hundred fifty thousand perished in just that region alone. Since the persecution raged as fiercely in northern Egypt, Asia Minor, and Greece, where there were more than thirty major cities where executions probably took place, one might be led to reckon that more than seven hundred fifty thousand people were executed in that entire empire. This figure does not include the great numbers who perished in the mines. It is not unreasonable to assume that, throughout the empire, between 304 and 311, more than one million Christians were martyred, perhaps many more. When we realize that many of these martyrs could have saved their lives simply by going through a perfunctory ceremony of offering incense to the gods of Rome, or, in many cases, simply by allowing a sympathetic magistrate to certify falsely that they had done so, we are staggered by the deep commitment of those who willingly gave their lives for the name of Jesus.

As we have seen, the Great Persecution was imposed upon the empire unequally. The Christians who lived under the rule of Constantius and later Constantine in what are now France, Spain, Portugal, and Britain, were hardly touched, except when overzealous governors acted independently of the emperor. Those who lived in Italy and northern Africa west of Egypt suffered tremendously for about one year, until the abdication of Maximian. When Maxentius consolidated his power in that area, he carried out the edicts of persecution lackadaisically, when he did it at all.

Even so, the situation at Rome remained so bad that, after the martyrdom of Pope Marcellinus in 304, no bishop was elected for four years. Marcellinus had lost the respect of many of the faithful by complying, out of fear, with the imperial edict to surrender the extensive archives of the Church at Rome. It was perhaps because of this loss that we have so little documentation of the apostolic period. When, however, the decree went out that all Christians must sacrifice or die, Marcellinus proved faithful to his Lord and, along with hundreds of his parishioners, was executed.

In the eastern half of the empire, where first Diocletian and Galerius, and then Maximinus Daza and Galerius ruled, the killing of Christians continued unabated for seven years on an incredibly massive scale. Methods of torture and execution varied with the location. In what is now Jordan, victims were usually beheaded. Axe-blades, blunted from repeatedly crashing into cervical vertebrae, had to be changed several times a day. In what are now Syria and Iraq, Christians were strung upside down over a slow fire. In Pontus (northeastern Turkey) pointed reeds were driven under the nails of victims' fingers before they were killed by being coated with a "boiling, seething mass" of molten lead. In Asia Minor, magistrates vied with each other in their attempts at devising the most gruesome tortures. Physicians were employed by provincial governors for the purpose of inventing excruciating ways to put victims to death. Eusebius mentioned "shameful, merciless, and unmentionable tortures applied to the private parts" of those being tortured.

In Egypt, torturers delighted in chopping off Christians' hands, noses, and ears. Phileas, bishop of Thmuis, in northern Egypt, who was later himself to lose his life, wrote of the situation in his country.

He tells us that in attempts to force a renunciation of Christ, some believers were strung up by one hand, heaved high into the air, and dropped repeatedly for hours on end. Others were bound to pillars, facing inwards, with their feet off the ground and the weight of their bodies drawing them tighter and tighter.

If they proved obdurate, as most of them did, they were suspended from a wooden frame with their hands tied behind them while the executioners ripped their bodies apart from face to foot with metal combs.

In southern Italy, executioners would force together the trunks of two small strong trees that grew several feet apart. Stripped naked, men, women, and even little children were bound with one leg fixed to one bough and the other limb to the second trunk. Then the executioners permitted the boughs to fly back to their normal position, so that the victims would, in seconds, be ripped in half.[2]

In some places, martyrs were thrown to the beasts in the arena, but, as usual, this proved a very inefficient means of execution, for, as often as not, the animals were more afraid of their intended victims than the victims were of them. Eusebius recounted how, in some instances, three successive animals were turned loose on Christian prisoners without harming them.

He described the moving sight of the prisoners standing unfettered, extending their arms in the form of a cross, praying silently while bears and panthers rushed on them. Most of the time the frightened animals failed to kill the victims, who, mangled and savaged, had to be dispatched by gladiators.

It seemed that for every Christian who was killed, two pagans took his place through conversion. Eusebius recounted that no sooner had a group of Christians been sentenced to die than "others from every side would jump on the platform in front of the judge to proclaim themselves Christians." Unafraid of the brutal torture, they sang, laughed, and praised God until their last breath.[3]

In 308, some provincial governors, fearful of swift depopulation from the continued massacres, began to turn to the "lenient" practice of condemning Christians to a slow death in the mines. In that way, the state could at least make use of their services as well as provide for them a long and agonizing period for reflection. And so, for the next three years, especially in Egypt and Palestine, every day scores of prisoners could be seen being force-marched to the nearest metal mine, to wear their lives away there. Prisoners were normally allowed visitors there, but those bold enough to pray with the unfortunate victims betrayed themselves as Christians and were quickly sentenced to a similar fate. Sometimes when the guards saw that the Christians, despite their deep misery, continued to meet in prayer and convert pagan prisoners, they decided that it was unwise to wait for starvation and exhaustion to take its course, and resorted to mass executions in the prison camps.

The story of the Great Persecution can best be told not through statistics or generalities, but through the confessions and deaths of heroic men, women, and children. Perhaps the martyr who best symbolized the multitudes who went to their death unremembered is a young girl whose name is known only to God. In 1802 there were found in a burial niche in the catacomb of Priscilla in Rome the skeletal remains of a girl of about fifteen. Enclosed within the niche was also a vial of dried blood, which seemed to identify the girl as a martyr. The niche was apparently prepared in the time of the Great Persecution and was marked by the inscription, "Peace be with you, Philomena." In 1805 the relics were given to the parish priest of Mugnano, near Naples, and, within a few years, numerous graces and miracles were being attributed to "Saint" Philomena. Devotion to her was immensely popularized by Father Jean-Baptiste Marie Vianney, of Ars, France, "the world's best-beloved parish priest." Pope Gregory XVI authorized a feast day — August 11 — in Philomena's honor in 1837, and in 1855 Pope Pius IX approved a proper Mass and Office for her feast.

In later years archaeologists became convinced that the bones found in the niche were placed there long after the inscription to Philomena had been carved, and that Philomena and the martyred girl whose bones were taken to Mugnano were two different people. Because of this and because of the total absence of information about her, "Saint" Philomena was removed from the Calendar of Saints by the Sacred Congregation of Rites in 1961. Yet, the young martyr, whoever she was, must surely hold a place in the hearts of subsequent generations of Christians similar to that of an Unknown Soldier — as a Christian, representative of the myriads of others, who gave her life for her faith, but whose true identity and history is known only to God.

One of the best loved heroines of the Church is St. Agnes. St. Jerome wrote that "the tongues and pens of all nations are employed in the praises of this saint, who overcame both the cruelty of the tyrant and the tenderness of her age, and crowned the glory of chastity with that of martyrdom."[4] All that we know for sure about St. Agnes is from the inscription in the church erected in her honor fifty years after her death, which described her as a "virgin" and "victorious." Medical examination of her relics revealed that she was about thirteen years old at the time of her death. We are not even certain that the given name of this "Patroness of Purity" was really Agnes. Some feel that "Agnes," which came from the Latin word for lamb, was associated with this martyr (whose real name was forgotten) because, like a pure and spotless lamb, she gave her life as an offering to Christ.

According to most versions of her life, Agnes was a beautiful girl belonging to one of the wealthiest and most aristocratic Roman families. Her parents were pagans, but Agnes and her stepsister Emerentia had secretly embraced the Christian faith, and, as many girls did at the time, vowed themselves to eternal chastity. When Agnes was thirteen, the age when Roman girls were normally married, the son of a prominent senator sought her hand in marriage, only to have her tell him that she was already engaged. When asked to whom she was affianced, Agnes, perhaps repeating some sort of formula learned by those who pledged themselves to eternal virginity, replied melodramatically, "He has already pledged me to himself by His betrothal ring, and has adorned me with precious jewels. He has placed a sign upon my brow that I should have no other lover but He. He has showed me incomparable treasures, which He has promised to give me if I persevere. Honey and milk have I drawn from His lips, and I have partaken of His body, and with His blood He has adorned my cheeks. His Mother is a virgin and His father knew not woman. Him the angels serve, His beauty sun and moon adore, by his fragrance the dead are raised and by His touch the sick are healed. His wealth never fails and His abundance never grows less. For Him alone do I keep myself. To Him alone in true confidence do I commit myself, whom, loving, I am chaste, whom, touching, I am clean, whom, receiving, I am a virgin."

Agnes' rejected suitor reported this curious conversation to the girl's father, who began to think that his daughter was going insane. When he questioned her about her refusal to marry, and she admitted that she was a Christian, he was aghast. He had no idea that his own household had been infected by what to him must have been a loathsome superstition. In the meantime, the senator's son reported the conversation to his father, Symphronius, who was concerned about the safety not only of the girl but of her family as well. He asked Agnes and her parents to come to his home and there he urged her to marry his son.

When Agnes declared her intention of remaining a virgin, Symphronius told her, "If that is what you wish, then become a Vestal Virgin and serve the goddess in chastity. That is perfectly acceptable, but do not endanger your life and that of your parents and sisters by falling for this misguided superstition. You know that it is treason against the emperors to embrace this forbidden religion."

"If I would refuse your living son of flesh and blood," replied the serious-minded girl, "how could you think that I could possibly dedicate myself to gods made of sticks and stones that really do not exist?"

"Now, don't be stubborn, my child," said the senator. "What right have you to say that the gods of our fathers do not exist? What right have you to question the commandments of our revered emperors? You are awfully set in your ways for so young a girl!"

Rather pompously, Agnes told him: "Faith does not dwell in the years but in the heart."

"My dear, do you know what will happen to you if they find out that you are a Christian?" asked the senator. "They will imprison you in a house of prostitution, and what will become of your vaunted chastity then? And when every ruffian in Rome has had his way with you, then they will take you out and cut off your head, or burn you alive!" Agnes replied that, whatever happened, God would protect her and preserve her in chastity. And so the conference ended.

Agnes was soon recognized as a Christian by the police, arrested, invited to sacrifice, and, upon her refusal, sentenced to become a prostitute. This was a punishment that many pagan governors and prefects loved to impose upon Christian girls. Taken to a brothel, Agnes was, like the other women, stripped naked, but she loosened her hair, which was long and abundant enough to cover her entire body. "You may expose my virtue to insult," she said, "but I have my angel for my defense. Jesus will protect me."

All of Agnes' "clients" were so taken with this little girl, covering herself with her hair, kneeling, chanting psalms, and praying aloud for God's protection, that not one of them so much as ventured to lay a hand on her. Eventually, her rejected suitor, undaunted by her prayers, burst into the brothel determined to rape her. Agnes evidently put up such a struggle that the youth fell to the ground and was knocked senseless. When he came to his senses, enraged, he went to the authorities and accused the poor girl of using witchcraft.

Agnes was taken before a magistrate who again insisted that she sacrifice. Upon her refusal, she was sentenced to be burned alive. As she was bound to the pyre, Agnes prayed, "Almighty Father, I give Thee thanks for my escape from the threats of the profane tyrant. I thank Thee that I have passed, unstained, through the filthy sty of lust. I now come to Thee. I have loved Thee, I have sought Thee. I have always longed for Thee. I bless, I glorify Thy Name, world without end." As the fire was kindled, Agnes prayed, "I bless Thee, Father of my Lord Jesus, that I am permitted to come to Thee through the flames. What I have believed, I now see. What I have hoped for I now embrace. I confess Thee with my lips and with my heart. I altogether desire Thee. I come to Thee, my God, who reignest through ages of ages."

Before Agnes was dead, the fire went out, and so the officials ordered that the girl be dispatched with a stroke of the sword. The executioner was so taken with the sight of the dying girl, whose lips were still moving in prayer, that he had trouble wielding his instrument of death. When he managed to give Agnes the *coup de grace*, the martyr's parents took the body to their villa outside the city for burial. A crowd of Christian believers, despite the grave danger to their safety, followed. At the villa they were met by a mob of pagans, who massacred them. Among the slain was Agnes' step-sister Emerentia. According to the Christian poet Aurelius Clemens Prudentius, who wrote about a century later, eight days after her death Agnes appeared to her mother in a vision and led her to Christ. She had a pure white lamb in her arms and was surrounded by legions of angels.[5]

Many Christian women found themselves in the same predicament as Agnes. Not all of them acted as heroically. The Emperor Maxentius himself set his eyes on a lady named Sophronia. Her husband, who was a high official, told the emperor, "You are welcome to her." When the police came to fetch the unhappy woman, Sophronia asked permission to excuse herself to dress suitably for the occasion. She then went into her room, closed the door, and committed suicide.[6]

Many Christians, by keeping a low profile, might have escaped, but were recognized when, like the group who accompanied Agnes' corpse, they attended a martyr's funeral or shouted words of encouragement at a trial or execution. Others were recognized when they visited other Christians in prison. This was the case with Januarius, bishop of Benevento, a town near Naples. When two of his deacons and several lay Christians were arrested and imprisoned at Pozzuoli, Januarius came to see them. He gave himself away when he prayed with them, and was arrested. Sentenced to death with the others by Governor Timotheus of Campania and taken to Nola, he was exposed to the wild beasts in the stadium there. When the terrified creatures refused to harm the men, Januarius and his companions were beheaded.

We know nothing about the life of Januarius except for these few facts about his death. He would scarcely be known to posterity at all except for the alleged miracle that occurs to this day in connection with his blood. Januarius was buried near Pozzuoli, but soon afterwards his bones were disinterred and moved back and forth to various places in south-central Italy until, in 1497, they were placed in the cathedral at Naples. Since that time, a curious phenomenon has been observed. The relics of St. Januarius consist of part of his skull, which is kept in a reliquary, and a vial partially filled with a dark, opaque substance which is alleged to be his blood. Eighteen times a year, on various feast days, the vial with the blood is brought out and held by a priest in the presence of the reliquary containing the skull. As the congregation prays, often loudly and vociferously, the priest turns the reliquary up and down. If nothing happens within a few moments, members of the congregation have been known to shout in prayer, "Boil! Boil! Boil, damn you!" Usually, within an hour's time, the dark mass liquefies, turns bright red, and bubbles up to fill the glass vial. It has been demonstrated that the phenomenon is not a trick, and no satisfactory scientific explanation has ever been proffered. On those occasions when the blood has failed to liquefy, the congregation has interpreted this as a sign of the saint's displeasure. For example, when the blood failed to boil during an exposition during the 1970s, some of the faithful were convinced that it was because Naples had recently elected a communist mayor.

We know more about Nicander and Marcian, who were soldiers stationed in southern Italy who were brought before the Governor Maximus on suspicion of being Christians. Daria, the wife of Nicander, accompanied the two soldiers to the place where the men were to be interrogated. She took what normally would have been a lethal step when she publicly encouraged her husband not to sacrifice. "Do not sacrifice to the dumb idols! Look up into heaven and remember what a prize is laid up for you there."

The governor, a humane man who was simply carrying out orders, chided Daria for risking her life and forfeiting that of her husband. "Stupid, why do you want the death of your husband?"

"So that he might live in God."

"That can't be the real reason. You must want to get rid of him. You're looking for a second husband."

"If you think that, kill me instead of my husband."

Although he was obligated by the imperial edict to kill Daria along with her husband, the governor did no more than threaten to arrest her. Telling Nicander not to pay any attention "to the idle talk of that woman," he urged him to go home, take three days to think the matter over, and "Don't be crazy enough to force me to sentence you to death."

"The time is past," rejoined Nicander. "I have had three days to consider before I was brought here, and I am resolved on my safety."

"Ah, the gods be praised!" sighed Maximus, who thought Nicander was about to offer the perfunctory sacrifice required of him. He was horrified when Nicander explained that his idea of "safety" was the salvation of his soul in heaven.

A legal assistant said to Nicander, "It seems to me that you have chosen death."

"No," replied Nicander. "I have chosen eternal life. Do to my body whatever you please. But I tell you once and for all, I am a Christian."

Maximus turned to Marcian and asked, "What do you say, Marcian?"

"I say the same as Brother Nicander."

The exasperated governor ordered both soldiers to prison for time to reconsider. After twenty days they were again taken before Maximus, who urged them to obey the emperor or suffer the consequences.

"We do not fear your torments, but press towards the prize which God has prepared for those who love Him. Dispatch us speedily, so that we might be with the Crucified, whom you have blasphemed."

Maximus was offended by what struck him as an attitude of insulting superiority. "It is not I who am persecuting you," he said. "You are not opposing me, but the emperor, and you are forcing me to carry out his mandates." Visibly shaken and with tears in his eyes, Maximus sentenced Nicander and Marcian to death. He added, "I hope you go where you desire, and may all your hopes be fulfilled."

Nicander and Marcian bade Maximus an affectionate farewell. "Peace be with you, kind governor."

Marcian's wife, unlike Daria, was completely unreconciled to her husband's martyrdom. Following him, weeping and sobbing, to the place of execution, she begged him not to make her a widow and their little son an orphan through his "obstinacy." A man named Zoticus, obviously a Christian, took Marcian's hand, telling him, "Be courageous. Fight the good fight and win your crown." Marcian told him to take the hand of his distraught wife and hold her back. "Keep her away until it is all over," he told Zoticus. "She must not see me die." Then, taking up his little son, whom his wife had thrust at his feet, be handed the child to Zoticus. "Lord God Almighty," he prayed, "take this child into Thy special care."

Marcian's wife, still shrieking and sobbing bitterly, was led away with difficulty by Zoticus. Daria, however, followed her husband, Nicander, encouraging him until he and Marcian were blindfolded and beheaded. She was not arrested and was allowed to bury her husband at their home in Venafro. Marcian was buried at Atina.[7]

We can see from the example of Saints Nicander and Marcian that the persecution was not carried out with equal rigor throughout Italy. A great deal depended on the local magistrates. We see that Maximus was a kind man who tried his best to avoid the imposition of capital sentences. He gave the two soldiers every opportunity to save their lives. He subjected neither of them to torture, nor did he order the arrest of either Daria or Zoticus, who made no secret of their Christian faith. In other parts of Italy it was a different story. In many places, such as in Rome, as we have seen, Christians were lynched by angry mobs even before they had a chance to be brought to trial. In the town of Imola in northern Italy, public sentiment reached such a fever pitch against Christians that even young children joined in the bloodbath. An elderly teacher named Cassian was cornered in his classroom by his elementary school-aged boys, who demanded to know whether he was a Christian. When he replied that he was indeed, the boys immediately set on him like a pack of wild dogs, kicking him, beating him, and slashing him with the points of their metal pens until the old man sank dead in a pool of his own blood.[8]

The most grisly incident that occurred in the western empire was recorded by one St. Eucherius, bishop of Lyon, who wrote about a century after the event. Fairly early in the Great Persecution, there was a legion of soldiers from Egypt, commanded by an officer named Maurice, stationed in Agaunum, in what is now Switzerland. Unknown to the Emperor Maximian, most of these fifty-five hundred soldiers were Christians or Christian sympathizers. When Maurice received orders from the emperor to exterminate all the residents of that predominantly Christian region, both he and his legion refused to carry out the order. Furious that the Theban Legion was in a state of mutiny. Maximian ordered a decimation. That is, every tenth man in the Theban Legion was seized and executed with the sword. When five-hundred fifty men were slain, the survivors still showed no inclination toward carrying out their orders. Maximian ordered a second decimation. When the soldiers still refused to move against the local people, the emperor ordered his loyal troops to Agaunum to slaughter all the survivors of the legion before carrying out his command to exterminate the inhabitants.

Even Christians in the domains of the tolerant Constantius

were not entirely safe. The emperor could not be everywhere at once, and governors hostile to Christianity often took the initiative into their own hands. Dacian, governor of Tarraconensis, was, like his predecessor Aemelianus, extremely anti-Christian. One of his victims was Valerius, the aged bishop of what is now Zaragoza, who, along with his priests and deacons, was arrested and force-marched one hundred miles without benefit of food or rest to Valencia, where they were tried. The bishop, who had suffered a stroke and was unable to speak intelligibly, delegated his deacon Vincent to speak for him. When it was clear that the old man remained adamant, he was taken off and killed. Dacian spoke to Vincent, who was a younger man, about his family and the "sweet joys of youth which still lie before you." When Vincent refused to sacrifice, Dacian ordered the deacon jailed and stretched on the rack and torn with iron hooks, but to no avail. Vincent would not renounce his faith.

When led again before Dacian, Vincent was told that his life would be spared if only he handed over the Christian books. When the deacon refused, he was chained on an iron frame with sharp bars running across it, a device similar to that on which St. Laurence had suffered fifty years before. Beneath it the fire was kindled until the frame was red-hot. As his flesh was roasted, Vincent gazed heavenward. He uttered neither shriek nor moan, but moved his lips softly in prayer. After several hours of this torture, Vincent was carried, still alive, back to his cell, where his naked, burned body was placed on a floor strewn with pieces of broken pottery. That night Vincent's guards heard no groans, but the sound of the singing of God's praises. The next morning the prisoner told one of the jailers that an angel had appeared during the night to comfort him. That impressed the guard to such an extent that he accepted Christ on the spot. That same day Dacian, perhaps after checking with Constantius, freed Vincent. Christian friends were allowed to take him back to Zaragoza, where he died of his burns a few days after reaching home.[9]

Dacian was especially severe with Christians who went out of their way to proclaim their faith without being summoned to sacrifice. By hunting down Christians he could run afoul of Constantius, if the emperor found out, but Dacian was clearly within his rights in venting his wrath against Christians who had the temerity to proclaim themselves as such without having been called upon to do so. One such person was a young farm girl from central Spain named Eulalia, the daughter of Christian parents, who slipped from her home one night to make her way to the town of Merida (where Dacian happened to be at the time) to declare publicly that she was a Christian. The governor dealt mercilessly with the girl. He had her flogged, stretched on the stocks, torn with iron combs, and burned with torches. Eulalia died praying, "Lord Jesus Christ, hear my prayer and perfect Thy work in me, and bid me be numbered among Thine elect in the rest of life eternal." Dacian suspended her body from a gibbet three days as a warning to other Christians so reckless as to be inclined to proclaim their religion in public.[10]

The persecution seems to have been felt most lightly in Gaul and Britain, where Constantius spent a great deal of time. In Britain there was only one reliable tradition of martyrdom. This concerned a Roman Briton by the name of Albanus, or Alban, who lived in the town of Verulamium, which was later renamed in the martyr's honor. Alban was a pagan, but sheltered a Christian priest and was so impressed by the man's devotion to God that during the time the clergyman was hidden in his home, Alban received instruction from him and was baptized.

Eventually soldiers knocked on Alban's door, seeking the fugitive priest. Alban dressed in the priest's clothing and told the soldiers that he was their man. In the meantime, the clergyman escaped to safety. When the local magistrate ascertained that Alban was not the fugitive priest, he ordered the prisoner to sacrifice or suffer death. When Alban refused to sacrifice, he was asked, "Of what family and race are you?"

Alban replied only that he was a Christian. Believers were apparently instructed to give as little information as possible to the authorities, so as to ensure the safety of Christians who had escaped official notice.

"What is your name? Tell it immediately!" insisted the magistrate.

"I am called Alban by my parents, and I worship and adore the true and living God, who created all things."

"If you want to enjoy eternal life, do not hesitate to sacrifice to the great gods."

Alban answered, "These sacrifices, which are offered to devils, are of no avail. Hell is the reward of those who offer them."

The magistrate ordered Alban scourged in hopes of breaking his will. When the Christian still refused to sacrifice, the magistrate sentenced him to death. The martyr walked to his execution with crowds of the curious lining the road. He and his military escort had to wade through a stream because there were so many onlookers crowded onto the bridge that passage across it was impossible. Alban was marched to the top of a green hill covered with flowers. There the executioner refused to carry out his orders, throwing down his sword and proclaiming himself a Christian. Another soldier was ordered to execute both Alban and the convert, and both were decapitated together.[11]

Except in Tarraconensis, where Dacian carried out the edict from Nicomedia despite the emperor's reluctance to have it enforced, there was little bloodshed in the domains of Constantius. This mildness in the West was, however, more than countervailed by the incredible violence carried out in the East.

# 13

# 'Fear not the punishment which is but a moment': The martyrs of the East

As we have seen, in the eastern half of the Roman Empire, Christians were hunted down and killed in huge numbers; yet there were still instances in which individuals were subjected to orderly trials and executed either individually or in small groups. For some of these martyrs, accounts survive of their passion and death.

The story of three courageous sisters in Thessalonica, Greece, has come down to us. After the edict in 303 which commanded the destruction of all copies of Scripture, three sisters, Agape (Charity), Irene (Peace), and Choine (Snow) hid many copies of the sacred writings in their home and fled to the mountains. For some time they lived in the open, eating whatever herbs and berries they could find in the wild. After some time (for reasons that are not clear), they returned to their home, where they were arrested and taken before the governor of Macedonia, whose name was Dulcitius. Along with a man named Agatho and three other women, Cassia, Philippa, and Eutichia, they were charged with being Christians and ordered to sacrifice.

"What madness is this of yours," asked Dulcitius, "that you will not obey the most religious commands of our emperors and caesars?" He then interrogated each of the prisoners, all of whom were steadfast in their adherence to Christ. He noticed that Eutichia was pregnant and inquired after her husband. When she told him that he had died six months ago, the governor was incredulous, refusing to believe her pregnancy was so far advanced.

"By whom are you bearing this child then?"

"By the man whom God gave me," she replied.

"How then do you find yourself with child, if, as you tell me your husband is dead?"

"No one may know the counsels of the omnipotent God," she answered. "This is the will of God." Actually Eutichia was only in the early stages of pregnancy, as Dulcitius rightly suspected. Her first husband had died six months earlier, but she had immediately remarried, and was trying to cover for her new husband, who was the father of the unborn child. Since Roman law protected expectant mothers, Dulcitius did not order Eutichia's execution, but ordered her to prison, from which nothing more was heard from her again.

Dulcitius questioned Agape and Chione, asking whether they had any "books of the impious Christians" in their possession. They replied that their library had already been confiscated and they had nothing. When it was clear that the two sisters would not renounce their faith, the governor had them burned at the stake. Their sister Irene, along with Eutichia, Agatho, Cassia, and Philippa, was kept in prison.

Later, after a thorough search of the sisters' house, more Scriptures were found. Irene, brought again before Dulcitius, was confronted with this fact and also with an offer of clemency if she would simply eat a bit of meat which had been sacrificed to the gods of Rome.

"My answer is no, by the omnipotent God who created heaven and earth, the sea, and all things that exist," Irene declared. "The dreadful punishment of eternal fire is especially reserved for those who have denied Jesus, the Word of God."

Dulcitius asked Irene who had convinced her to hide the Scriptures in her home. "It was God," said Irene. "He requires us to love Him even unto death and to allow ourselves to be burned to death rather than hand them over."

"Who beside yourself knew that these writings were hidden in your house?"

"No one else," said Irene, "as God sees me, except the omnipotent God who knows all things; other than He, nobody. We consider our own people indeed worse than our enemies, for we fear that they may betray us. Therefore I showed them to nobody."

After further interrogation about the details of her flight to the mountains with her sisters, Dulcitius decided that there was left to him no other alternative but to sentence Irene to death. He decided that death by fire was too easy a death. "I will not see that you end your life quickly, as your sisters did. I command that the guards and Zosimus, the public executioner, expose you naked in the brothel. Every day you will be given a loaf of bread from the palace and the guards will see that you do not escape." Dulcitius warned the guards that if Irene left the brothel for but a moment, their lives, like hers, would be forfeit.

As in the case of St. Agnes, according to the account of her trial and death, "Not one person dared to approach Irene or to do or say anything wicked to her." When it became apparent that Irene's virtue could not be compromised, she was brought to the governor, who asked her if she still persisted in her "temerity."

"It is not temerity, but divine piety," Irene replied. "In that I still persist."

Dulcitius thereupon ordered Irene burned to death, like her sisters. And so she perished on April 1, 304. Agatho, Cassia, Phillippa, and Eutichia were still in prison at the time. Presumably they perished, too, but no account of their end has survived.[1]

One of the most touching accounts of martyrdom concerns a young girl named Febronia. Although it would be several centuries before convents and monasteries were organized around formal rules, by the beginning of the fourth century there were groups of Christians committed to lifelong celibacy and a life given totally to the service of their Lord, who chose to pool their resources — physical, financial, and spiritual — to withdraw from society to live in community. Febronia, who was eighteen in 304, lived in one such community in Sibapte, Syria, composed of fifty women and headed by her aunt, "The Great Mistress" Bryene. Febronia was evidently an orphan and had been reared since the age of two in the community, where she had come to be loved for her physical as well as spiritual beauty. "Nourished from infancy among the sisters, reading the Holy Scriptures, fasting, praying, chanting psalms with them," Febronia "became full of heavenly thoughts and her understanding in divine things was much wondered at." Women from the town came to hear her interpret Scripture, and she was credited for the conversion of Hieria, the widow of a Roman senator.

Selenus, governor of Syria, was violently anti-Christian and rigorously enforced the imperial edict, traveling from town to town to undertake personally the extermination of Christians. He was accompanied by a physician, who supervised the torture of the prisoners, and by two nephews, Lysimachus and Primus, who privately deplored the old man's cruelty and sent word secretly to the towns that the governor planned next to visit so that the Christians there might have an opportunity to flee. When word was received that Selenus was on his way to Sibapte, the bishop there gave orders that all the faithful should flee. A serious problem presented itself to Bryene. Febronia was ill and unable to travel. The Great Mistress decided to dismiss all the ladies under her direction, but chose to remain with Febronia. Two other women, Thomais and Procla, also elected to stay behind.

Febronia heard her aunt sobbing and asked Thomais why the Great Mistress was weeping so bitterly. "My child," answered her aged friend, "she is anxious at heart about you. We are old and ugly, and all that can befall us is death; but you are young and fair, and there are things we fear for you of which you know nothing. We need not say more to you, dear child, than bid you be very careful how you accept any offers of the governor, however innocent they may seem — ease, riches, happiness — a danger is hidden beneath them you little dream of."

The next morning the soldiers broke down the door and were on the verge of slaughtering Bryene, when Febronia got up out of bed and threw herself between the men and her aunt, begging them to kill her instead. Just then Primus, the governor's nephew, arrived and sharply reprimanded his men for their violence and ordered them to leave the house. "You had plenty of warning," he chided Bryene. "While I withdraw my soldiers, take the opportunity to fly." Almost immediately, however, Selenus arrived in person and ordered Febronia brought to him the next day.

Febronia, still sick and supported by Thomais and Bryene, was brought before the governor, who held court in the public square. Thomais and Bryene begged to be condemned along with her. "They're old and ugly," snarled Selenus. "Send them back."

As Bryene was led away, Febronia said to her, "I trust in God that as I have always been obedient to you, so may I be faithful to your exhortation here before all the people. Go and pray for me, but first give me your blessing."

Her aunt extended her arms and prayed, "Lord Jesus Christ, who didst appear to Thy handmaiden Thecla in her agony to comfort her, stand by this lowly one in her great contest." She embraced Febronia and kissed her until the soldiers dragged her away.

Selenus ordered Lysimachus, whom he knew to have pro-Christian sympathies, to examine the girl. Barely able to control his true feelings, the younger man asked, "Tell me, young lady, what is your condition in life?"

"I am a servant."

"Whose servant?"

"I am the servant of Christ."

"What is your name?"

"I am a humble Christian."

"Give me your *name*, young lady. What is your *name*?"

"The good mother always calls me Febronia."

Selenus broke in and snapped, "We'll never get through if we proceed in this fashion. Get to the point at once. Febronia, I swear by the gods that I have no wish to hurt you. Here is my nephew, a fine young man. You take him as your husband and forget your false religion. I had other plans for him, but that doesn't matter, because I have never seen a sweeter face than yours and I am ready to accept you as my niece. I am a man of few words. Accept my offer, or, by the living gods, I shall make you regret you refused my offer."

Febronia replied, "I have a bridegroom in the heavens, eternal, with all His celestial glory as His dower!"

Selenus, in a rage, ordered Febronia stripped naked, then given a tattered cloak as a partial covering. "Why, you're not even resisting!" the governor taunted. "Where is your maiden modesty, you impudent little hussy?"

Febronia retorted that since she had lived in her aunt's religious community from the age of two, she had never even laid eyes upon a man until that very day. "Do I seem lost to shame?" she asked. "No, but I am stripped as a wrestler in the games to strive for victory. I do not fear you."

Selenus gave orders that the torture should begin. He loved to roast his victims slowly over a fire of coals. Surrounding the fireplace were four large stakes. Febronia was fastened upsidedown over the fire with each of her limbs bound to one of the stakes.

After the fire was kindled, the victim was flogged by soldiers until her blood hissed into the fire. By now a large crowd of pagans had gathered, but, far from gloating in the agony of the young girl, they began to express their outrage. There were shouts to Selenus to have pity on the innocent girl who had done no wrong except to hold firm to her convictions. "Stop it! Stop it!" they cried. This only incited the governor to order his soldiers to redouble their blows.

When cries of horror and disapproval increased, Selenus had Febronia removed from the fire. "Well, girl, how did you like this first taste of justice?" he asked. When Febronia, still conscious, declared, "My resolution is invincible," Selenus ordered her attached upright to the four stakes. Then he ordered his soldiers to put aside their whips and make use of their iron combs. As her sides were being raked open, Febronia prayed, "O Lord, make haste to help me. Do not leave me in this hour of anguish!"

"Cut out her tongue!" bellowed the governor. This was too much for the crowd, which was now fully in sympathy with the victim, so much so that menacing voices were heard raised against the governor. As a concession to their sensibilities, he instructed the surgeon to undertake a less radical operation. Instead of amputating Febronia's tongue, the doctor was ordered merely to extract her teeth, one by one. After he had drawn seventeen teeth, Selenus bade the physician stop. "Cut off her breasts!" he commanded.

This order brought an uproar from the crowd. The surgeon at first refused to perform the mastectomy. "Coward, go on, cut!" roared Selenus. With one sweep of his razor, the surgeon sliced off the girl's right breast. Febronia screamed, and prayed, "My Lord! My Lord! My God, see what I am suffering, and receive my soul into Thy hands!" She spoke not another word after that.

After the surgeon removed the other breast and cauterized the wounds with fire, the crowd went wild, breaking into a roar, "Cursed be Diocletian and all his gods!" As the dying girl was unbound and allowed to sink in a heap on the ground, Hieria, the senator's widow, who had been in the crowd, approached the governor, shouting, "You monster of cruelty, shame on you! Shame! Shame! You have outraged your own mother in the person of this poor girl! God, the Judge above judges, will make a swift work of you, and cut it short, and root you out of the land of the living."

Selenus ordered the arrest of Hieria, but the town fathers warned him that if he killed a senator's widow, one, moreover, who was widely known and respected, not only would he have a riot on his hands, half the city would be confessing Christ. Selenus released Hieria, but ordered the hands, feet, and finally the head of the unconscious Febronia to be hacked off.

When he returned to his home, Selenus was aware that he had incurred not only the ill-will of the entire town, but the hatred of his nephews as well. Instead of eating, he paced his room, storming and raging against his nephews, the people, and the world in general. That night he slipped and struck his head against a stone pillar, suffered a concussion, and died the next day.

Lysimachus and Primus, the nephews of the late governor, ordered that the body of Febronia be carried to the house of Bryene. There the whole town thronged to see the mangled and burned body of the young girl who had suffered so heroically. Lysimachus and Primus, among many others, publicly renounced the gods of Rome and requested baptism as Christians. Both men went into hiding and survived the persecution to become leaders of the Church.[2]

Some victims had less constructive reactions than Febronia. In Antioch, which had a large Christian population, thousands of victims were burned at the stake, but some believers who felt that they could not endure the agony of flame when they heard the midnight knock committed suicide by jumping off their roofs. One wealthy lady, named Domina, who was seized along with her three unmarried daughters at their villa outside of Antioch, marched past a body of water en route to Antioch and execution, and asked the guards for a few minutes to attend to necessity. Instantly, the four leaped into the water and drowned themselves.[3]

Eusebius, in his work *The Martyrs of Palestine*, recounted the exemplary courage of several of the thousands of Christians slaughtered in the small province of Palestine. As far as he knew, the first victim of the Great Persecution to die in Palestine was a lector and exorcist named Procopius, arrested in June 303, when he refused to hand over copies of the Scriptures. A native of Jerusalem, Procopius was living in Baishan. Ascetic to the point of eccentricity, having taken a vow of chastity as a little boy, every few days he whipped himself, or "took the discipline," in an attempt to defend himself against unclean thoughts, buffeting himself so violently that he frequently fainted from his self-inflicted blows. He ate, at most, three or four times a week — sometimes going more than seven days without nourishment — and even then he partook only of bread and water. Most of his time he spent in prayer, meditation, and study of Scripture.

When taken to Caesarea and ordered to sacrifice by Governor Flavian, Procopius asserted, "There is but one God, the creator and maker of the universe." Flavian said that he agreed with him, but added that they were both under the obligation to go through the formality of sacrificing to the four emperors. When Procopius stood fast, he was taken out and beheaded on July 7.[4]

By the summer of 303, nearly all the Church leaders in Palestine were under arrest for holding services of worship and refusing to surrender copies of Scripture. Even before the edict for a general massacre went out in 304, some of these men were put to death. On November 17, 303, two prominent Church leaders were brought before Flavian and ordered to sacrifice. Zacchaeus was a deacon from Gadara. His given name has been forgotten, but he was called "Zacchaeus" because his tiny stature and enthusiasm for Christ reminded people of the tax collector mentioned in the Gospel who climbed a tree because he was too short to see Jesus through the crowds. Alphaeus, a lector and exorcist, came from a wealthy family in Eleutheropolis and was renowned as a great preacher, and was credited with many conversions of pagans. Both men refused to sacrifice. "We know one God alone, the king of all." Zacchaeus had been held in prison for months with an iron collar around his neck. His flesh had been torn with iron combs and his legs had been forced apart until torn out of joint on the rack. Alphaeus had been flogged pitilessly and also stretched on the rack. When, after all their tortures, both men remained firm, Flavian ordered both of them beheaded immediately.

That same day, a deacon and exorcist from Caesarea, Romanus by name, was killed in Antioch in the presence of Diocletian. There were several Christians with him who agreed to sacrifice, but Romanus protested, shouting, "What are you doing? Do you want to hurl yourselves into the abyss of hell? Lift up the eyes of your mind on high and think of God and the Saviour of all the ends of the world, and do not abandon the commandment entrusted to you." The judge ordered Romanus to be burned at the stake, but Diocletian overruled him, saying that this was too easy a sentence, instructing the physician in attendance to first cut out the deacon's tongue. The surgeon bungled the job and removed only part of Romanus' tongue, leaving the deacon able still to exhort his companions to trust in Christ alone. He was hurried back to his prison cell, where he was strangled to death after all his limbs were broken on the rack.[5]

Flavian had been succeeded as governor by Urban when, in 304, the order went out that all Christians were to sacrifice. Instead of resorting to mass executions, Urban normally sentenced non-sacrificers to the mines, saving a select few to be thrown to the beasts at the public games or tortured publicly as an example. One such victim was a lay leader named Timothy of Gaza, who was publicly flogged in Caesarea until his back was torn to ribbons. After his sides were torn with the iron comb and he still refused to renounce Christ, Timothy was burned alive over a slow fire.[6]

A man named Apphianus did not wait for an official summons to sacrifice. Twenty years old in 306, he was one of Eusebius' roommates. A native of Gagae in Lycia (in what is now southwestern Turkey), Apphianus came from a respected pagan family, and, along with his older brother Aedesius, had embraced Christianity. Apphianus had studied at Beirut and was "the very embodiment of self-control, goodness, absolute chastity, and sobriety." One day, eluding the bodyguards, Apphianus rushed up to Urban as he was offering sacrifice and seized the governor's hands, begging him to stop. "It is not permitted that men should turn from the one and only true God and sacrifice to lifeless idols and evil spirits."

Instantly Apphianus was seized by Urban's bodyguards, who punched him in the face, knocked him down, and kicked him repeatedly as he lay bleeding on the ground. After a night in prison in which his legs were dislocated on the rack, Apphianus was taken before Urban and urged to sacrifice. When he refused, the governor ordered him strung up and torn with metal combs until his intestines were hanging out of his body. Then he was flogged in the face until his countenance was an unrecognizable mass of lacerated flesh. Again taken before Urban, Apphianus was asked, "What is your name? Where do you live? Where were you born?" Apphianus replied only, "I am a Christian and a slave of Christ."

Urban ordered Apphianus strung up by his hands and, his feet swathed in cloths soaked in oil, set afire. His flesh "melted and flowed like wax" as the fire "penetrated to the bones as if they were dry reeds." The young man was now a "fearful sight to see," his face almost entirely torn away, his body ripped wide open, and his legs nothing but charred bones. Again Urban demanded, "What is your name? Where do you live? Where are you from?" Again Apphianus replied, "I am a Christian. My father is God."

The broken youth was again thrown into a prison cell and the next day carried once more into the presence of the governor. When he still refused to sacrifice, he was sentenced to be tied with weights and dumped into the Mediterranean Sea. On that day — April 6, 306 — there was a severe earthquake and a small tidal wave, which cast Apphianus' mutilated remains back on shore to lie, "a sinister sight," in full view of the inhabitants of Caesarea. The grisly cadaver was seen by many pagans and the story of the courage of Apphianus led many of them to declare their faith in Christ, even though they knew that it meant death in the mines, or worse.

Apphianus' older brother Aedesius was then living in Alexandria, and was renowned as an authority on the Greek and Latin classics. He had been sentenced to a two-year term in the mines in 304, and had been one of the few prisoners who lived to complete his sentence. His experience did not dim his commitment to Christ, and when he learned that Christian girls were being condemned to the brothels, he hobbled up to the judge, Hierocles, and punched him in the face, knocking him to the ground. Aedesius was immediately arrested, and after being subjected to further tortures, was, like his brother, drowned.[7]

That same year, 306, Maximin Daza came to Caesarea and spectacles were staged in honor of his birthday. One of the Christians selected to be killed for the occasion was a man named Agapius. Daza offered him one last chance to sacrifice and save his life. "It is not for any trivial cause that I come to this conflict," Agapius said. "I am a witness to the true doctrine of God and I bear witness to you all, so that you too might know and worship the one and only God, creator of heaven and earth. Everything that has come upon me has happened for the sake of His name, and I accept it joyfully. I have not been brought here against my will. I am fighting for my faith, so that I might give courage to those younger than I that they too might despise death and follow eagerly after life, scorning Hades, so that they might arrive safely in the everlasting kingdom . . . and so that they might not fear the punishment which is but for a moment, but rather fear those flames of fire which are not quenched."

After hearing this public testimony, Daza ordered Agapius exposed to the wild beasts. Agapius literally ran up to meet them. In Eusebius' words, "A savage bear rushed foaming upon him and tore him with its teeth." Agapius, bleeding, but still alive, was carried off to prison and the next day was drowned.[8]

Another Christian singled out for extraordinary punishment was an eighteen-year-old girl named Theodosia who, like Febronia, was a member of a religious community. She had somehow been overlooked in the general roundup of Christians and was recognized only when, visiting Christians in the copper mines, she was overheard to say, "Remember me when you have reached your goal." Immediately she was arrested and taken to Urban, who commanded sacrifice. When Theodosia refused, Urban ordered the girl's breasts torn off with iron claws and her sides ripped open until her internal organs were exposed. During all this torture Theodosia did not murmur or groan, but her face was "alight with joy." Once again ordered to sacrifice, she refused. Before she was sealed in a bag and thrown into the sea, she declared, "Don't you know that I am experiencing what I have prayed for, and now I have been worthy to join the company of the martyrs of God?"[9]

Eusebius, who spent most of the period from 303 to 311 in hiding, wrote of just an hour in the typical life of the governor of Palestine in 308. First a physician named Dominus was led before Urban. He had been a very large, strong man, and for this reason had survived his term in the mines. It was now impossible to tell that he had once been handsome. Urban gave him an opportunity to save his life, but Dominus boldly confessed Christ and was sentenced to burn at the stake. Next Urban sentenced three young Christian boys to box each other in the arena. (Later, when he learned that the boys refused to box, he sent them to the mines.) A "grave and saintly old man" named Auxentius he ordered thrown to the wild beasts. He had several young men publicly castrated and sent to the mines at Phaeno. Then a group of women was sentenced: the young ones were condemned to the brothels and the older to the mines. It was all in a day's work.

Urban was deposed and executed by Daza in 309 for not being tough enough, and his successor, Firmilian, proved even more zealous in rounding up Christians to be sentenced to the mines. Firmilian began his administration by questioning a Christian woman named Ennatha, whom he crucified and had ripped open with iron claws. Still living, she was taken down and placed on the rack, where her legs were torn out of their sockets. Ennatha's sister Valentina appeared, hysterically ranting at the governor for "mangling my sister." Firmilian ordered Valentina arrested and commanded her to sacrifice. When Valentina kicked over the portable altar, Firmilian, insane with rage — "like a wild beast" — had Valentina "combed without mercy." Then he ordered both Ennatha and Valentina bound together and burned at the stake.[10]

Firmilian decided to be lenient with many wealthy and influential converts to Christianity. He first tried to soften them by sentencing them to care for government horses and camels. Then, if they proved stubborn, he sentenced them to the mines. Although most prisoners were still sent to the mines at Zoar and Phaeno, Firmilian killed many more victims immediately after their trial than his predecessors. Eusebius recorded that all over the city of Caesarea and its suburbs "fowls of heaven were tearing human flesh" and, in the very downtown areas, "bones and human entrails" were visible every day in the public squares where executions were held.[11] Some were burned at the stake, others were crucified, still others were hacked apart.

In the mines, Christians met together to pray. People from the neighboring districts were drawn to the camps and, sneaking them food, stayed to pray with them and even receive instruction in the faith. Roman officials noted that in Phaeno and Zoar, where most of the prisoners were Christians, the inmates behaved as though they were part of "a festive gathering," singing, praying, and laughing.[12] When Firmilian heard of this, he ordered the execution of the prison ringleaders. On September 19, 310, at Phaeno, Egyptian Bishops Peleus and

Nilus, Bishop Silvanus of Gaza, the lector John, and two Egyptian laymen, were burned at the stake. John was blind and had memorized the Scriptures by heart. Despite his condition, he had still been subjected to the usual torture of having one of his eyes burned out with a red-hot poker. From that day on, Firmilian burned or beheaded up to forty prisoners a day at Zoar and Phaeno.

The governor also undertook to execute the various Christians whom Urban had kept languishing in prison. The most distinguished of these, by far, was Pamphilus, a priest and scholar whom Eusebius characterized as "the most wonderful man of our time." A native of Beirut, in what is now Lebanon, Pamphilus was the scion of a wealthy and distinguished Christian family sent to study at the famous Catechetical School of Alexandria under Pierius, a pupil of the then recently deceased Origen. Pamphilus returned to Palestine, where he set up the School of Sacred Literature at Caesarea. He spent huge sums of his considerable wealth in acquiring books from all over the world, documenting the history of the Church, thus creating the most extensive Christian library of his time. Not only was Pamphilus noted for his learning and scholarship, but for his humility, self-control, and concern for the poor, for whose welfare he spent lavishly. By the time he was arrested, Pamphilus had almost completely exhausted the vast fortune he had inherited from his family.

Pamphilus had been held in prison since 307, along with several other Church leaders from Caesarea. During this time these men had been flogged, combed, and stretched on the rack, but none of them had broken down and renounced Christ. Firmilian, upon taking office, summoned Pamphilus, along with Valens, an aged deacon, and Seleucus, a respected lay leader. Despite their years of imprisonment and torture, the prisoners impressed bystanders with their "bright" and "smiling" faces. When asked their place of residence, Pamphilus and his colleagues alarmed Firmilian when they replied, "Jerusalem." The fact is that most people were ignorant of the fact that the Palestinian city of Aelia Capitolina had long ago borne that name. The name "Jerusalem" was totally new to

Firmilian, and he thought that Christians were setting up a colony by that name somewhere in the desert, without authorization by the government. So now the men were held guilty of treason as well as of being Christians. On February 16, 309, Pamphilus and nine other Christian prisoners were killed. Pamphilus was ripped apart by iron combs. Two catechumens were burned at the stake, another was crucified, and the remaining prisoners were beheaded. Firmilian was outraged when he saw one of his own slaves, an old man named Theodulus, give one of the condemned men the kiss of peace, thus revealing himself as a Christian. Immediately Firmilian had the slave crucified.

Firmilian's wrath was not spent. A house servant of Pamphilus, a boy of seventeen named Porphyry, asked if his master's body might be released for burial. The youth was not known to be a Christian, but Firmilian wanted to be sure, so he demanded that Porphyry sacrifice. He refused. "Torture him and tear his whole body to the very bone!" screamed the governor. When the relentless maceration of the iron combs failed to impel the boy to sacrifice, Firmilian gave orders that Porphyry was to burn to death on a slow, smoldering fire. The youth went to his death "smiling and cheerful," directing his friends how to dispose of his affairs "with undisturbed and sober consideration, as if he had nothing to trouble him." When the flames engulfed him, he murmured "Jesus" and seemed actually to try to inhale the flames.

By the evening of the sixteenth of February there were eleven charred or mangled bodies lying in the public square of Caesarea as a warning to all who might be so foolish as to embrace the Christian faith. That evening a Christian named Julian, who had been in hiding, went up and began to kiss the dismembered fragments. Immediately he was seized and taken to the governor and condemned to death over a slow fire. "Bounding and leaping and with a loud voice rendering thanks to God who had thought him fit to receive such blessings," the meek and gentle Julian gave up his spirit.[13]

So, until the spring of 311, the persecutions raged throughout the eastern half of the empire. Although bishops made it clear that Christians must not, under any circumstances, sacrifice or surrender copies of Scripture, they also made it plain that it was inadvisable to court martyrdom by seeking arrest, and urged those who could to flee. Eusebius, who admired his mentor Pamphilus so much that he took "Pamphili" ("of Pamphilus") as his surname, was one of those who survived during these years by going into hiding. Thus, in this way and through numerous conversions by pagans who were moved by the commitment of the Christian martyrs, the Church survived the determined efforts of the Roman government to extirpate it from the face of the earth.

# 14

# 'In this sign you will conquer': The peace of the Church

Christians were by no means the only people to suffer in the years of terror during the prolonged civil war. After he had been in power for a time, Maxentius ceased murdering Christians in Italy, at least on account of their faith, but his reign was by no means a time of peace or humane government. Maxentius was just as much a mass murderer as Galerius and Daza. His motives were, however, political and social rather than religious.

Maxentius was a short, balding, swarthy man, probably in his late thirties. According to all contemporary accounts, he was a depraved, paranoid egomaniac, very much in the tradition of Caligula, Nero, Commodus, and Elagabalus. Eusebius, seconded by less partial contemporaries, reported that Maxentius was "plunged into every kind of depravity, and there was not one filthy, dissolute act of which he was innocent, given up as he was to adultery and sexual corruption in all its forms." Heavily involved in witchcraft, Maxentius directed that pregnant women be seized and ripped open so that their unborn babies might be dissected for the purpose of augury and divination. In addition, Maxentius slaughtered lions and performed "unspeakable rites" to invoke demons and appease the gods of war.[1]

As for the subjects of Maxentius, they lived in a constant state of war waged on them by their prince. In order to obtain their financial assets, Maxentius killed hundreds of wealthy citizens and confiscated their estates. Insanely fearful of opposition, he massacred scores of senators, frequently on irrational suspicions. Eusebius recounted that all Rome trembled before him, rich as well as poor. On the slightest of pretexts, he ordered his bodyguards to murder enemies real and imagined. The death toll in the city alone was said to have been in the thousands, as the emperor's death squads, in full military dress, were active with fire and sword around the clock. The combined effects of this continuous bloodbath and the ongoing civil war led to food shortages in Italy so severe as to reduce the common people to the point of starvation.[2]

Although Maximin Daza was Maxentius' rival, he was very similar in character. In the Middle East, Daza also murdered his wealthy subjects to confiscate their money and property. Daza was also a lecher and a drunkard. Eusebius recorded that in his frequent orgies he often drank until he was like a raving madman. He often conducted official business in a state of total intoxication, and later regretted decisions he did not realize that he had made. Unlike Maxentius, however, Daza, a fanatical pagan who "could not bring himself to move a hair's breadth" without divinations and oracles,[3] pursued his policy of Christian extermination with singleminded ferocity and religious zeal.

Daza's undisciplined armies left a trail of devastation wherever they went, looting and plundering, killing and raping Christians and pagans alike. In whatever towns and villages his troops entered, Daza ordered his men to search out and kill all those suspected of being Christians. Doubtless, among the thousands he put to the sword, burned at the stake, crucified, drowned, or saved for the beasts in the arena, among those who were castrated, blinded, branded in the face and then thrown into dungeons or sent to the mines, there were hundreds of hapless people who suffered as "Christians" only because their enemies who wished their destruction denounced them as such.

By the end of the first decade of the fourth century, conditions all around the Mediterranean were in a state of total chaos. Travel was virtually impossible. Ships were, with frightening regularity, attacked by the navies of one or another of the warring emperors. The cargoes were confiscated and the passengers seized, to be crucified or burned at the stake on the pretext that they might be enemy spies. Trade and commerce were disrupted and the only industries not in a state of collapse were the shipbuilding business and the manufacture of swords, shields, javelins, and other weapons. Because of the food shortages, the empire was swept by epidemics.

The common people were not the only ones to sicken. By the spring of 310, the dreaded Galerius, now sixty-eight, was gravely ill. Ulcers teeming with pus broke out on the unmentionable parts of his body. His physicians, in a series of painful operations, cut away much of that area, but his entire body became affected. The slightest movement brought on hemorrhaging. The rectum and urethra were destroyed by the proliferating abcesses and the contents of the bowels and bladder were discharged "indiscriminately" through fistulae, which ate themselves through the body wall. According to Lactantius, Galerius' "bowels came out" and his entire pelvic area "putrefied." The intestines became gangrenous and the vile-smelling discharge was filled with "swarms of worms." Raging with unbearable pain from head to toe, the old tyrant bellowed in agony "like a wounded bull."[4]

As news of the sufferings of the detested prince leaked from his palace at Sofia, Christians and pagans alike gloated over the agonies of the man who had caused others so much suffering. Like Shakespeare's Macbeth, the despised old man must have reflected that "I must not look to have" . . . that which "should accompany old age, as honor, love, obedience, troops of friends . . . but in their stead, curses, not loud, but deep. . . ."

By April 311, even Galerius' family could scarcely abide the stench of the sickroom. In his pain and rage, the emperor ordered his physicians executed.[5] Once enormously corpulent, Galerius was now shrunk to a near-skeleton, his "ghastly-looking skin . . . settled . . . deep among his bones." His legs alone were an exception; they were "distended like bladders with no appearance of joints." Dissolved into "one mass of corruption" and raging with pain,[6] Galerius, perhaps through the efforts of his wife, Valeria, whom he had always suspected of being a secret Christian, suddenly fell under the conviction that he was being punished by the Christian God. To everyone's amazement, he turned to Christ for mercy and issued an order on April 30, bringing an end to the persecution.

The man whose official title was the absurdly pompous appellation "Emperor Caesar Galerius Valerius Maximianus Invictus Augustus, Pontifex Maximus, Germanicus Maximus, Egyptiacus Maximus, Thebaicus Maximus, Sarmaticus Maximus five times, Persicus Maximus twice, Carpicus Maximus six times, Armeniacus Maximus, Holder of the Tribunician Authority for the twentieth time, Imperator for the nineteenth, consul for the eighth, Father of the Fatherland," declared, in his own name and that of the other emperors, that he had always tried to act for the "advantage and benefit of the nation." He admitted that "many" Christians had been "punished with death in many forms." He had, however, been led to such extreme measures out of concern for "law and order." Christians had "abandoned the convictions of their forefathers" and refused to "follow the path trodden by earlier generations," making "their own laws to suit their own ideas and individual tastes." In other words, Christians had been jeopardizing the welfare of the state by not worshipping the gods of their fathers and thus incurring the wrath of those spirits who were expected to protect and prosper the state.

Galerius, however, admitted that his measures had failed. His attitude toward Christians was now, "If you can't beat them, join them." After years of violent coercion, Christians still were refusing to worship the "gods of heaven." So, "in consideration of our [benevolence] and our [established] custom, by which we are want to extend pardon to all, we have determined that we ought most cheerfully to extend our indulgence in this matter also; that they might again be Christians, and may rebuild the conventicles in which they were accustomed to assemble, on condition [that they do nothing contrary to public order]." He concluded his order with a request that Christians pray to their God for him, for the state, and for themselves, that peace and brotherhood might reign on earth.[7]

Eusebius recounted that it was "as if all at once a light [was] shining out of a dark night. In every town could be seen crowded churches, overflowing congregations, and the appropriate ceremonies duly performed." Everywhere prison doors were opened. From the mines throngs of men, women, and children hobbled back to their homes. They "pursued their journey along the highways and through the marketplaces praising God with hymns and psalms." Despite their tortures and mutilation, they were "beaming and joyful," full of "pleasure and boldness which cannot be expressed in words." So moved were the pagans that "even those who had been athirst for our blood, when they saw this unexpected wonder . . . congratulated us."[8] Many of them lined the roads, welcoming the freed captives, shouting, "The God of the Christians alone is good and true!" As for Galerius, almost as soon as he issued his edict, his pains vanished. A few days later, commending his wife and son to Licinius, he peacefully died.

Maximin Daza, however, searched for ways of minimizing the edict of Galerius in his domains. He refused to authorize the rebuilding of Christian houses of worship or even permit the meeting of believers in cemeteries. On the other hand, he did everything in his power to revitalize the old National Religion. He rebuilt pagan temples in all cities and provinces under his control, creating a hierarchy of pagan priests patterned on the hierarchy of the Christian Church. To combat the faith, he circulated a forgery called the *Memoirs of Pilate*, a work containing "every kind of blasphemy against Christ."[9] This tract was handed out in public squares and given to schoolchildren to be learned by heart. Prostitutes were rounded up and induced, under torture, to sign statements that they were Christians and could vouch for the existence of immoral and obscene practices among the faithful.

Daza urged local officials, such as his friend Theotecnus, city sheriff of Antioch, to make official complaints against Christians as a public menace, begging the emperor to save their people from these perverse and impious folk who had the temperity to renounce the old gods. Then, claiming to be responding to popular demand, Daza renewed the persecution.

A letter written to the city fathers of Tyre, in what is now Lebanon, illustrated the attitude of this archpagan, who sincerely believed that only wholehearted devotion to the old gods would restore prosperity to the realm. He extolled Jupiter, "who preserves your ancestral gods, your wives and children, your hearth and homes from every destructive pest and decay." A failure to reverence the old gods had been responsible for two calamities that had lately befallen the empire. Like his predecessors throughout the years, Daza maintained that earthquakes, hurricanes, wars, and famine were the result of "the irreverence of the impious followers of the New Religion, who came near to destroying the whole world through their blasphemous neglect of the old gods."

During the summer of 311, the weather had been better than it had been for years, and this Daza attributed to the recent policy of genocide. Now that myriad thousands of Christians had been liquidated, he urged his countrymen to

> look at the standing crops already flourishing with waving heads in the broad fields, and at the meadows glittering with plants and flowers, in response to abundant rains and the restored mildness of the atmosphere.

Let men rejoice "that through our piety, our sacrifices, and our veneration, the might of the most powerful and terrible Mars has been propitiated."

Daza declared clemency for those who acknowledged their "blind error," returning to the worship of Jupiter and other National Gods, as if they had been rescued from a grave illness. Those, however, who persisted in their "damnable folly" were to be severely punished.[10] So once again Christians, many of them returned only a few weeks from mine and prison, were arrested. Christian men and boys were punished by the amputation of their noses, ears, and hands, and the removal of their remaining eye. Christian women were subjected to a worse fate than death by imperial police. Killings were renewed, but on a limited scale. This time the victims were chiefly members of the clergy, like Silvanus, the aged bishop of Emesa, Phoenica, and Peter, bishop of Alexandria.

Peace and prosperity did not last. During the winter, the expected rains failed and a deep famine followed the drought. On the heels of this came a deadly epidemic, called "The Carbuncle." This was a "malignant pustule" which spread throughout the entire body. By spring hundreds were dying in the cities and thousands in country villages. Many villages were completely depopulated. Eusebius recounted that some

> desired to dispose of their most precious things to those who were better supplied, in return for the smallest morsel of food, and others, selling their possessions little by little, fell into the last extremity of want. Some, by chewing wisps of hay and recklessly eating noxious herbs, undermined and ruined their constitutions.

Rich people begged for food in the streets. Everywhere miserable folk "wasted away like ghosts and at the very point of death, stumbled and tottered here and there, and, too weak to stand, fell down in the middle of the streets; lying stretched out at full length they begged that a small morsel of food might be given them, and with their last gasp they cried out, 'Hunger,' having strength only for this last painful cry."[11] Dead bodies lay unburied in the streets for days on end, bloating and festering, until they were eaten by dogs. Cities were soon forced to order the extermination of all dogs, "for fear they might go mad and begin devouring [the living]."[12]

As in the great natural disasters of the past, Christians distinguished themselves by their courage and love. In the midst of the calamity, "Everyday some continued caring for and burying the dead, for there were multitudes who had no one to care for them." Wealthier Christians contributed a large portion of their supplies to their local congregation for the purpose of sharing it with the needy. Fearless of the dangers of recognition, lay leaders gathered a "huge number of skeleton-like famine victims, distributing bread to all of them, with the result that many pagans came to glorify Christ and openly declare that of all the people on earth Christians alone are truly pious and religious."[13]

As the suffering citizenry became more and more impressed by the deportment of the persecuted Christians, they became more and more disgusted by the persecutor, who, in the midst of the famine spent most of his time eating, drinking, and fornicating. Daza incurred almost universal opprobrium by his treatment of the dowager Empress Valeria, whom he attempted to marry. Valeria, who was Daza's aunt by marriage, rejected his proposal of marriage as indecent and obscene, reproaching the emperor for wanting to divorce his faithful wife for a hapless widow of whom, as in the case of his other women, he was soon bound to tire. In a rage, Daza banished Valeria to exile in the Syrian desert. Diocletian sent messengers to Daza, begging him to release his daughter and send her to him. The former emperor was now a nonentity, and Daza ignored his request. Valeria was kept in exile for several years, until, after the fall of Daza, she and her mother, the dowager Empress Priscilla, were beheaded on order of the Emperor Licinius.

The long civil war was now heading to its climax. By the middle of 312, a showdown was near in the West between Constantine and Maxentius, and in the East between Licinius and Maximian Daza. Maximian was now out of the picture. After allying himself with the ascendant Constantine by giving him his daughter Fausta as a bride, he gave up his bid to regain the throne in 308. Soon, however, he began to plot against Constantine, and was imprudent enough to disclose his plans to murder him to Fausta, whom he expected to support her father against her husband. Fausta, when she learned of her father's plans to have Constantine murdered in his bed, informed her husband, who, on the designated night, commanded a slave to repose in his chamber. Constantine hid in a corner of the room and watched as one of Maximian's minions slipped in and stabbed the hapless bondsman. When the murderer cheerfully announced the death of the "tyrant" to Maximian, who was in the hallway, Constantine appeared with his bodyguards and ordered the culprits arrested. Shortly afterwards, Maximian was found hanged in his prison cell.

Now, in the autumn of 312, Constantine's army swept south from the Alps to engage that of Maxentius outside of Rome. Constantine had an army composed of Gauls, Germans, and Britons consisting of 40,000 men, but Maxentius' force numbered more than 100,000. The night before the expected battle, Constantine had a dream that was to alter the history of mankind. He dreamed that he saw Christ, who pointed to a cross of light shining in the heavens and said, "In this sign you will conquer."[14] Then, as directed in the dream, Constantine marked his soldiers' shields with a symbol known as the "Chi-Rho," consisting of the Greek characters for "Ch" and "R" entwined together.[15]

Constantine met Maxentius on October 28, at Red Rock, a town five miles outside of Rome. Maxentius had consulted his fortune-tellers, who told him, "On this day the enemy of Rome shall perish." Of course, he assumed that Constantine was the "enemy of Rome." Maxentius was routed and forced into headlong retreat across a pontoon bridge over the Tiber River. The structure collapsed, plunging hundreds of men into the river. The defeated emperor, in full armor, tried desperately to clamber up onto the bank, but sank beneath the waves. Constantine entered Rome, slaughtered Maxentius' son and all his supporters as well as the survivors of his army, and, when the body of Maxentius was recovered, ordered the head removed and placed on the end of the pike, to be paraded around Rome.

Meanwhile, six months later, on April 30, 313, Daza was defeated by Licinius in what is now Bulgaria, and was forced to retreat into Asia Minor. He now turned against his pagan priests. Convinced that in his attempt to resurrect the Old Religion he had been backing the wrong horse, Daza now followed Galerius' example and proclaimed an end to the persecution of the Church. In an edict issued almost two years to the day of his uncle's proclamation, Daza affirmed complete religious freedom. Everyone was to have the freedom, "without any fear or suspicion," to worship according to his conscience.[16]

Daza tried to regroup his army, but by now he was deathly ill, driven nearly mad with "intolerable pain." By late spring he was bedridden, dashing his head against the wall in agony, his flesh seemingly "consumed by an invisible fire." According to Eusebius, "The whole appearance of his frame was changed, and there was left only . . . a skeleton of dry bones."[17] Now blind and in delirium, he "imagined that he saw God, with His servants arrayed in white robes, sitting in judgment on him." He moaned like a man being burned alive, begging for death. Having confessed all his sins to the Lord, he died praying, "Christ, have mercy on me!"[18]

On June 13, 313, a policy of religious toleration was proclaimed throughout the empire. In the Edict of Milan, issued by Constantine and Licinius, it was announced, "Freedom of worship shall not be denied. Every man, according to his own inclination and wish, shall be given permission to practice his religion as he chooses." It was specified that Christians and non-Christians alike "shall be allowed to keep the faith of their own religious beliefs and worship." All confiscated property was to be restored to the Church.[19]

What sort of person was this man Constantine, who now shared the Roman world with his elderly drunken brother-in-law Licinius? Flavius Valerius Constantinus had been born February 27, 274, most likely at Naissus, in what is now Yugoslavia. His father was Constantius, and his mother was Helena, or Helen, whose origins are obscure. Some claimed that she was a British princess, the daughter of the "Old King Cole" of legend. More reliable sources assert that she was of much more humble origins, a peasant girl from what is now Bulgaria and a waitress in the inn where her father tended bar when Constantius met her. Some historians feel that Helen was only a concubine and not the principal wife of the old emperor. She was later to become a fervent Christian, and, in the decade before her death at eighty in 330, she traveled throughout the Middle East, erecting churches at sites associated with Jesus' ministry.

At any rate, we know that Constantine was educated at the court of Diocletian in Nicomedia, and that at any early age he embarked upon an illustrious military career. After being proclaimed emperor by his troops at York, England, on the death of his father, Constantine spent several years fighting the Alamans and Franks. He gained the reputation of a good administrator, working on internal improvements, fortifying borders, building bridges, restoring cities, and building schools. Not only did he forebear to enforce the imperial edicts, but made no secret of his sympathy for Christians.

Constantine has been described as a powerfully built man

of medium height with a ruddy complexion, a hooked nose, thinning hair, and penetrating eyes. Many of his contemporaries spoke of the "majestic beauty" of his face and his "piercing bright eyes." A man of great physical strength and vigor, at fifty he would still maintain his "invincible strength," and, at sixty still possess "a sound and vigorous body, free from all blemish and of more than youthful vivacity; a noble mien and strength equal to any exertion, so that he was able to join in martial exercises, ride, endure the fatigues of travel, and engage in battle."[20]

Although Constantine was considered benign and merciful in his day, at least for a Roman emperor, according to Christian standards he was frequently cruel and ruthless. We have seen the slaughter he wrought in Rome after the defeat of Maxentius. Later, for reasons unrecorded, he killed his eldest son, Crispus, and shortly thereafter his wife, Fausta, whom he ordered impaled in her bath and held under scalding water. On the other hand, unlike the case of most of his contemporaries, the violent side of his nature was under control most of the time. Why, or even when, he accepted Christ has never been fully explained. Long before his dream in October 312, he had expressed sympathy for the faith in much the same way that Alexander Severus and Philip the Arab had in bygone days. Will Durant advanced the theory that Constantine became a Christian at least partially because it was in the best interests of his bid for power and his attempt to bring stability to the Roman world:

> He had seen in his lifetime the failure of three persecutions, and it was not lost on him that Christianity had grown in spite of them. Its adherents were still very much in the minority, but they were relatively united, brave, and strong, while the pagan majority was divided among many creeds, and included a dead weight of simple souls without conviction or influence. Christians were especially numerous in Rome under Maxentius and in the East under Licinius. Constantine's support of Christianity was worth a dozen legions against these men.

> [Moreover, Constantine was impressed] by the comparative order and morality of Christian conduct, the bloodless beauty of Christian ritual, the obedience of Christians to their clergy, their humble acceptance of life inequalities in hope of happiness beyond the grave; perhaps this new religion would purify Roman morals, regenerate marriage and family, and allay the fever of class war. The Christians, despite bitter oppression, had rarely revolted against the State; their teachers had inculcated submission to the civil powers, and had taught the divine right of kings. Constantine aspired to an absolute monarchy; the hierarchical discipline and ecumenical authority of the Church seemed to offer a spiritual correlate for monarchy. Perhaps the marvelous organization of bishops and priests could become an instrument of pacification, unification and rule.[21]

Roland Bainton, on the other hand, maintained that "politically speaking, his course must have appeared sheer folly," since Christians were still outnumbered by pagans. The only explanation that seemed likely to the gentle Yale professor was that Constantine was sincerely converted.

Although, like many people of his time, Constantine elected to be baptized only in his final illness (in 337), there is much evidence to suggest that, by the time of the Edict of Milan, he was sincerely committed to the "struggle for deathlessness," as he called Christianity. Spending long hours in prayer in his chapel, Constantine gave up all the claim to divinity that had been advanced by his predecessors and, as early as 314, spoke of Christ as "My Lord and Saviour," insisting, "My chief work in life is to glorify Christ."[22] His dream was that of a Roman world prospering under one sovereign, one law, and one religion.

While permitting religious freedom, Constantine immediately began to act in favor of the Christians. Restoring to the Church all confiscated property, he subsidized the building of houses of worship. Furthermore, he gave bishops the authority of judge within their dioceses, exempted clergy from taxation, and made Christian associations "judicial persons," thus allowing them to own land and receive legacies. On the other hand, Constantine forbade magic, divination, crucifixion, rape, and premarital sex, removed the legal penalties against the single and the childless, dating from the time of Augustus. He made Sunday a national holiday. Moreover, Constantine ended the life-and-death authority that Roman men had over their wives and children (although, as we have seen, he continued to exercise this authority over his own family), and forbade the separation of slave families. He contemplated abolishing slavery altogether, but took no action to do so. The gladiatorial games, however, Constantine did abolish.

Despite Constantine's vigorous support of Christianity, the Church was still not at peace in the territories controlled by Licinius. Though married to a sister of Constantine, Licinius soon turned against his brother-in-law and the Christians who were that emperor's most enthusiastic supporters. Licinius fired all Christians on his staff and decreed that all soldiers in the territories under his control must sacrifice to the gods of Rome or be imprisoned. During the second decade of the fourth century, a number of Christians, mostly clergy and soldiers, were imprisoned, but few were killed. Several bishops were "hacked with a sword and carved up like butcher's meat,"[23] but the worst atrocity under Licinius appeared to have been the martyrdom of forty members of the Twelfth Legion, which was stationed in Sebastea, in what is now eastern Turkey. These men refused to obey the imperial command to sacrifice and, after a long period of imprisonment, were sentenced to die by being exposed at night in the middle of winter on an artificial lake in front of the public baths. The entrance to the baths was left open to show the prisoners that safety was just steps away, if they chose to renounce Christ. For hours nothing happened. Then one of the men dragged himself toward the lighted door and renounced Christ, only to die of hypothermia shortly afterwards. When this happened, one of the guards decided to take his place. Proclaiming himself a Christian, he stripped off his clothing and took his place on the ice. By morning only one soldier was alive, a young man named Meliton. His mother was in the crowd that watched the frozen bodies being heaped onto a cart to be taken for incineration, and noticing that he was still breathing, took him in her arms, where he shortly died. After the bodies were burned, the ashes were thrown into the river.

In the fall of 324, Constantine defeated Licinius in battle, and shortly afterwards ordered his execution. Constantine had now realized his dream of a Roman world with one ruler. Now he was free to pursue his pro-Christian policy without opposition anywhere in the empire. It was in his attempt to solve the various divisions which had appeared in the Church and to unite all believers into the Holy, Catholic and Apostolic Church that he called the Council of Nicaea, in which Christian bishops from all over the world formulated a basic treatment of belief, binding upon all believers, which is known as the Nicene Creed.

Eusebius noted that, upon the defeat of the "besotted old dotard" Licinius, Christians "kept dazzling festival." "Everything was filled with light and those who before we downcast beheld each other with smiling faces and beaming eyes. With dances and hymns, in city and country, they glorified God the Universal King. . . ."[24]

# Conclusion

The "Peace of the Church" certainly did not bring an end to the phenomenon of Christian martyrdom, much less terminate the troubles of the Church. Throughout the ensuing sixteen hundred years, Christians have continued to give their lives for their faith, often unhappily, as in the shameful religious strife that swept Europe in the sixteenth and seventeenth centuries at the hands of other "Christians." It has been said that the twentieth century has seen more martyrdoms than all the other centuries since the time of Christ combined. One can recall the millions of Christian Armenians slaughtered by the Turks during the First World War, the untold millions killed by Lenin and Stalin in Soviet Russia, and the myriads of Christians who died in Hitler's death camps along with the Jews, Gypsies, and other minorities whose sufferings have been more publicized, as well as the untold number of Christian believers killed in the China of Mao Zedong.

What does it all mean? What is the purpose of exploring so bloody and gruesome a subject as that of the martyrdom of the early Christians? Is interest in the martyrs akin to a general interest in murders and fires, earthquakes and explosions? Is a person who reads the story of the martyrs no different from one who loves to pore over pictures of the charred and dismembered bodies of the victims of plane crashes and automobile accidents? Is the study of the martyrs simply an unusual form of necrophilia?

Some people would hold that remembering the martyrs is a way of ensuring that such an event will never happen again. However, we know that similar events did happen again after 325, and, barring an immediate return of Christ, they will happen again in the future. Others would say that the whole subject is meaningless and depressing, the story of innocent lives cruelly obliterated at the whim and caprice of fanatical madmen. Pointing to the martyrs as themselves examples of misguided fanaticism, who found death preferable to the recitation of a simple formula, such critics would say that a history of the martyrs reveals only that it is better to swallow one's convictions and follow the crowd rather than risk the chief of all evils, death.

The Church of Jesus Christ has always affirmed that the remembrance of the martyrs is a reflection not of an interest in death, but in life, a life in eternity with God — a destiny so glorious and desirable that to attain it rational and intelligent men and women throughout the centuries have in untold numbers willingly forfeited their liberty, property, and even their lives in this world, surrendering it amidst the most inhuman tortures. It reflects an interest not so much in the masters of death, the Neros, the Marci Aurelii, the Decii, the Galerii, the Stalins, the Hitlers, or the Maos, but in the Author of Life, who put aside His Godhead to become a Man and to offer up His lifeblood that all who put their trust in Him might win, as Constantine put it, the "struggle for deathlessness."

If this life is all there is, then the chapter of history that we have examined should be spoken of only with horror. If our days are but, as it were, a conveyor belt into everlasting blackness, if there is no succor to be expected save that within our feeble powers, if we wander, helpless, groping, in a bleak and dreary maze of chance, buffeted about through an absurd world without purpose or meaning, formed only through the chance perambulations of random atoms, then we might well shut our mind to the story of those who prized a "good" more highly than life. If the kingdom not of this world is but an illusion, a mirage upon a barren and desolate wilderness, if the City of God is but a phantasm of men's wishful imaginations, if the Words of Christ are false, then, as St. Paul suggested, "Let us eat and drink, for tomorrow we die."

If, however, the Word of Christ be true, then the martyrs give us the courage to live (and if need be, die) for our convictions, to live not for the admiration of men nor for the praise and laudation of the world, nor for the admiration of wealth nor for the attainment of power and honor, but for the accomplishment of the will of Jesus Christ. The martyrs tell us that the loss of our integrity is far worse than earthly suffering and pain, that the loss of heaven is infinitely more disastrous than the loss of earth. When we think of those who loved their Lord so much that they gave up everything for Him — family, friends, possessions, career, limb and life — we are reminded of the words of the English hymnist Isaac Watts:

> When I survey the wondrous cross,
> On which the Prince of Glory died,
> My richest gain I count but loss,
> And pour contempt on all my pride.

Thinking of the "sorrow of love" that flowed "mingled down" from the Sacred Head, Hands, and Feet, we are moved to declare with Watts:

> Were the whole realm of nature mine,
> That were an offering far too small;
> Love so amazing, so divine
> Demands my soul, my life, my all!

Many thousands of people who were put to death during the first three centuries after Christ, might have saved their lives if only they had denied their Lord. Yet they chose to stand by their convictions, to love and serve their Lord, and by losing this life, to gain a better one.

The lesson of the martyrs is total commitment and devotion to Christ. Many radio and television preachers stress only the benefits of being a Christian. I myself have attended religious meetings in which speakers, trying to entice nonbelievers to a commitment, have given the impression that the acceptance of Christ necessarily entails the fulfillment on earth of all one's desires for material prosperity. One sees books that tell one how being a devoted Christian fattens the bank account and slims the waistline, how it makes for success in school, in business, and on the athletic field, how it makes for a long, healthy, and honored life. This attitude is nowhere to be found in the Sacred Scriptures. Paul taught that it is "through many tribulations we must enter the kingdom of God" (Acts 14:22), that, as fellow heirs of Christ we must "suffer with him in order that we may also be glorified with him"

(Romans 8:17). Peter, likewise, tells us that it is our lot on earth to "share in Christ's sufferings" (1 Peter 4:13), and Our Lord taught that "in the world you have tribulation" (John 16:33), even though we have peace in knowing that He has overcome the world.

Although it is unfashionable to speak of sufferings, they are an important part of the Christian life, and we must be mindful of the meritorious nature of offering them to God as a sacrifice to Christ and a participation in His redeeming work. Paul tells us, "I rejoice in my sufferings for your sake, and in my flesh I complete what is lacking in Christ's afflictions for the sake of his body, that is, the church" (Colossians 1:24). It is not that Christ's death on the cross was insufficient or that He needs man's works, but that in offering our sufferings to Him these are joined to His own in the work of the redemption of all mankind. This was well understood by the early Christian martyrs. We can imitate them in making a total commitment of self to the Heavenly Sovereign, a commitment which holds back nothing — time, finances, health, opportunities — even life itself — in pursuit of God's kingdom and righteousness.

# Chapter notes

## Chapter 1

1. Francis X. Glimm, ed., *The Apostolic Fathers* (Washington, 1947), p. 171.
2. *Ibid.,* pp. 172-173.
3. *Ibid.,* pp. 173-174.
4. Philip Schaff, *History of the Christian Church,* Vol. II (New York, 1912), p. 355 (hereafter referred to as Schaff, *History II*) .
5. Gregory Dix, *The Shape of the Liturgy* (London, 1945), p. 38.
6. *Ibid.,* p. 42.

## Chapter 2

1. Flavius Josephus, *The Jewish War* (Hamondsworth, England, 1959), p. 399.
2. Alexander Roberts and James Donaldson, ed., *Anti-Christian Library; translations of the writings of the Fathers down to A.D. 325,* Vol. VII (Edinburgh, 1868-1872), p. 546 (hereafter referred to as ANF, followed by vol. no.).
3. Henry Wace and Philip Schaff, eds., *A Select Library of Nicene and Post-Nicene Fathers of the Christian Church, Vol. 7. Eusebius: Church History, Life of Constantine the Great, and Oration in Praise of Constantine.* (Oxford, 1890), p. 126 (hereafter referred to as W/S *Eusebius*).
4. *Ibid.*

## Chapter 3

1. Robert L. Wilken, *The Christians as the Romans Saw Them* (New Haven, 1984), pp. 91-92.

2. Michael Grant, *The World of Rome* (New York, 1969), p 158.
3. Clifford H. Moore, *Pagan Ideas of Immortality During the Early Roman Empire* (Cambridge, 1918), p. 32.
4. *Ibid.*, p. 37.
5. George C. Brauer, *The Age of the Soldier Emperors* (Park Ridge, N.J., 1975), p. 25.
6. Grant, *op. cit.*, p. 136.
7. P. Cornelius Tacitus, *The Annals of Imperial Rome* (Hamondsworth, England, 1956), p. 280.
8. Grant, *op. cit.*, p. 133.
9. Shirley Jackson Case, *Experience with the Supernatural in Christian Times* (New York, 1929), p. 53.
10. Schaff, *History II*, pp. 301-305.

## Chapter 4

1. Suetonius Tranquillus, *Lives of the Twelve Caesars* (New York, 1931), pp. 241-280.
2. Tacitus, *op. cit.*, pp. 362-364.
3. *Ibid.*, pp. 365-366.

## Chapter 5

1. Tacitus, *op. cit.*, p. 365.
2. Schaff, *History II*, p. 336.
3. *Ibid.*, p. 400.
4. Wilken, *op. cit.*, p. 18.
5. Henri Daniel-Rops, *The Church of the Apostles and Martyrs* (London, 1960), p. 169.
6. Eusebius, *The History of the Church* (Hamondsworth, England, 1965), p. 105.
7. *Ibid.*, p. 126.
8. Anthony Birley, ed., *The Later Caesars* (Hamondsworth, England, 1976), p. 40.

9. *Ibid.*, p. 44.
10. Daniel-Rops, *op, cit.*, p. 173.
11. Birley, *op. cit.*, p. 44.
12. Wilken, *op. cit.*, pp. 12-13.
13. *Ibid.*, p. 16.
14. *Ibid.*, p. 22.
15. Fernand Hayward, *A History of the Popes* (New York, 1931), p. 20.
16. ANF, Vol. I, p. 130.
17. Glimm, *op. cit.*, p. 89.
18. *Ibid.*, p . 94.
19. *Ibid.*, p. 109.
20. *Ibid.*, pp. 109-110.
21. *Ibid.*, p. 110.
22. ANF, Vol. I, p. 131.
23. ANF, Vol. VIII, pp. 676-685.

## Chapter 6

1. Augustus Neander, *General History of the Christian Religion and Church*, Vol. I (Boston, 1848), p. 87.
2. Sabine Baring-Gould, *Lives of the Saints*, Vol. VI (London, 1898), pp. 127-129.
3. Birley, *op. cit.*, p. 97.
4. W/S *Eusebius*, pp. 188-192.

## Chapter 7

1. Wilken, *op. cit.*, p. 87.
2. *Ibid.*, p. 90.
3. *Ibid.*, p. 102.
4. *Ibid.*, p. 111.
5. Eusebius, *History*, p. 164.
6. Schaff, *History II*, p. 169.
7. Henry Bettenson, ed., *The Early Christian Fathers* (London, 1969), p. 58.

8. *Ibid.*
9. *Ibid.*, p. 62.
10. *Ibid.*, pp. 61-62.
11. *Ibid.*, p. 62.
12. Birley, *op. cit.*, p. 135.
13. *Ibid.*, p. 119.
14. *Ibid.*
15. Wilken, *op. cit.*, p. 82.
16. ANF, Vol. I, p. 306.
17. Baring-Gould, *Lives*, Vol. I, pp. 4-5.
18. Daniel-Rops, *op. cit.*, pp. 187-189.
19. W/S *Eusebius*, pp. 212-217.
20. Malachi Martin, *The Decline and Fall of the Roman Church* (New York, 1981), p. 16.
21. Eusebius, *History*, pp. 206-207.
22. ANF, Vol. X, p. 285.
23. Birley, *op. cit.*, pp. 161-162, 166.
24. Eusebius, *History*, pp. 209-210.
25. Daniel-Rops, *op. cit.*, pp. 201-202.
26. Schaff, *History II*, p. 75.

## Chapter 8

1. W/S *Eusebius*, p. 239.
2. Edward Gibbon, *The Decline and Fall of the Roman Empire* (Hamondsworth, England, 1962), p. 129.
3. ANF, Vol. III, pp. 699-705.
4. *Ibid.*, pp. 693-694.
5. W/S *Eusebius*, p. 251.
6. *Ibid.*, p. 253.

## Chapter 9

1. Joseph C. Ayer, ed., *A Source Book for Ancient Church History* (New York, 1913), p. 152.
2. J. Eugene Reed, ed., *The Lives of the Roman Em-*

*perors and Their Associates* (Philadelphia, 1889), p. 154.
3. W/S *Eusebius*, p. 269.
4. Reed, *op. cit.*, p. 165.
5. Ayer, *op. cit.*, p. 153.
6. *Ibid.*
7. *Ibid.*
8. Martin, *op. cit.*, pp. 15-17.
9. Daniel-Rops, *op. cit.*, p. 400.
10. Neander, *op. cit.*, p. 127.
11. ANF, Vol. V, p. 269.
12. *Ibid.*, pp. 580-581.
13. *Ibid.*, pp. 584-585.
14. Daniel-Rops, *op. cit.*, p. 377.
15. Ayer, *op. cit.*, p. 210.
16. W/S *Eusebius*, p. 283.
17. *Ibid.*
18. ANF, Vol. V, p. 582.
19. *Ibid.*, p. 288.
20. *Ibid.*
21. *Ibid.*
22. Daniel-Rops, *op. cit.*, p. 383.
23. W/S *Eusebius*, p. 284.
24. Schaff, *History II*, p. 61.
25. W/S *Eusebius*, p. 275.
26. *Ibid.*, p. 273.
27. Baring-Gould, *Lives*, Vol. II, p. 136.
28. W/S *Eusebius*, pp. 284-285.
29. *Ibid.*, p. 285.
30. Baring-Gould, *Lives*, Vol. II, pp. 430-432.
31. *Ibid.*, pp. 287-289.
32. *Ibid.*, pp. 5-7.
33. *Ibid.*, pp. 319-320.
34. Brauer, *op. cit.*, p. 54.

## Chapter 10

1. W/S *Eusebius*, p. 293.

2. *Ibid.*, p. 305.
3. Robert Gottfried, *The Black Death: Natural and Human Disaster in Mediaeval Europe* (London, 1983), p. 6.
4. Gibbon, *op. cit.*, p. 149.
5. Thomas Burns, *A History of the Ostrogoths* (Bloomington, Ind., 1984), pp. 28-29.
6. Brauer, *op. cit.*, p. 71.
7. Baring-Gould, *Lives*, Vol. IX, pp. 16-18.
8. Ayer, *op. cit.*, p. 242.
9. *Ibid.*, p. 243.
10. W/S *Eusebius*, p. 298.
11. Baring-Gould, *Lives*, Vol. IX, p. 107.
12. *Ibid.*, pp. 109-110.
13. *Ibid.*, pp. 143-144.
14. *Ibid.*, Vol. I, pp. 234-235.
15. Gibbon, *op. cit.*, p. 327.
16. ANF, Vol. V, p. 273.
17. Baring-Gould, *Lives*, Vol. I, pp. 312-313.
18. Gibbon, *op. cit.*, p. 171.
19. Brauer, *op. cit.*, p. 147.
20. Gibbon, *op. cit.*, p. 171.
21. *Ibid.*, p. 172.

## Chapter 11

1. Gibbon, *op. cit.*, p. 186.
2. ANF, Vol. VII, p. 304.
3. *Ibid.*
4. *Ibid.*
5. Gibbon, *op. cit.*, p. 186.
6. Neander, *op. cit.*, p. 144.
7. Giuseppe Riciotti, *The Age of Martyrs: Christianity from Diocletian to Constantine*, trans. Anthony Bull (Milwaukee, 1959), pp. 37-38.
8. *Ibid.*, pp. 39-40.
9. Baring-Gould, *Lives*, Vol. I, pp. 304-305.

10. ANF, Vol. VII, p. 309.
11. Dix, *op. cit.*, pp. 25-26.
12. David Ayerst and A.J.T. Fisher, ed., *Records of Christianity, Vol. I, In The Roman Empire* (New York, 1971), p. 133.
13. W/S *Eusebius*, p.325.
14. *Ibid.*, p. 328.
15. *Ibid.*, p. 335.
16. ANF, Vol. VII, p. 307.
17. *Ibid.*, p. 309.

## Chapter 12

1. W/S *Eusebius*, p. 330.
2. *Ibid.*, pp. 330-331.
3. *Ibid.*, p. 330.
4. Baring-Gould, *Lives*, Vol. I, p. 317.
5. *Ibid.*, pp. 317-321.
6. W/S *Eusebius*, p. 337.
7. Baring-Gould, *Lives*, Vol. I, pp. 231-234.
8. *Ibid.*, Vol. IX, p. 130.
9. *Ibid.*, pp. 331-332.
10. *Ibid.*, Vol. III, p. 277.
11. *Ibid.*, Vol. IV, pp. 296-298.

## Chapter 13

1. Riciotti, *op. cit.*, pp. 122-126.
2. Baring-Gould, *Lives*, Vol. VI, pp. 343-351.
3. Eusebius, pp. 342-343.
4. Eusebius, *The Ecclesiastical History and the Martyrs of Palestine*, Vol. I (London, 1954), pp. 331-333.
5. *Ibid.*, p. 135.
6. *Ibid.*, p. 340.
7. *Ibid.*, p. 356.
8. *Ibid.*, p. 357.

9. *Ibid.*, p. 359.
10. *Ibid.*, p. 361.
11. *Ibid.*, p. 357.
12. *Ibid.*, p. 396.
13. *Ibid.*, pp. 380-386.

## Chapter 14

1. W/S *Eusebius*, p. 336.
2. *Ibid.*
3. *Ibid.*, p. 337.
4. ANF, Vol. VII, p. 315.
5. W/S *Eusebius*, p. 338.
6. ANF, Vol. VII, p. 315.
7. W/S *Eusebius*, pp. 339-340.
8. *Ibid.*, p. 358.
9. *Ibid.*, p. 359.
10. *Ibid.*, p. 361.
11. *Ibid.*, p. 362.
12. *Ibid.*
13. *Ibid.*, p. 363.
14. John Holland Smith, *Constantine the Great* (New York, 1971), p. 103.
15. ANF, Vol. VII, p. 318.
16. W/S *Eusebius*, p. 367.
17. *Ibid.*, p. 377.
18. ANF, Vol. VII, p. 321.
19. W/S *Eusebius*, pp. 379-380.
20. Philip Schaff, ed., *A Select Library of Nicene and Post-Nicene Fathers of the Christian Church*, Vol. I (New York, 1890), pp. 421-422.
21. Will Durant, *Caesar and Christ: A History of Roman Civilization and of Christianity from Their Beginnings to A.D. 325* (New York, 1944), p. 656.
22. Roland H. Bainton, *The Penguin History of Christianity*, Vol. I (Hamondsworth, England, 1967), p. 116.
23. Schaff, *A Select Library . . .* , p. 433.
24. W/S *Eusebius*, p. 387.

# Index

*NOTE: The names in italics are those of martyrs.*

*St. Barnabas* (1st cent.) (apostle), 31
*St. Basilides* (d. 203, Alexandria), 115-116
*St. Besas* (d. c. 250, Alexandria), 131
*St. Biblis* (d. 177, Lyon), 92
*St. Blandina* (d. 177, Lyon), 92, 93, 94-95
Bryene (4th cent.) (abbess), 185-187
Caligula (Gaius) (12-41) (Roman emperor), 17-18, 27-28, 43, 44, 154
*St. Callistus I* (d. 222) (bishop of Rome), 120
Caracalla (188-217) (Roman emperor), 116, 117
*St. Cassianus of Imola* (d. 304), 179
*St. Cassianus of Tangier* (d. 298), 159
Cassius Dio (4th cent.) (governor of Africa), 156-158
Castula (4th cent.), 160
Catacombs, 90, 99-100, 143-144, 147
*St. Cecelia* (d. c. 177, Rome), 89-91
Celsus, Aulus Cornelius (1st cent.) (philosopher), 78-79
Cerdo (1st cent.) (theologian), 79
*St. Cerealis* (d. c. 120, near Rome), 70-71
*St. Chione* (d. 304, Thessalonica), 183-184
*St. Cittinus* (d. 180, Carthage), 97-98
Claudius I (10 B.C.-A.D. 54) (Roman emperor), 18, 27, 38, 43
Claudius II (c. 214-270) (Roman emperor), 150, 153
Clemens, Flavius (1st cent.), 53, 57
*St. Clement I* (d. c. 101) (bishop of Rome), 56, 62
Commodus (161-192) (Roman emperor), 69, 98-99, 102
*St. Concord* (d. c. 175, Spoleto), 87-89
Constantine I the Great (274?-337) (Roman emperor), 2, 55, 167, 206-207, 208-211, 212, 214
Constantius Chlorus (c. 245-306) (Roman emperor), 151, 152, 153, 166, 169, 179, 208
Cordianus (2nd cent.), 87
Council of Nicaea, 2, 212
Crescens (2nd cent.) (philosopher), 85
*St. Cronion* (d. c. 250, Alexandria), 131
Cybele, cult of, 38, 44
*St. Cyprian* (c. 200-258) (bishop of Carthage), 122-124, 129, 138, 140, 141, 142, 146, 147
Dacianus (4th cent.) (governor of Tarraconensis), 179, 182
Decius (c. 195-251) (Roman emperor), 124-126, 127, 136-137, 138
*St. Denis* (or Dionysius) (d. c. 250) (bishop of Paris), 129 Diocletian (c. 245-c. 313) (Roman emperor), 151-152, 153-156, 158, 159-162, 164, 165, 166, 167, 169, 189, 191, 206, 208

*St. Silvanus* (d. 310) (bishop of Gaza), 196
*St. Simeon of Jerusalem*, (c. 86 B.C.-A.D. 107) (bishop), 57, 62-63, 71
Simon Magus (1st cent.) (cultic leader), 55
*St. Sixtus (or Xystos) II* (d. 258) (bishop of Rome), 143-144
Socrates, 81
Sophronia (d. c. 304), 175
*St. Speratus* (d. 180, Carthage), 97-98
*St. Stephen* (d. 37) (deacon, protomartyr), 25-26
*St. Stephen I* (d. 257) (bishop of Rome), 141, 143
Suetonius Tranquillus, Gaius (c. 68-c. 140) (historian), 43, 44, 53
Symmachus (2nd cent.) (theologian), 79
Tacitus, Cornelius (c. 55-c. 120) (historian), 38, 39, 47, 48, 53, 56
*St. Tharsicius* (d. c. 258, Rome), 144-145
Tertullian, Quintus Septimius Florens (c. 150-c. 240) (theologian), 17, 80, 101, 104, 113-114, 120, 121-122
*St. Theodosia* (290-308) (d. Caesarea), 194
*St. Theodulus) (d. 309, Caesarea), 196*
*St. Theophilus* (d. c. 250, Alexandria), 132
Tiberius (43 B.C.-A.D. 37) (Roman emperor), 17
*St. Tiburtius* (d. c. 175, Rome), 89-90
*St. Timothy of Gaza* (d. 304, Caesarea), 192
Titus (39-81) (Roman emperor), 53, 56, 57
Torquatus (2nd cent.) (governor of Umbria), 88-89
Trajan (53-117) (Roman emperor), 58-60, 61-62, 63-64, 68, 103
Urban (4th cent.) (governor of Palestine), 191, 192, 194-195
*St. Valens* (d. 309, Caesarea), 196
*St. Valentine* (d. 308, Caesarea), 195
Valeria (c. 270-c. 315) (Roman empress), 156, 161, 165, 201, 206
*St. Valerian* (d. c. 175, Rome), 89-90
Valerian (c. 195-c. 260) (Roman emperor), 139, 140, 142, 143, 144, 148-149
*St. Valerius of Zaragoza* (d. 304) (bishop), 179
Vespasian (9-79) (Roman emperor), 52-53, 54, 57
*St. Vestia* (d. 180, Carthage), 97-98
*St. Vettius Epagathus* (d. 177, Lyon), 91
St. Vincent (d. 304, Zaragoza) (deacon), 179-180
Watts, Isaac (1674-1748) (hymnist), 215
Worship, early Christian, 8, 10-11, 30-31, 60, 82-83, 86, 100, 155
*St. Zacchaeus* (d. 303, Caesarea) (deacon), 191
St. Zeus (d. c. 250, Alexandria), 132